The Life of Torah

THE RELIGIOUS LIFE OF MAN
Frederick J. Streng, Series Editor

The Life of Torah

Readings in the Jewish Religious Experience

Jacob Neusner

Brown University

DICKENSON PUBLISHING COMPANY, INC.

Encino, California and Belmont, California

ISBN–0–8221–0124–6
Library of Congress Catalog Card Number: 73–91731

Printed in the United States of America

Printing (last digit): 9 8 7 6 5 4 3 2

For
Joel and Ann Zaiman
Ilana Beth
Sarina
Ari Lev
Rafael

contents

general editor's foreword

The power of religious life is often self-evident to the participant, but very difficult to communicate to the uncommitted observer. Therefore, in an attempt to allow students to understand the thoughts, feelings, and attitudes of participants in the major religious traditions, we present companion volumes of readings in the Religious Life of Man Series.

The aim of this series of readings is to introduce the literature of a tradition, and provide sympathetic interpretations and descriptions of important activities which expose the dynamics and some of the concrete variety in a religious tradition. Every book of readings is selective in the material it includes, and the focus here is on religious life, in the past and present, that defines the religious options available today. The selections seek to reveal the goals, experiences, activities, symbolic imagery, and community life of a religious tradition. Hopefully the reader can thereby imaginatively participate in some of the feelings and experiences which are exposed.

Each of the volumes is edited by a university or college teacher who is also a specialist in the major languages and cultures of a religion. Several volumes have new translations of material made especially for them, and each reading is introduced with a brief comment about its place in the tradition and its general religious significance. Further background is found in the companion textbook in the Religious Life of Man Series; at the same time, these books of readings might well be used in combination with other books and media.

Frederick J. Streng
Series Editor

preface

The *Way of Torah: An Introduction to Judaism, Second Edition,* provides an account of Judaism from the perspective of history of religions. The primary problem is to define and describe Judaism as a religious tradition characteristic of Jews of all stages of society, from the most sophisticated to the uneducated, and of both the classical or archaic and modern situations in human culture. Here I propose to offer for reflection and discussion an account of the primary motives of Judaic religious life, to provide a portrait of Jewish piety. I therefore concentrate on the prayers and religious observances, the heroes and value-determining authorities, the organized movements in modern American Judaism, and similar evidences as to the dominant themes in the life of Jewish spirituality. These constitute the guideposts which mark out and illuminate the way of Torah.

The relationship of *Way of Torah* to the present anthology is threefold.

First of all, I have supplemented and enriched the data provided in *Way of Torah.* Prayers alluded to are here provided in detail; many aspects of the liturgical life, expressive of the mythic structure of classical Judaism (*Way of Torah,* Part I) are added.

Second, I have introduced important aspects of contemporary religious life in Judaism which are ignored in *Way of Torah.* The entire discussion of the major organized movements of modern Judaism, both in the Western countries and in the State of Israel, introduces materials not considered in detail within the theoretical framework of *Way of Torah.*

Third, I have tried to give the concept of "Torah" more breadth and specificity by introducing substantive discussions of the message of Torah, the synagogue's response to its specific teachings, the exegesis of its literature, the rabbis as vivid personalities, not merely as religious types, and the way Torah gives shape and meaning to life.

In general, the correspondence between the two works is as follows: *Way of Torah,* Part I: "The Mythic Structure of Classical Judaism" may be read in conjunction with Parts II–IV of *Life of Torah; Way of Torah,* Part II: "Torah —A Way of Living" is elaborated by Parts V–VII, *Life of Torah;* and *Way of Torah,* Part III: "Continuity and Change in Modern Times" is greatly expanded in Parts I and VIII–X, *Life of Torah.*

The theory of *Way of Torah* and of *Life of Torah* is that one may describe even so varied and complex a set of religious phenomena as are yielded by Judaism, and that this is to be done not so much through theological or creedal formulations as through the examination of the imaginative and pious life of the people of the Torah, of the spirituality of the Jews as Judaists. To put it differently, the way of Torah is defined by the norms of *halakhah,* of Jewish law, which constitute the axioms of the Judaic tradition and the way in which theology and myth alike are embodied. This is the theory which explains the emphases of the present anthology. It is not offered, therefore, as a description of the traits of "Jewish culture" or of the meaning of "Jewish history"—which I should regard as primarily theological efforts, internal to the discourse of the believing community itself—but as an account, as accurate and responsible as I am capable of making it, of what constitutes Judaism as a *religion* in the context of the study of religions.

Two interesting movements in Jewish spirituality are, unfortunately, not represented here. The first is the life of the extreme Orthodox Jewish world, that is, that part of contemporary Judaism which has not entered into discourse with modernity at all. This Jewish life is important in the State of Israel and significant in American and European Judaism as well. Its stress on study of Talmud in *yeshivot* and on the separation of authentic Jewish life from all forms of modernity is an important testimony to the condition of modern Judaism. I was not able to find satisfactory accounts of the life of the most traditional expressions of Orthodoxy, such as the Yeshiva at Lakewood, New Jersey, and similar institutions in other cities in America and Western Europe. This is not surprising, considering the primary commitment of such expressions to a separation from modernity. A second omission is Hasidism, which, because of its mystic color and exotic qualities, is of special interest. My problem here is not that we do not have apt descriptive materials. We have, on the contrary, many efforts at capturing the meaning of Jewish mysticism in general, and of Hasidism in particular, perhaps an overabundance. For in addition to the writings of contemporary Hasidim, much of it translated into English, we have the philosophical descriptions by Martin Buber and his followers, on the one side, and the imitative efforts of guitar-playing, self-styled holy men, whether Reform or Orthodox rabbis, on the other. The problem, therefore, is to locate what is authentic and to interpret and understand the development of what is imitative, also authentic in its own way, but *not* to classical Hasidism. This seemed too special, and to involve too few people, to warrant attention.

It is fairly simple to locate accurate accounts of the nature and problems of Reform, Orthodox, Reconstructionist, and Conservative Judaism. It is far more complicated to represent all the phenomena called Hasidism, from the Lubavitch Movement centered at 770 Eastern Parkway, Brooklyn, and spreading through the whole of the Jewish world, on the one side, to the House of Love and Prayer in San Francisco, on the other—not to mention the Hasidic circles of Jerusalem and New York which do maintain the old forms in the old ways and in the classical spirit. I can recommend, in addition to the pertinent writings of Martin Buber, Gershom G. Scholem, "Martin Buber's Hasidism: A Critique," reprinted in Judah Goldin, ed., *The Jewish Expression* (New York, 1970: Bantam Books), and especially Herbert Weiner, *9 1/2 Mystics. The Kabbala Today* (New York, 1969: Holt, Rinehart, and Winston).

This work is dedicated to my friend, colleague, and rabbi, Joel H. Zaiman, and to his family. Rabbi Zaiman embodies for me everything vital in the rabbinic tradition in Judaism. He is authentic to the tradition and an exemplar of both its relevance to the contemporary condition and its wisdom. My respect for him as a rabbi makes all the more precious the friendship and intimacy which unite our families.

The artwork was originally contributed by my wife, and rendered for publication by artist Tom Martin.

Jacob Neusner
Brown University

introduction

The Life of Torah is a source book intended to convey, so far as it is possible through the experience of merely reading a book, some of the meanings contained within the Jewish religious tradition. I believe that classical Judaism is accessible through three sources, of which we shall draw on two: first, the pages of Jewish liturgy, second, the classical literature of the rabbinic sages of all times, and third, the reflections of living men and women whose lives are shaped by, and in response to, the tradition. In the readings that follow are the first and the third sorts of evidence. The second is omitted because of the difficulty of gaining immediate access to, and accurately interpreting, the writings of premodern men and women. To approach the classic literature in its own setting and not mediated through the mind and expression of twentieth-century men and women is exceedingly difficult, for one has to know a great deal about the cultural and philosophical context in which that literature was created. A surer path into the classical tradition is through the ways in which it is described by contemporary writers for contemporary readers, particularly by those writers who also are scholars and are able to express in a clear and authentic way what the classical literature has to say. The liturgy, on the other hand, still lives in the synagogue and preserves the capacity to speak directly to modern men and women. One does not need to be a scholar to appreciate its power. Indeed, to know who wrote a particular prayer and where he lived in no way illuminates the full meaning of that prayer. To know only that when facing God Jews say these particular words is to know a great deal about Judaism.

I therefore have tried to represent the inner life of Jewish piety through very extensive quotations from the Jewish prayerbook. These serve to illustrate the theology and moral perceptions of the Judaic tradition. They do so better than do theological writings, for the prayers are said by all pious Jews and speak both to and for their situation. Obviously, people who do not affirm the message of these prayers are not going to grasp all of what they say in behalf of people who do. But the presentations of the liturgical forms and personal piety are to express the spirit of Judaism in its most authentic and idiomatic language. If you want to know what it means to be a Jew, this is the best way.

Sacred literature of course occurs throughout the liturgy, and Psalms and many Scriptural passages are cited as they appear in important and dramatic moments in the life of prayer. Nearly every writer who appears in this anthology draws extensively, whether explicitly or not, upon the Hebrew Bible, the Talmud, the writings of philosophers, mystics, and sages. But, again, for our purpose it would be misleading to approach the Hebrew Bible or the Talmudic sources outside of the context of Judaic piety, for it is only that context which today gives them meaning and makes them significant for the description of classical and

1

contemporary Judaism. The problem of such a description is not historical, chronological, or cultural. If you want to know about the history of the Jews, then you will ask about the historical Yoḥanan ben Zakkai or the name of the person who wrote the Twenty-third Psalm. If you want to know about the meaning of Judaism, such historical information will be useless. You rather will inquire about the meaning of Yoḥanan ben Zakkai to the living faith, the place, interpretation, and significance of the Psalm in the life of the synagogue. The tradition speaks for itself—as it is expressed by its modern and contemporary masters. That is why living men and women are called upon to tell us, in prose and in poetry, what being Jewish means to them.

What I offer here is the chance to enter into the imaginative religious life of the pious Jew. I want you to know how Jews pray—or, at least, the words they say; how they confront Torah in synagogue worship and in response to its message; how they examine their souls on the Days of Awe and celebrate the Sabbath and festivals of the Jewish year. I want you to know what it means for a Jew to live according to the Torah and its *halakhah,* its way, to share the joy and hopefulness and transcendent pleasure of life in conformity with its sacred disciplines. I present glimpses into the lives of some of the great rabbis, for those lives are part of the Torah and constitute its most vivid exemplification. But I also want you to take seriously the vitality and complexity of Judaism in the West and in the State of Israel, to learn about the great religious movements—all of them claiming to be true to the Torah—created in Europe and America, deeply modern and profoundly Jewish at the same time. What does it mean to be a Jew who lives in the way of Torah? Here are brought together various and authentic answers —although not all possible ones—to these questions.

It is inevitable that you will feel like an onlooker, that you will find this book confessional and inner-directed. If you do, then I shall have succeeded in my goal. For my purpose is not to tell you what Judaism should mean to you or how Judaism may speak to the great issues confronting "all mankind." Judaism has all too often been represented in its universal aspect, as a religion and ethical system relevant to everyone everywhere. That is because Jews in the West are a minority and are acutely sensitive to their status as people in some ways apart from the Christian or post-Christian majority. They therefore tend to address the world in the language of the world and to focus upon issues of common concern to their neighbors and friends. In so doing they do not attempt to report what they are not certain will be understood or even taken seriously: what is unique to Judaism and ultimately not wholly accessible. The festivals, for example, will be explained in their universal significance. Passover is the festival of "human freedom." That is so, but it is the season of *our* freedom, of us, the Jewish people. The so-called high holy days, the Days of Awe in the autumn, are dimly perceived by the outside world as days of penitence. But the intense, personal character of these days, their extraordinary hold on Jews in other respects remote from traditional life—this is hardly explained by reference to penitence in general. Elsewhere you can hear what Jews say when they speak to the world at large. But nearly every writer in this book sees himself or herself as speaking to Jews as Jews, who are reading a Jewish book or praying a Jewish prayer or thinking about a Jewish hero or, so commonly, arguing about a narrowly and parochially Jewish issue. I shall not apologize, therefore, for the confessional and narrowly Jewish framework of selection and discussion that follows. If you want to know what it means to be a Jew, you should not ask a Jew to *tell* you. Rather, you should listen to what one Jew has to say to another Jew about Judaism.

The readings are organized in the following way. The first part introduces the topic as a whole. The writers explore in general terms what being Jewish means. Their intent is not descriptive. They propose, rather, to explain to Jews why *they* in particular should be Jewish. What is important to you are the sorts of apologetic arguments adduced, the way in which the question is phrased and answered. The second part takes up the central religious affirmation of Judaism —the assertion that God is one. This is the sole theological proposition we shall examine, and we consider it not as it is spelled out by theologians, but rather how it is *prayed* in the life of the community. It is no less theological because it is phrased at the cutting edge of piety: in prayerful address to God himself. The third part then takes up Torah in four aspects: first, the Torah as a sacred scroll, a physical object, and how it is received in the synagogue; second, the Torah as it is preached to the believing Jew, presented in a single example of a great exposition of the substance of Torah; third, the Torah as it is responded to in the heart of a Jewish poet; and fourth, an overview of the ways in which Torah has lived through the exposition and exegesis of Judaism over the centuries.

From our consideration of the great assertion of Torah—that God is one— and of Torah as teaching, we turn to the effects of Torah. First come three rabbis who lived at the seedtime of classical Judaism, and who exemplify in their lives as much as in their teachings what the Torah is supposed to mean. Then we study at length what Torah means in the life of the people, for Judaism has always understood itself not as a creed but as a way of living, as a mode of forming culture and creating civilization. Torah as a way of life begins with the general attitude of Jews within its discipline, the attitude of joy. Then we deal with some specific modes of Torah, and last, with Torah in time, as a way of organizing the passage of the days into meaningful, consecrated moments.

The last important question is, What has happened to Torah in the modern world? To answer this question we deal with the specificities of the religious movements in contemporary American Judaism, for they all claim to constitute the true outcome of the classical tradition. We want to know two things. First of all, what is the claim of a specific movement? How is it defined by its authentic spokesmen? And second, what are the central issues confronted by each move- ment? How are these issues defined by people loyal to the movement? In this same setting we ask two further questions related to the State of Israel. First, what is the role of Torah in the life of the Jewish State? Second, what is the role of the Jewish state and of Zionism in the life of Torah, in the piety and imaginative world of Judaism? For one commitment shared by nearly all pious Jews has to do with Zionism and the State of Israel, and this commitment is understood in other than narrowly political terms. If you want to understand what it means to be a Jew anywhere in the world, you must face up to the role of Jerusalem, to the meaning of Zionism and the State of Israel, of the Zionist commitment, characteristic in one way or another of nearly all Jews who regard themselves as religious, as of nearly all who do not.

We move, therefore, from the general to the specific, from the theological to the concrete, and from the classical to the contemporary aspects of Judaism. Just as the religious Jew will see himself or herself as Orthodox or Reform or Conservative, so we must ask what this identification means; just as the religious Jew will observe the Sabbath and festivals and holy days, so we inquire as to what these say in the life of the observant and faithful Jew. Above all, just as the religious Jew will fill his days with prayers, so we must listen to those prayers and inquire after their significance. At the outset comes the unavoidable problematic: Why do people do it? What arguments are adduced in behalf of the tradition?

I try to serve as a reliable and honest guide, for I am showing my home, the house of Israel. I live within the tradition and speak from its midst. This source book is meant to document the living religion of the Jewish people and to invite men and women of good will to share in some of the joys of that religion, at least to learn about them. I regard the teachings of Judaism as truths available to contemporary men and women and as important for their understanding of the world and of God. To be sure, I have insisted that you listen to our people as they today talk with one another. But I shall have succeeded if at the end you both understand the complex situation of the contemporary religious Jew and appreciate the promise for mankind contained within that very particular and intensely concrete, highly idiomatic mode of being human, of living the life which here is called "the way of Torah." And even if you do not appreciate or admire that way but nonetheless *understand* it, I shall have achieved my purpose.

My own position may be stated briefly. I grew up in a Reform Temple and remain committed to the Reform approach to the classical tradition. I received my rabbinical education at The Jewish Theological Seminary of America and am a Conservative rabbi and member of the Rabbinical Assembly. I worship at an Orthodox *minyan* and try to observe as best I can the Orthodox interpretation of Jewish law. I am a Zionist, but choose to make my life in America. And, finally, I respect and revere the commitments and self-understandings of Jews who regard themselves as secular, as much as those who call themselves religious. I am at home, therefore, in every room in the House of Israel.

part one

the jewish heritage

What makes it easy to study Judaism is this: You are likely to know, and certain to know about, Jews, who are to be found throughout the English-speaking world, in the fifty American states, every Canadian province, Great Britain, South Africa, Australia, New Zealand, and elsewhere. What makes it difficult to understand Judaism is the rich variety of ways in which Jews interpret what it means to be Jewish, and, in the case of the religious sector of Jewry, practice Judaism. The range of self-understandings is broad. The forms of religious expression defy reduction to simple and one-dimensional descriptions.

We therefore have at the outset to ask simple questions: What is a Jew? Who is a Jew? Surely, despite the diversity and complexity of data pertinent to these queries, we should be able to find answers.

Two answers are before us. The first is an effort to describe the Jewish situation in its essentially particular elements and to locate in the ordinary experience of any person exactly these same elements. The argument is that being Jewish is a particular way of being a human being.

The second comes from Ludwig Lewisohn, a novelist, literary critic, and Jewish thinker over the first half of the twentieth century. Lewisohn was a professor at Brandeis University at the time of his death, and, in his lifetime, was one of the most eloquent and dedicated advocates of Judaism among the creative writers of his time. He writes with passion and appeals for belief; his problem is not one of description but of advocacy. And this itself should alert you to part of the problem of defining "being Jewish": the problem, or lingering crisis, of identity and identification confronting the contemporary Jew. For the Jew sees himself as having to choose whether to be a Jew, and that means two things. First of all, he perceives the alternative of dropping out of the "Jewish situation," on the one side; he also understands "being Jewish" as a problem, as something somehow external to his essential character, on the other. Ludwig Lewisohn writes with passion because he knows his reader, and he sees that reader as asking the question others need never face: Why should I be what I am?

Lewisohn tells us what a Jew should be, and this is something a neutral description could not have provided. At the same time the tone and claims may offend, for historians might take exception to some of the claims made or implicit in his statements, and the stridency and emotion of his claims might put off someone who is unacquainted with the heat and passion of Jewish discourse. But for we who want to enter into the situation of the Jew and understand his or her piety, Lewisohn's mode of expression as well as his ideas are more reliable evidence than might be gained from objective and dispassionate scholars.

I.

the human situation of the jew

jacob neusner

From *History and Torah,* by Jacob Neusner (New York: Schocken Books, 1965), pp. 7–12.

The Jewish situation endows me, first of all, with a long and formidable perspective. It forces me to see myself as part of a continuum of time and of space, as heir of some of the most sublime and most foolish men that have ever lived, and as friend and brother of men who, in days past, lived almost everywhere men have been. I cannot therefore accept provinciality, either temporal or spatial, or see myself as rooted forever in one culture or in one age.

Thus the Jewish situation is international and cosmopolitan, and never wholly part of one place or time. This is both a blessing and a curse. It is a blessing because it assures me of ultimate detachment, of a capacity to contemplate from without, to think less fettered by rooted attachments than other men. It forces not only detachment, but to some measure, an act of selection and judgment also, for, not being fully committed anywhere or ever, I am forced to perceive what other men may stand too close to see, and in perception, to respond, to judge. I must therefore learn to love with open arms, to know that this land, this people are mine, yet not wholly so, for I belong to Another as well. Thus to be a Jew means in a historical and more than historical sense to be always homeless in space and in time, always aware of the precariousness of security, of the possibility, by no means remote, that I may have to find another place.

But the Jewish situation of homelessness, of detachment, has provided me, secondly, with the awareness that what is now is not necessarily what was, nor what must always be. Being able to stand apart because of an inherited and acquired perspective of distance, I realize that men have choices they may not themselves perceive, that there have been and are now other ways of conducting life and living with men, of building society and creating culture, than those we think are normative. Being able to criticize from the perspective of other ages and lands, I am enabled to evaluate what others may take for granted, to see the given as something to be criticized and elevated.

Third, the Jewish situation of living with a long perspective imposes upon me a terrible need to find something meaningful, truly eternal in human affairs. If I see that all things change, and that only change is permanent, then I need all the more a sense of what abides in man, of what endures in human civilization. If one says, with Sinclair Lewis' men of Gopher Prairie, that to build the emporium that is ours, Washington weathered the rigors of Valley Forge, Caesar crossed the Rubicon, and Henry stood at Agincourt, then one declares his faith that what is here is truly the Zenith and the end of Western history. But we Jews know differently, for we know of cities once great and now no more, of civilizations—and we too have built civilizations—that prospered and were wiped out in time. We ask, therefore, because we need to ask: what abides, what is permanently meaningful in life? We want to know where history is moving, because we know that history does, indeed, move.

Fourth, out of this need, this thirst for meaning in kaleidoscopic life, we Jews have learned that something in man is indeed eternal. We use the words of Scripture, and say that man is "made in the image of God," but underlying these words is a mute and unarticulated awareness that man prevails, and some of his achievements can endure. We know, moreover, what will live, namely, the intellect, the capacity of man to learn. We have, therefore, dedicated our best energies to the cultivation of the mind, to study, enrichment, and transmission of man's insights and ideas through the ages. We have held that that part of man which may think, know, believe, hope, love—that part is divine and endures, and whatever part of it endures from another age is ours to know, love and cherish. Therefore, in other ages, our monuments have been books, the school house, and our heroes have been men of learning and of mind.

Fifth, because I am a Jew, I understand how important to the world are compassion, and man's capacity to transcend his animal base through acts of love and fellowship. The Jewish situation imposes this understanding in two ways. First, because we were slaves in Egypt, we know how important is an act freely done, freely given, that at its most elevated is represented by compassion. Because we have suffered in history, we have learned how important is the opposite of cruelty and oppression, namely, kindness and love. Second, because we see ourselves as men, neither animals nor God, neither wholly objects of nature and history nor wholly subjects of nature and history, we see our human duties and capacities as neither wholly passive nor on the other hand entirely active. We know, therefore, that man may *do* little, but that he may *do:* and what he may do as an act of his own will is to act decently, compassionately, justly, for his free will permits him to choose compassion. The larger part of his life may be 'conditioned,' and outside of his power, but that precious corner of freedom to act by one's own will remains, and *will* at its most virtuous is goodwill, in Hebrew *hesed* (in the abstract, compassion) and *gemilut hasadim* (in the concrete, acts of compassion).

Sixth, more concretely, the Jewish situation imposes upon me an intensity of human relationship, best embodied in the family and people, that others see as clannishness. Seeing the world as we do, a lonely, insecure, transitory place, we look within it for places of security and evidences of permanence, and these we find, as I said, in the abstract in compassion, and in the concrete, in human relationships of love and deep acceptance. We know that death is always near, and that each man goes his separate way to death. But we find in this knowledge not only separateness, but also union of the generations. Death is the experience that brings together the generations that have gone before and those that will come; it is the one experience we share in common, and the Jewish forms of death —the sanctification of God's name on this one stark moment when we are forced to recognize His power and His will—abide to unite the generations. This is the source of veneration of our past, and our capacity continually to live in it, and the foundation of our love for our people, wherever and whenever they are found.

Finally, the Jewish situation has at its foundation a continuing confrontation with the reality of God. Until now, one may have wondered where is the "theology" of the Jewish situation. Beyond the theologies of Jewish religion, and before them all, is the simple sentence, "In the beginning God created the heaven and the earth." That is our fundamental affirmation, and all else must be built on that fact. We affirm that God, who made the world, did so purposefully, and ultimately that purpose is revealed in the course of human history. All that I have said about our long and formidable perspective, our awareness of the frailty and transitory quality of man, our thirst for permanence, through dedication to the mind and reason, to love and compassion, in the abstract and in concrete terms —all this is founded upon our fundamental attitude toward the world and ourselves, both of which we see to be the objects of divine concern, divine purpose, divine compassion. Both men and nature are objects, not subjects, of reality, both are profane, and the only sanctity lies beyond the world and man. Hence our concern for history and its movement, for man and his conduct in society arises out of our awareness that in the objects of creation we see in pale reflection a shadow of the Subject.

Because of this awareness, we are not ashamed of our history, of our frailty and inconsequentiality as a small and insignificant people among the peoples of mankind. We know that those great nations that ruled the world like God perished like men, while we who have patiently endured in hope endure today. Therefore we do not reject our tragic past.

Very little has been said here to distinguish Jews from other men. It is hardly necessary to be a Jew to understand the Jewish situation. The existential qualities I have described are those that Jews may know best and longest, but that others know too. We have words for our situation, such as *Galut,* exile, *Rachmanut,* compassion, *Yosher,* righteousness, and *Bitahon,* faith, trust in God; and these words, though ultimately not translatable into any other language, are in fact shared existentially by every other people today.

In a sense, therefore, just as, on account of Hiroshima, we are all murderers, so, on account of Auschwitz, we are all Jews. Just as we men incinerated entire cities in our fury, so we men were incinerated, shot, gassed, starved, destroyed in our frailty. An age that is threatened by the total destruction of entire civilizations knows what it means to be Jews, who suffered the destruction of their entire European civilization in our time. An age that knows no security knows what it means to be Jews, who have lived for thousands of years without security. An age that finds itself almost powerless to change the course of history, in which individuals find they are almost impotent to affect events, knows what it means to be Jews, who have lived as outsiders, standing always on the wings of history and never in the spotlight. An age that suddenly realizes it is in the grip of past events, knows what it means to be Jews, who have seen themselves forever in the grip of events they have not caused, and ultimately, in the hand of Providence. An age that now knows the danger of nationalism and provinciality knows what it means to be Jews, who have lived internationally before there were nations.

If this is so, perhaps others will learn from us the affirmative lessons of our situation: our quest for meaning in events, our consecration to the human intellect and capacity to think, to create and preserve culture; our appreciation of the preciousness and sanctity of man's slender treasure of compassion and of love, in the abstract and also in day-to-day human relations in which, after all, we do retain considerable power; and, finally, our awareness of the reality, immediacy, and centrality of God's will, our knowledge that in the end, it is not we but God who determines the history of men and nations, not we but God with whom men must strive for blessing.

2.

what is a jew? who is a jew?

ludwig lewisohn

From *What Is This Jewish Heritage?* by Ludwig Lewisohn (New York: Bnai Brith Hillel Foundations, 1954), pp. 1–6. © 1954 by Bnai Brith Hillel Foundations, Inc., and reprinted with their permission.

What Is a Jew

What is a Jew? What is it to *be* a Jew? Are Jews a religious community, like the Roman or Greek Churches? Or are Jews an ethnic group, like the Negroes? Or are they a secular community, formed by historic forces, which is a vague enough term, like the Danes or the Dutch?

A little accurate thinking will show that each one of these analogies breaks down hopelessly as soon as it is pressed.

No merely religious community ever had a specific homeland nor an authentic language created by itself as the expression of its unique character nor, above all, thousands of passionate adherents who are indifferent to religion or even hostile to it.

An ethnic group, on the other hand, has or is supposed to have definite physical characteristics, such as skin pigmentation or hair texture or eyeshape. Trivial as even these marks are, Jews do not possess them. Even the so-called Jewish nose is at least as prevalent among "Indo-European" Armenians as it is among "Semitic" Jews. So it is clear that Jews are neither a *merely* religious body nor an ethnic group.

Our trouble becomes even acuter when we seek to define Jews as a mere national community, shaped by historic forces, like the Danes or the Dutch. Danes and Netherlanders, relatively late converts to Christianity, leaders in the Protestant revolt, have no autochthonous religion—none, that means, which they themselves originated. Jews have. When these Nordic peoples leave their own lands, they merge easily with the peoples and the cultures of their new environment. What are the Dutch of New Amsterdam but a shadow and a pleasant legend today? In what specific sense was Franklin Delano Roosevelt a Dutchman? But though the Jews were driven from their recently recovered homeland eighteen-hundred years ago, a distinguished American public servant, like Mr. Mordecai Joseph Ezekiel, whose family has been on these shores nearly as long as the Roosevelts, is by name and fame, by spiritual configuration and outer destiny, a Jew.

In view of these facts, too simple and obvious to be denied, it is not surprising that responsible thinkers have described and defined the Jewish people not only as a unique group, but as one torn out of the general context of history. Modern historians are fond of attributing a pattern to the existence of peoples. Each people and its culture arises, flourishes, declines and disappears from the scene of history. The Jewish people made its historic appearance, as we shall see, in quite a normal fashion. Yet the pattern of its history is violently abnormal. It never flourished greatly in terms of power. It knew defeat and desperate catastrophe over and over again. Yet from each historic grave it re-arose; it survived; it lived to re-affirm its changeless character and historic function.

What was the source within history of that power of survival and renewal which has taken place from age to age down to that birth of the State of Israel from the ashes of the six-million martyrs, an event within the memory of the youngest Jew now living and seeking to interpret his destiny and its meaning? So far as human insight extends, the source of that perpetual life and perpetual power of re-birth must be, cannot but be, in that transcendent experience at the foot of Sinai which welded a group of rude clans and fugitives from oppression into a people whose fundamental character was stamped and moulded then.

Petulant men with minds frozen thirty years ago will call this explanation "mystical" in the illiterate usage of that word as anything beyond the grasp of the most mechanical and empty understanding. Mature and unbiased reflection will show that this explanation and this alone, precisely this, like any respectable hypothesis in the sciences, serves to account for the historic phenomena which no one denies. This hypothesis alone *works*. It alone explains the character, the history, the ever recurrent fate of the Jewish people.

Who Is a Jew

It is clear, then, that the question: what is a Jew, is an intricate one. Though it may seem a purely theoretical question, the answer given to it has very concrete consequences in the conduct of life. But in America today there are even more searching and immediate questions, questions that involve what William James used to call living options or choices. And these questions are: *Who is a Jew?* And: *What does it mean to be a Jew?*

People with lazy minds use verbal rubber-stamps to keep the facts of life at a distance. And one of these verbal rubber-stamps by which they seek to evade reality is "the accident of birth." Now the word "accident" is in itself invariably an evasion or a confession of ignorance. We call "accident" any fact or event for which we cannot account. Those who use the word do not ever pretend to give up the notion of cause and effect. They know that a universe without the category of causality would fall to pieces. Without the chain of cause and effect there would be no science, there would be no observational knowledge nor the laws, those statements of recurrence, which science derives from such knowledge. In other words: there are no "accidents." There are only facts and events, of which the causes are unknown to us.

Birth, however, has been called an "accident" out of quite impure motives. There is no event—no result or issue—of which the causes are more clearly known. If you are known as a Jew and if you acknowledge yourself to be one, it is so because a chain of cause and effect arising in an immemorial antiquity has not been broken. If you are known as a Jew and know yourself to be a Jew, you have two Jewish parents and four Jewish grand-parents and eight Jewish great-grandparents and sixteen Jewish great-great-grandparents. Around the year 1700 you had 512 Jewish ancestors and around the year 1670 you had 1024. Pursue this chain of arithmetical progression. No aspect of human destiny can be more deeply rooted in either nature or history than the destiny of birth.

Let us repeat these words: one's birth is destined by both nature and history. Yet the universe is not one of inescapable determinism. At any point the ancestral chain could have been broken. It could have been broken by apostasy or by intermarriage or by both. But had the chain been broken in your case, had a single one of your direct ancestors abandoned the community of Israel, you would no more be a Jew nor would you be known as a Jew nor know yourself to be one. The slightest observation of the contemporary scene, as well as of historic scenes, confirms this. Apostasy or intermarriage without the conversion of the Gentile spouse still leaves him who practices either a recognizable Jew. But the character of his children is already blurred and his grandchildren are no more known as Jews nor know themselves as such.

Now from this circumstance there arises a fact, a truth, of the very highest moral import. All of that great group of men and women, of fathers and mothers, who begot and bore you—all *willed* to be Jews; all affirmed their humanity within and through their Jewishness and clung to their Judaism in good and evil days. Blank escape from medieval Ghetto and later community was always possible and was practiced from time to time. Until the appearance of Hitler all the prizes of the world were in many lands open to the apostate. Not one of that great and venerable company of *your* fathers and mothers dreamed of avoidance and escape.

Hence, if today you are known as a Jew and know yourself to be one, you are what you are not only within the order of nature and biological descent, but within the order of moral freedom, of willing and of choice, of loyalty to a historic reality and to a set of inherent values of transcendent worth.

3.

the form of the heritage

Clearly, Lewisohn must now explain the "argument from history" so important in his earlier claim. What he asks is that the Jew understand himself not as an isolated individual, but in the context and setting of the history of the Jewish people. The individual identifies himself with that history. The religious role of the history of the Jewish people is laid forth in every stage in the unfolding of Judaism. The Israelites' Exodus from Egypt is accompanied by the demand, made in the Passover celebration, that forever afterward the Jews must see themselves as *being* redeemed from Egyptian bondage. History is not in the past, but in ourselves. At Passover the Jew does not celebrate what happened a long time ago, but what happens now, in this generation as in every earlier one. This is not a historical argument at all, but an interpretation of the meaning, the very being, of Judaism. Lewisohn's account is written in the past tense, but his purpose is utterly contemporary, and history here serves the cause of theology. To understand how this works, just realize that virtually every Jew in the world knows that had he or she been in Europe between 1939 and 1945, Auschwitz would be not a symbol or a code-word, but a reality. No Jew can forget that if he or she had been there, he or she would have perished. No one is exempt from the fate of the people as a whole. That ever-present awareness even now is what makes the history of the Jewish people into the story of one's own self. Lewisohn takes account of that fact in phrasing the argument as he does.

From *What Is This Jewish Heritage?* by Ludwig Lewisohn (New York: Bnai Brith Hillel Foundations, 1954), pp. 18–28. © 1954 by B'nai B'rith Hillel Foundations, Inc., and reprinted with their permission.

Let us look at the form, the outer manifestation of Jewish history. It has three strange characteristics: the first is its *endurance* or length. The second is its *recurrence.* The third (which is a direct consequence of the second) is its *ever-presentness* in and to each generation. Let us look at these three characteristics in order.

Let us confine ourselves for the moment to the hard facts of secular history, to the ascertainable and ascertained. The tribally united *B'nei Yisrael* the children of Israel, took possession of Cana'an and settled in the land in (roughly) 1250 before the Common Era. This occurrence, namely, the conquest of Cana'an by Joshua bin Nun and the men of Israel, has its world-wide analogues. Aryan-speaking peoples came from the North and conquered the Indian sub-continent and stamped it as their own; Hellenic tribes came from the East and took possession of the lands of which they were to make Hellas or Greece; Angles and Saxons invaded Celtic Britain which then became forever England.

Neither the Torah nor the Prophetic books of Israel nor Homer nor the plays of Sophocles nor the works of Chaucer or Shakespeare or Milton were written by the ultimate aborigines of the lands that gave them birth. They were all written by conquerors who transformed Cana'an into Eretz Yisrael, the land of Israel; the easternmost peninsula and islands of Europe into Hellas; and Britain into England.

Thus the beginning of Israel's secular history conforms to a pattern not unknown or unfamiliar. But the 3303 years that have elapsed since the walls of Jericho fell, seeing that modern archaeology has proven their fall, present a quite other and quite abnormal spectacle. The commonwealth or state or kingdom or kingdoms established by the children of Israel was, from the time of the Judges on to its final extinction by Rome, a strange and an unquiet one. This particular people disliked and feared governmental authority from the start. It yearned for the rulership of God; it was frightened of the idolatry of the state from its most primitive period on. . . .

Powerful empires threatened this small, turbulent people with its troubled conscience. When Babylon conquered it and destroyed both Jerusalem and the Temple and deported (note the aptness of that modern term) the majority of the inhabitants of the land of Israel to strange places, that should normally have ended its history. Here then we have the first great deviation and here the first unconscious aspiration toward perpetuity. Not all the Israelites in Babylon retained character, faith, sense of destiny. Not all. But a core and remnant did here, as it has done everywhere and always, so that when Cyrus the Persian permitted the return of the exiles, there was a people ready to return; there was a scribe and prophet, Ezra, ready to lead them to return; there were those ready to rebuild the Temple, trowel in one hand, sword in the other, even as the sons of Israel rebuilt the broken land into a State, while fighting off the Arab armies in our own immediate day.

It is difficult, clearly, to keep the theme of endurance, of perpetuity, disentangled from the theme of the living Jewish people, up to that slow spiritual attrition practiced by the Soviets and culminating almost on the day on which these lines are written by the unleashed fury of the trials in Prague.

Yet we are here!

Jews are here. And we are more than merely here. The establishment of the State of Israel; the consolidation of the great American Jewish Community, of which this essay is a small sign and symbol; the intensification of Jewish life in other, smaller corners of the wide dispersion—all these phenomena bear witness to the unique perpetuity and will to live of the people Israel.

It has already been said how hard it is to keep apart the survival of the Jewish people from the recurrences of Jewish history. But it may be clear by now that Jews survived attacks that were always identical in ultimate motivation, however various they seemed in the rationalizations behind which the evil conscience of the world withdrew. From Cicero and the Alexandrian anti-Semites, concerning whom Josephus reports, on to the neo-Pagan butcheries and deportations of the Twentieth Century, the ultimate motivation of attack against the Jewish people was one and the same: to eliminate that threat and reproach to the world's inveterate pagan instincts which the very existence of the Jew embodies and incarnates.

Even the formula scarcely changes. "If the Jews are Alexandrian citizens," asked that Apion against whom so long ago Josephus wrote, "why do they not worship the gods of the city?" The worshippers of the one transcendent God could not ever worship the idols of any city, any *polis,* any state, neither of Alexandria nor of Rome, neither of the mediaeval empires nor of the contemporary ones.

Therefore, from Apion of Alexandria to Lenin the attempts, whether by persuasion or menace, were always the same: to force Jews into the idolatry of the gods of a particular city. Lenin wrote as early as 1913:

> Half the Jews live under conditions favoring maximum assimilation . . . Jewish national culture is the slogan of rabbis and bourgeois . . . Jewish Marxists who merge with Russians, Lithuanians, Ukrainians contribute their share.

Assimilation here, as nearly everywhere, does not mean a reasonable sharing of the cultures of the peoples among whom Jews dwell. It means worshipping the idols of the city. It means the extinction of Jewish identity. But the Jewish people has not been able to will deliberate extinction in the mire of the Pagan world. Hitler perhaps saw that most clearly and therefore attempted the last resort of physical obliteration. And that, too, failed.

Thus nothing new ever happens to Jews. The new things are illusory.

Our civic emancipation was to eliminate the Jewish problem. It brought forth other phenomena of the intensification of that problem. Nor was that all. It subtly turned the attack inward and began to gnaw away the spiritual substance of the Jewish people. And so, for the first time in history, there began to appear Jews who, though sharing all aspects of Jewish destiny, began to lose knowledge of and faith in the inner and eternal reasons; they became Jewish anti-semites and began to declare that Jews survived only by virtue of the recurrence of antisemitism, forgetting the glaring fact that, had Jews been able wholly to disappear, antisemitism could not have survived. The one thing it needs to feed on is Jews, living and recognizable.

Hence it is clear that it is the destined and inextinguishable Jewish will to live that forever re-evokes the resistance of the fury of the Pagans and their rebellion against God and good. Thus it comes about that whenever that fury re-arises the deluded wanderers of the house of Israel return to the core and matrix of their people. And they return, like the eminent philosopher Henri Bergson so recently, not slinkingly, not shame-facedly, not with gloom but with a liberating incandescence in their proud, tragic and repentant hearts. . . .

part two

the unity of god

The first and most important dogma of Judaism is that there is one God and that he is unique, creator of nature and sovereign over history.

How does the Judaic tradition express this dogma? It is not primarily through philosophical or theological discourse. It is not given the form of a creed or dogma which all are expected to recite and confess. It comes down through the prayers of the synagogue, going back for more than twenty-five centuries. We therefore shall find our way into the meaning to the Jew of the unity of God by considering the prayers through which he expresses that meaning.

They are collectively called *the Shema* ("Hear"), from the first word of the sentence, *"Hear,* O Israel: The Lord our God, the Lord is One."

But the proclamation of God's unity consists of much more than that single sentence. It is contained within a group of prayers, recited morning and evening. These prayers declare God to be creator of the world, revealer of his will and instruction—the Torah—to Israel, and redeemer. The three constants in Judaic thinking—creation, revelation, redemption—thus form the framework in which God as one and unique is confessed and blessed.

We shall consider this group of prayers one by one, in the order in which they occur in synagogue worship. But it should not be thought that these prayers are said only, or primarily, in the synagogue. Jewish worship is intensely personal. One is expected to pray three times a day, whether in the synagogue or not. Many pious Jews say their prayers at home, except on the Sabbath-day. The chief reason that one must pray in the synagogue on the Sabbath has to do with certain religious rites which are possible only in a congregation or *minyan,* meaning quorum. A congregation consists of ten male Jews; Reform and Reconstructionist Jews include women for a *minyan.* It is only when such a group is assembled that you may take the Torah-scroll from its ark and read from it, on the one side, and say certain prayers of Sanctification, on the other. The Torah-scroll is read on the Sabbath-day, Saturday, and on Monday and Thursday, as well as on certain holy days and festivals—the New Moon, the intermediate days of festivals, and the like. But for the ordinary days of the year, these prayers will be said as much in the home or office or factory as in the synagogue. And

they may be said without the presence of the Torah or other sanctifying objects.

Many Jews who do not pray every day take very seriously the obligation to
recite the Sanctification prayer, or *Qaddish,* in memory of a deceased relative.
This is expected daily for a year after burial. They therefore will take up the
discipline of daily prayer at that time, and, since the Sanctification can be said
only in a quorum, will seek out a *minyan* not only in the morning, but in the
later afternoon and after sunset as well.

Yet how are prayers said in the classical synagogue? No prayer-leader has
a special right to say one prayer or another. Every male Jew is equally permitted
to carry out every action of worship, provided he is sufficiently learned to do
so. Rabbis have no role whatever in synagogue worship, except as ordinary
Jews. Further, the mode of praying is individual rather than collective among
Jews of European origin. That means each person essentially says the prayers by
himself, not in unison; yet he does so along with others who are praying by
themselves, at approximately the same point in the liturgy. Only a few prayers
will be said at the same time. The net impression in a classical service, therefore,
is a kind of quiet chaos. There is a kind of subdued buzz—the mumbling or
davening (a word which simply cannot be translated) of the prayers. And,
significantly, "to pray" is "to *daven*"—to say the liturgy aloud yet quietly and
privately. Each one prays by himself, and all come together only at a few points
in the service. The prayer-leader performs the function of saying the prayers on
behalf of the entire congregation—that is what he is there for—and he will repeat
the opening or closing words of a prayer simply to keep the congregation
informed as to where in the service one ought to be. A delicate balance is
maintained between the individual and the community.

In Reform and most Conservative synagogues, on the other hand, prayer is
primarily collective; much of the service is read by the rabbi of the Reform
Temple, with the congregation responding in unison at certain points or saying
prayers together. The rabbi takes a dominant role unknown to the *shaliah sibbur,*
or "agent of the community," of the classical synagogue.

In the recent past many Jews in the West have come to reject the Western
liturgical customs, following chiefly along Protestant lines, adopted in the modern synagogues. They have found these modes contrary to the needs of "true
worship." Yet it must be observed that if you visit an Eastern rite Christian
church, a Greek Orthodox or Russian Orthodox service, for example, you will
not regard the classical Jewish mode of worship as entirely without its affinities
and parallels. Rejecting the Protestant mode of worship does not guarantee the
discovery of something quintessentially Jewish. What is essential to Judaism are
the words which are said.

4.

lord of creation

From *Weekend Prayer Book,* edited by Jules Harlow (N.Y.: Rabbinical Assembly of America, 1962), pp. 42–45. © 1961 by The Rabbinical Assembly of America. Reprinted by permission of the Rabbinical Assembly.

Praised are You, O Lord our God, King of the universe.
You fix the cycles of light and darkness;
You ordain the order of all creation.
You cause light to shine over the earth;
Your radiant mercy is upon its inhabitants.

In Your goodness the work of creation
Is continually renewed day by day.
How manifold are Your works, O Lord!
With wisdom You fashioned them all!
The earth abounds with Your creations.

O King, who alone is exalted from of old,
Praised and glorified since the world began,
Eternal God, our shield and our protection,
Lord of our strength, and Rock of our defense,
With Your infinite mercy, continue to love us. . . .

He is the Lord of wonders;
His goodness is for all time;
Daily He renews the work of creation.

So sang the Psalmist: Give thanks
To Him who made the great lights,
For His loving kindness is everlasting.

O cause a new light to shine on Zion;
May we all soon be worthy to behold its radiance.
Praised are You, O Lord, Creator of the heavenly bodies.

5.

revealer of the torah

From *Weekday Prayer Book,* edited by Jules Harlow (New York: Rabbinical Assembly of America, 1962), pp. 45–46. © 1961 by The Rabbinical Assembly of America. Reprinted by permission of The Rabbinical Assembly.

Deep is Your love for us, O Lord our God;
Bounteous is Your compassion and tenderness.
You taught our fathers the laws of life,
And they trusted in You, Father and King.

For their sake be gracious to us, and teach us,
That we may learn Your laws, and trust in You.
Father, merciful Father, have compassion upon us;
Endow us with discernment and understanding.

Grant us the will to study Your Torah,
To heed its words and to teach its precepts.
May we observe and practice its instruction,
Lovingly fulfilling all its teachings.

Enlighten our eyes in Your Torah,
Open our hearts to Your commandments.
Unite our thoughts with singleness of purpose
To hold You in reverence and in love.

Then shall we never be brought to shame.
We will delight and exult in Your help;
In Your holiness do we trust.

Bring us safely from the corners of the earth,
And lead us in dignity to our holy land.
You, O God, are the Source of deliverance;
You have chosen us from all peoples and tongues.

You have drawn us close to You;
We praise You and thank You in truth.
With love do we thankfully proclaim Your unity,
And praise You who chose Your people Israel in love.

6.

hear, o israel!

From *Weekday Prayer Book,* edited by Jules Harlow (New York: Rabbinical Assembly of America, 1962), pp. 47-49. © 1961 by the Rabbinical Assembly of America. Reprinted by permission of the Rabbinical Assembly.

Hear, O Israel: The Lord our God, the Lord is One.

Praised be His sovereign glory for ever and ever.

You shall love the Lord your God with all your heart, with all your soul, with all your might.

These words which I command you this day shall be in your heart. You shall teach them diligently to your children. You shall talk about them at home and abroad, night and day.

You shall bind them as a sign upon Your hand; they shall be as frontlets between your eyes, and you shall inscribe them on the doorposts of your homes and upon your gates. (Deut, 6:4–9)

Heed the Commandments

If you will earnestly heed the commandments which I give you this day, to love the Lord your God, and to serve Him with all your heart and with all your soul, then I will favor your land with rain at the proper season—rain in autumn and rain in spring—so that you will have an ample harvest of grain and wine and oil. I will assure grass in the fields for your cattle. You will eat to contentment.

Take care lest you be temped to forsake God and turn to false gods and worship them. For then the wrath of the Lord will be directed against you. He will close up the heavens and there will be no rain; the earth will not yield her produce. You will soon disappear from the good land which the Lord is giving you.

Therefore, keep these words of Mine in your heart and in your soul. You shall bind them as a sign upon your hand; they shall be as frontlets between your eyes.

Teach Your Children

You shall teach them to your children. You shall talk about them at home and abroad, night and day. You shall inscribe them upon the doorposts of your homes and upon your gates.

Then your days and the days of your children will be as many as the days of the heavens over the earth on the land which the Lord swore to give to your fathers. (Deut. 11:13–21)

Remember the Commandments

The Lord said to Moses: Tell the children of Israel that, throughout their generations, they shall make fringes on the corners of their garments, and add a thread of blue to the fringe of each corner.

When you look upon these fringes you will be reminded of all the commandments of the Lord and fulfill them. You will not be led astray by the inclinations of your heart or the allurements of your eyes.

Then you will remember and fulfill all My commandments and be holy before your God.

I am the Lord your God, who brought you out of the land of Egypt to be your God. I, the Lord, am your God. (Num. 15:37–41)

7.

saviour and redeemer

From *Weekday Prayer Book,* edited by Jules Harlow (New York: Rabbinical Assembly of America, 1962), pp. 49–52. © 1961 by The Rabbinical Assembly of America. Reprinted by permission of The Rabbinical Assembly.

You are our King and our fathers' King,
Our Redeemer and our fathers' Redeemer.
You are our Creator, our victorious stronghold;
You have ever been our Redeemer and Deliverer.

There can be no God but You.

Our Protector

You have been our fathers' protector of old,
Shield for them and their children,
Our Deliverer through all generations.

Though You dwell in the highest heights,
Your just decrees reach out everywhere.
They extend to the very ends of the earth.

Happy the man who obeys Your commandments,
Who lays to heart the words of Your Torah.

You are, in truth, Lord of Your people,
You are their Defender and mighty King.

You are the first and You are the last;
We have no King or Redeemer but You.

You, O Lord our God, rescued us from Egypt;
You redeemed us from the house of bondage.
The first born of the Egyptians were slain,
The first born of Your children were saved.

You split apart the waters of the Red Sea,
The faithful You rescued; the wicked drowned.
The waters engulfed the enemies of Israel;
Not one of the arrogant remained alive.

Then Your beloved sang hymns of thanksgiving;
They extolled You with psalms of adoration.

They acclaimed the King, God on high,
Great and awesome Source of all blessings,
The everliving God, exalted in His majesty.

He humbles the proud and raises the lowly;
He frees the captive and redeems the meek;
He helps the needy and answers His people's call.

Praises to the supreme God, ever praised is He!
Then Moses and all the children of Israel
Sang with great joy this song to the Lord:

Who is like You, O Lord, among the mighty?
Who is like You, so glorious in holiness?
So wondrous Your deeds, so worthy of praise!

The redeemed sang a new song to You;
They sang in chorus at the shore of the sea,
Acclaiming Your sovereignty with thanksgiving:

The Lord shall reign for ever and ever!

Rock of Israel, arise to Israel's defense!
Fulfill Your promise to deliver Judah and Israel.

Our Redeemer is the Holy One of Israel,
The Lord of hosts is His name.
Praised are You, O Lord, Redeemer of Israel.

part three

four aspects of torah

"Torah" clearly is the recurrent, central image in Judaism. It refers to many aspects of the Jewish tradition.

First, "Torah" means *the* Torah—the sacred scrolls kept in an ark in the synagogue, which contain the five books of Moses, or the Pentateuch: Genesis, Exodus, Leviticus, Numbers, and Deuteronomy. The Torah in this sense contains the fundamental teachings of Judaism: the doctrines, laws, and sacred narratives, which are regarded as the foundation of the tradition as a whole. The Torah-scroll is removed from its ark only to be carried in solemn procession around the synagogue and among the congregants. It is then read, in a beautiful and exact melody which goes back to antiquity. Afterward it is held up and displayed, and everyone affirms, "This is the Torah which Moses laid before the children of Israel on God's command." Finally, it is carried once more in procession and returned to its ark. These are the most dramatic moments in synagogue liturgy.

Second, while Torah refers to the Pentateuch, the Torah comes to include the entire Hebrew Scriptures, called in Judaism *Tanakh*—a word which includes the first letters of the three components of the Hebrew Bible, *Torah,* revelation; *Nevi'im,* prophets; and *Ketuvim,* writings; thus *TaNaKh.* These together correspond to what Christians call "the Old Testament."

Third, Torah means study of Torah, meditation, reflection upon the meaning of the Scriptures and traditions of Israel as these have accumulated over many centuries. Beyond meditation, however, is response in terms of one's contemporary situation to the meaning and message of Torah.

Fourth, Torah means interpretation of Torah, the intellectual processes of carrying on the study according to the issues and disciplines of one's own time. The Torah is claimed to be the basis for all truth, and therefore each generation has had to interpret the Torah in terms of the values of its own time. The task of interpretation, explanation, and exposition of the message of Judaism always begins in the sentences of Scripture.

We shall consider Torah in all four aspects.

8.

taking up the torah

Imagine entering the synagogue to witness the display of the Torah-scrolls and to hear the beautiful, precise reading of the pentateuchal lection. On the eastern wall of the synagogue, as the focus of all eyes, you see an ark, closed and covered by a richly embroidered velvet curtain. While all else may be in somber colors, the curtain will be bright, in red or yellow or blue. On it will be Hebrew words, Scriptural verses or, sometimes, the name of the person who gave the veil. Open the ark and before you will be not one but several, sometimes many, Torah-scrolls, each covered in velvet, often with silver or gold shields and crowns in richly filigreed design. Lift the Torah and you will hear bells, for the crowns contain small silver or gold bells, and when the Torah is moved, these tinkle. The procession with the Torah-scroll will be accompanied by the sound of bells. When the Torah is brought to the reading desk, its garments—crown and coverlet—will be removed, and the scroll will be unrolled. A pointer is supplied, for one does not touch the Torah-scroll itself. Look into the Torah and you will see long, wide columns of beautifully written Hebrew letters, each inscribed according to requirements laid down many centuries ago. The words are written on animal-skins, not on parchment, and these will last a very long time.

If you come on a Monday or Thursday, you will hear the words of the following selection as the Torah is carried around the congregation. Many of the congregants will reach out and touch the scroll, usually with the fringe of the prayer-shawl, and then kiss the fringe. Thus the Torah-scroll is displayed before all, then read, and finally, returned to its ark. These are the words recited during the dramatic processions.

From *Weekday Prayer Book*, edited by Jules Harlow (N.Y.; Rabbinical Assembly of America, 1962), pp. 82–90. © 1961 by the Rabbinical Assembly of America. Reprinted by permission of the Rabbinical Assembly.

On Opening the Ark

When the ark was carried onward, Moses exclaimed: Arise, O Lord, that Your enemies be scattered and those who would deny You be put to flight. For out of Zion shall go forth the Torah, and the word of the Lord out of Jerusalem.

Praised is He who in His holiness
Gave the Torah to His people Israel.

A Scroll of Torah

Reader:

Proclaim the greatness of the Lord;
Together let us exalt His glory.

Congregation:

Yours, O Lord, is the greatness and the power and the glory. Yours is triumph and majesty over all heaven and earth. Yours, O Lord, is supreme sovereignty.

Exalt the Lord our God, and worship Him for He is holy. Exalt and worship Him at His holy mountain. The Lord our God is holy.

Father of mercies, be merciful to us whom You have always sustained, and remember the covenant with the patriarchs. Deliver us from hours of darkness. You, who have upheld us, restrain the evil impulse within us and graciously grant us enduring deliverance. Answer our petition; grant us an overflowing measure of mercy and help.

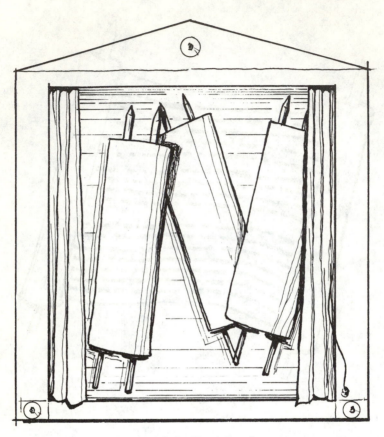

An Ark for Torah-Scrolls

On Raising the Torah Scroll

This is the Torah that Moses set before Israel.
This is the Torah given by God, through Moses.

It is a tree of life to those who hold fast to it;
All who uphold the Torah are blessed

Its ways are delight; its paths are peace.
In its right hand are length of days;
In its left hand are riches and honor.

The Lord, because of His righteousness,
Exalts the Torah and renders it glorious.

On Returning the Torah Scroll

Reader:

Praise the glory of the Lord; His glory is supreme.

Congregation:

His glory is high over heaven and earth. He exalts His people and extols His faithful, the sons of Israel who are close to Him. Halleluyah!

The Earth is the Lord's

A Psalm of David

The earth is the Lord's, and its fullness;
All the world, and all its inhabitants.
He founded it upon the seas;
He set it firm upon flowing waters.

Who may ascend the mountain of the Lord?
Who may stand in His holy place?
He who has clean hands and a pure heart,
Who takes not His name in vain, swearing falsely.

He will receive a blessing from the Lord,
A just reward from the God of his deliverance.
Such is the generation of those who seek Him,
Who, like Jacob, long for His Presence. Selah.

Lift high your lintels, O you gates;
Open wide, you ancient doors!
Let the King of glory enter.

Who is the King of glory?
The Lord, strong and mighty,
The Lord, triumphant in battle.

Lift high your lintels, O you gates;
Open wide, you ancient doors!
Let the King of glory enter.

Who is the King of glory?
The Lord, strong and mighty,
The Lord, triumphant in battle.

On Replacing the Torah Scroll

When the ark was at rest, Moses said: Return,
O Lord, to the myriads of the families of Israel.
Return, O Lord, to Your sanctuary,
You, and the ark of Your glory.

Let Your priests be robed in righteousness;
Let Your faithful sing with joy.
Do it for the sake of David, Your servant,
And do not reject Your anointed one.

Precious instruction do I give you:
Never forsake My Torah.

It is a tree of life to those who hold fast to it;
All who uphold the Torah are blessed.
Its ways are delight; its paths are peace.

Lead us back to You, and we shall return;
Renew our glory as in days of old.

9.

the message of torah: amos versus amaziah

shalom spiegel

How do Jews receive the message of the Torah? First of all, in the synagogue they hear Pentateuchal and prophetic writings read to them from week to week. If they know Hebrew, or if, as in Reform and some Conservative congregations, the passages are translated, they will hear and understand the sacred words. But it is primarily through the teachings of rabbis and other learned men and women that the message of the Torah is brought home to the people. For merely hearing the words hardly carries with it their message to each and every situation of life, to the actualities of a given time and place. The words of Torah have to be explained and carefully applied, so that their meaning will be made clear and exact.

Professor Shalom Spiegel of The Jewish Theological Seminary of America here gives a remarkable and imaginative account of one central teaching of Torah: justice is God's supreme command. Spiegel spoke these words on a dramatic occasion. It was a Sabbath luncheon, after morning worship, the Seminary professors and students assembled in honor of Chief Justice Earl Warren of the United States Supreme Court. Unexpectedly, President Harry Truman joined the assembly to honor the Chief Justice. Spiegel himself is a great man, and was perceived by his students as very great; he spoke with dignity and solemnity, yet with humor and grace. Everyone was aware of the meaning of the moment: What is Torah to say to the great men of the age, men deeply respected and admired by all present, and what is it to say that is profoundly and uniquely Jewish? Spiegel spoke without notes. Only later were his words transcribed, from his memory, and yet those present were sure this is, word for word, what was said.

This address is great because it was appropriate to the occasion and captures exactly what was fitting to the hour. Before reading, you would be wise to reread the entire Book of Amos. Then you will understand how Spiegel captures and gives life to the meaning of Amos's words for that particular hour.

From *Amos Versus Amaziah,* by Shalom Spiegel (New York: Herbert H. and Edith A. Lehman Series of the Hebrew Institute of Ethics, The Jewish Theological Seminary of America, 1957), pp. 10–24, 32–34, 39–44. This address was first given at The Jewish Theological Seminary of America Convocation on Law as a Moral Force, September 14, 1957. © 1957 by The Jewish Theological Seminary of America. Reprinted by permission of the author and The Jewish Theological Seminary of America.

The scene is Bethel in northern Israel, in the second half of the eighth pre-Christian century, a generation or so before the ten tribes of that kingdom were trampled in the dust or scattered to the winds by the fierce onslaught of Assyria. Amos, a shepherd from Tekoa, across the border in Judah, stirred up a commotion when, in a crowded assembly, perhaps in the temple of the realm, he told of dire visions his Lord had shown him:

> Thus He showed me: Behold, the Lord was standing beside a wall built by a plumbline, with a plumbline in His hand.
> And the Lord said unto me: "Amos, what do you see?" And I said, "A plumbline."
> Then the Lord said: "Behold, I am setting a plumbline in the midst of My people Israel, and I will never again pass by them. The high places of Isaac shall be desolate, and the sanctuaries of Israel shall be laid waste, and I shall rise against the house of Jeroboam with the sword."
> Then Amaziah, the priest of Bethel, sent to Jeroboam, king of Israel, saying: "Amos has conspired against you in the midst of the house of Israel; the land is not able to bear all his words. For thus Amos has said: 'Jeroboam shall die by the sword, and Israel must go into exile away from his land.' "
> And Amaziah said to Amos: "O seer, go, flee away to the land of Judah, and eat bread there, and prophesy there; but never again prophesy at Bethel, for it is the king's sanctuary, and it is a temple of the kingdom."
> Then Amos answered Amaziah: "I am no prophet, nor a prophet's son; but I am a herdsman, and a dresser of sycamore trees, and the Lord took me from following the flock, and the Lord said to me: 'Go, prophesy to My people Israel.' " (Amos 7: 7–15)

Amaziah at once instituted legal proceedings for the deportation of an undesirable alien. The Judean prophet promptly challenged his authority to deprive him of the right of free domicile and free speech in a sister state of the union. Fervently Amos declared that he had been summoned by the Lord to prophesy to His people Israel, a people one and indivisible whose union and covenant could not be lawfully dissolved by action of separate tribes or states, or even by their secession.

It stands to reason that the case *Amos vs. Amaziah* attracted wide attention in its own time and remained a *cause célèbre* to be discussed in law classes and debated in moot courts for generations. Unfortunately, Amaziah left no records of his own, or at least they have not survived. But the indictment of the prophet by the people and priests of Bethel, and the brief of argument prepared by the council of experts, were probably widely studied and excerpted in the textbooks and schools of antiquity. Maybe some day a fortunate discovery by the spade of an archeologist, in the warm sand dunes in the Judean desert or in a cave of the Dead Sea region, will turn up a tattered scroll with information now lost. Until such day or find, we must try to reconstruct the case of Amaziah solely on the basis of the scriptural account, the book of Amos. Still, we must remember that this book is but the deposition of the aggrieved party, a victim of expulsion, and that we owe his opponent, the priest of Bethel, a fair and full opportunity to state his version of the encounter with the seer of Tekoa.

It seems best to start with one initial assumption: that throughout the trial Amaziah never chose to challenge the accuracy of the transcript of public addresses as left by Amos himself or submitted on his behalf by his disciples, in short, essentially the record as preserved in Scripture. Only such a premise would make re-enactment of the trial at all possible in our day, in the absence of any other documentation. But even in his own day, Amaziah could reap thereby two advantages. He could considerably speed up all legal procedures, and if successful, could have the prophet condemned by his own mouth, as it were—a legal master stroke. Astutely, therefore, Amaziah would begin by reading from the speeches admittedly delivered by Amos, for example, the passage spoken in the sanctuary while the priests were offering sacrifices and the people beseeching Heaven to accept their alms and chants with favor:

> I hate, I despise your feasts, and I take no delight in your solemn assemblies.
> Even though you offer me burnt offerings and meal offerings, I will not accept them, nor will I look upon the peace offerings of your fatted beasts.
> Take away from Me the noise of your songs, and let Me not hear the melody of your harps.
> But let justice roll down like waters, and righteousness as a mighty stream.
> Did you bring to me sacrifices and offerings the forty years in the wilderness, O house of Israel?
>
> (Amos 5: 21–25)

The words, as rehearsed on the lips of the priest, did seem unmistakably a disturbance of public peace and interference with the rights of free worship. Such unwarranted provocation could not but throw any assembly, however orderly or decorous, into panic and pandemonium, in grave disregard of the fire laws, a clear and present danger to the life and limb of a throng of worshippers. Indeed no better case could be made, anywhere at any time, for immediate action by the police.

It was now up to the court to consider the measures taken by the temple police, and to review the validity of the prophet's banishment from Bethel. Naturally, Amaziah saw to it that his cause was buttressed by a formidable array of experts and leading representatives of public opinion.

The acknowledged head of religion in the realm, Amaziah spoke first, as was expected of him. In measured language, he voiced grave concern over the theological implications in the teachings of Amos, fraught, as he saw them, with hazard and heresy. This was the more dangerous precisely because some of Amos' tenets seemed plausible or even laudable, as, for example, his zeal for justice, and his commiseration with the needy and the poor. These were virtues which the just king Jeroboam and his priests at Bethel enjoined on all citizens, invariably urging pilgrims to the shrines to remember the destitute and help the disinherited. For they were indeed basic requirements of the covenant, primary duties of man to fellowman.

However, beyond and above these, extend the obligations of man to God, among them foremost regular ritual and worship in the sanctuary, which brought as a sweet savor to the Lord the gifts of His children, and implored for all of them the bounty of heaven: rain in season from above and springs in abundance from below, rich fields and teeming flocks, the fruit of the body and the fruit of the earth.

To be sure, in normal times, there need never arise a conflict between the claims of men upon each other and the claims of God upon men. However, should such collision of duties ever occur, there cannot be the slightest doubt which of the two demands must take precedence. Certainly what we owe to creature can never compare to what we owe to the Creator. If neglect of man be sin, neglect of God is sacrilege. This Judean seer, however, would have us turn the tables perversely. So long as men clamor for justice, he would forbid all acts of devotion in the sanctuary. Unless the needs of the poor be supplied, he would have us shut up all the establishments of the cult. But "the poor will never cease out of the land" (Deut. 15:11), which means that all the venerable rites in the temple as practiced by our ancestors from time immemorial, will have to be suspended, and the sacrifices stopped, and religion as known to us abolished from the face of the earth. It is a reckless doctrine, ruinous to worship and to the welfare of the commonwealth. For what are the solemn performances of ritual if not exercises in piety and patriotism? Indeed, what is sacrifice if not learning to give up for the common good? It is through such acts of renunciation—of food, of valuable possessions, of the inordinate part of our wills—that men are led to conform with the will of God and the requirements of religion. The rich and the rapacious are weaned of their selfishness and taught to share with the poor at least a part of their crop or wealth. Greed is thus subdued and charity towards the poor secured precisely through the observances and ordinances of organized religion.

Abolish altars and discontinue sacrifices, would not the lost and miserable be the first to suffer? It is the discipline of temple worship which trusts fear of the Lord even into the hearts of the mighty, enjoining them to divide their goods with their less fortunate brethren. Without such restraints and donations of piety, would not despair overtake the weak, the widow, and the orphan?

Amos threatens us with an earthquake for our alleged iniquities and abominations. Should *his* view ever prevail, and the land be bare of its altars and shrines and—God forbid—the affronted heavens refuse to yield rain, and the soil be blighted with draught, and man and cattle suffer famine and death, as happens anyhow from time to time; should his view prevail, would not the wretched and the hungry be first to seize the unblest prophet and drive him out in scorn, or in rage fling his mangled body beyond the gates of Bethel, to lie there unburied like the carcass of an ass?

A hushed dread hung over the court and crowd, as the priest spoke of perils to a country bereft of the protection of its divine rites. Now, sure of his impression on the audience, Amaziah turned in conclusion to Amos, speaking forgivingly and almost entreatingly: "O seer, go! Starry-eyed dreamer, impractical idealist, for your own safety, for the peace of your own soul, to keep your virtue untainted and your illusions undamaged, go away of your own accord, flee to the solitude of your flocks and forests of Tekoa!"

If, however, the shepherd should prove obstinate and refuse to leave, Amaziah felt duty-bound to submit to the court an official request and recommendation for deportation, signed without dissent by all the members of the College of Priests at Bethel.

The next speaker was chosen to represent the Association of the Bar of the City of Bethel. Skilled in the arts of rhetoric, and following the custom of the ancients, he would begin with a deft compliment to the wisdom and honesty of the court whose true administration of justice was the firmest pillar of good government. He would then proceed to win the favor of the crowd by a play for laughter. He would ridicule the simplistic jurisprudence of the shepherd of Tekoa with his appeal to the old, good days and ways of the desert: "Did you bring to me sacrifices and offerings the forty years in the wilderness, O house of Israel?" Such return to primitivism would wipe out all the advances of civilization won by a proud and prosperous people in half a millennium since it left the wasteland.

After such preliminaries, the speaker would proceed to the heart of his argument. Examined closely, the new doctrines of Amos amount to arbitrary abrogation of an undisputed part of legal theory and practice regulating the procedure in the gate and the rites of ancestral worship. They break with the tradition of secular and sacred law as heretofore known in Israel. How irresponsible, at bottom, his invocation of justice, always a sign of the ignorant layman unschooled to think in legal terms.

By easy, hazy appeals to righteousness and the whole cluster of virtues, he would have us disestablish the uncontested basis of all common law, whose working rule must be *stare decisis:* to adhere to and abide by decided cases. Without regard, indeed, without reverence for legal precedent, the scales of justice can not be kept even and steady; there would be no stability, no predictability, no certainty in the law. The courts would be thrown open to chance and whim and aribtrariness. There would be no desire for knowledge of law or legal precedent, hence also no need for the practice of law as a profession, and no demand for lawyers. This is no selfish or narrow professional appeal on behalf of the Bar. Without the safeguards of statutory law, and the standards of common law, and the canons of holy law, who would be the first victims of unscrupulous and bribable judges? Certainly not the rich and the haughty who can buy or bully justice in the gate, but the helpless, the fatherless, the friendless would be abandoned to greed and the guile of the moneyed, and to magistrates unrestrained by legal principle or precedent. Would not the very poor in desperation band together against their would-be tribune and cast his maimed body to the dunghill? To forestall mob outburst and lynch law which would sully the good reputation of the country, the lawyers of Bethel in duly convoked plenary session unanimously voted to ask for an injunction restraining the stranger of Tekoa from harrassing the public peace, returning him to his native land, in protective custody if necessary, until he had safely reached the borders of Judea.

The third to speak in court was a lady, appearing on behalf of the Daughters of the Confederacy—that is, the Confederacy of the Tribes of Israel. She found the message of the Judean herdsman very disturbing: "Are you not like the Ethiopians to Me, O children of Israel? says the Lord. Did I not bring up Israel from the land of Egypt, and the Philistines from Caphtor, and Aram from Kir?" (Amos 9:7). This seemed ill-bred, ill-tempered, and altogether illogical. Are we not Israel, and thus, unlike the heathen, in a very special and intimate and incomparable relation to the God of Israel? Of course, of course, since there is but one God, He must be the God of the whole world. But does this necessarily imply that God cares no more for the people of the covenant which He freed from bondage than he cares for their inveterate enemies, the uncircumcised Philistines? Naturally lines of communication must be maintained between the one God of the universe and all the peoples of the earth. We, the Daughters of the Confederacy, neither question nor deny any race equal access to the Lord, but cannot such access to the Lord be made *equal but separate?* The doctrine of equal but separate for white Israel and for dark-skinned Ethiopians would secure facilities of religious uplift to all, keeping them universal yet not uniform. Provisions permitting or even requiring the separation of the races do not necessarily imply inferiority of either race to the other. It is a fallacy that such a doctrine would stamp the colored race with the badge of inferiority. If this be so, it is not by reason of anything in Israel's religion or law, but solely because the colored Ethiopians choose to put that construction upon it.

In any event, the lady speaker concluded, there is no reason in the world why this unmannered, unneighborly agitator should be suffered to abuse the traditional freedom and amity of the fair peoples of the North.

Similar disapproval was voiced in the name of the Hebrew Legion, on behalf of the Veterans of the Israelitish Wars of Independence. The spokesman, in a neat army uniform, called attention to the slur on patriotism and danger to good citizenship, if the ideas of Amos were freely to be advocated: "You only have I known of all the families of the earth; therefore I will punish you for all your iniquities" (Amos 3:2). Such notions are plainly subversive of all soldierly and civic virtue, a threat to the security of the nation which had just emerged victorious from a long struggle with Aram. Consider also statements worded with deliberate slipperiness: "Behold, the eyes of the Lord God are upon the sinful kingdom, and I will destroy it from off the face of the earth, except that I will not utterly destroy the house of Jacob, said the Lord" (Amos 9:8). The ambiguity seems designed, permitting two interpretations. Either it is sheer bias in favor of Judah, called here "the house of Jacob," which will escape destruction, while the "sinful kingdom" or our northern realm is threatened with death by this partisan propagandist of the South. Or, still worse, the last clause with its negative particle placed conspicuously out of its customary word order in Hebrew, would seem to suggest that like any other guilty people, sinful Israel, too, will be destroyed: why should the house of Jacob alone claim exception from divine justice? This insults the valiant heroes of the nation and her slain on the field of battle who defended to the very last what all deemed their honor and their duty: "right or wrong— my country."

Amaziah received many messages of support which he wisely kept un-heralded. An expert in public relations, he shrewdly avoided even the faintest suspicion of being swayed by the pressure of lobbyists for private or collective interests. This is why no mention was made of the protest of the Chamber of Commerce in Bethel and Gilgal, alarmed at what a stoppage of pilgrimages to their shrines might do to the tourist trade of those holy cities. Nor would Ama-ziah release for publication vehement attacks on the prophet because of his denunciation of sacrifices and rejection of all offerings in the temples, which roused the ire of the *Meat and Poultry Purveyors,* the *Dairymen's League,* and the *Consolidated Wholesale Florists of Northern Israel.* Similarly, he ignored frantic appeals made by powerful temple unions such as the *Congress of Liturgical Organizations* which warned of disastrous unemployment, if the sanctuaries be closed.

Amaziah made only one exception, and disclosed a communication received from the *Israelitish Society of Composers, Authors, and Publishers,* known popu-larly as *ISCAP.* It minced no words about the boorishness of the Judean shepherd as shown in an utterance incredible in this day and age if it were not well attested: "Take away from Me the noise of your songs, and let Me not hear the melody of your harps." Such hostility to music and psalmody, such hatred of art and culture, shows up the man for what he is, an uncouth rustic and fanatic who should promptly be returned where he belongs, to his sheep and sycamores in Tekoa.

One could go on; with the benefit of hindsight it is easy to laugh at lost causes and caricature the past. That so much wit can be implied in the Writ, shows not only the pertinacity of human traits, but also the pertinence and recurring appeal of Scripture.

In justice to the ancients, however, we must not lose sight of the amazing freedom of speech in the northern kingdom of Israel. After all, Amos was not burned at the stake, nor liquidated in a political witch-craft trial, nor even condemned to drink the cup of hemlock by an enraged citizenry. He was permit-ted peaceably to repair to his native Tekoa where he wrote his book, which after two years—because of an earthquake he was believed to have foretold—made him nationally famous, and ultimately a part of the most widely read book in civiliza-tion.

In short, the banishment of Amos from Bethel proved an act of folly very soon. The prophet was vindicated within his lifetime by his own generation and upheld by every subsequent generation, no one dissenting. The decision of the clergy or court at Bethel was repudiated by the people, and one can say in a very real sense that it was *repealed* by the inclusion of the book of Amos in the biblical canon. It is this unanimous verdict of history, not the blunder at Bethel, which we have in mind when speaking of the case of *Amos vs. Amaziah.* This is the verdict which haunts the memory, and will forever merit the attention of students of religion and students of law. . . .

What makes *Amos vs. Amaziah* significant is that here religion compelled a break with pre-scientific thought. It is precisely religion which prompted and induced the advance toward universal standards, valid and applicable everywhere. It is the genius of monotheism which drove the herdsman of Tekoa to pry deeper into the difference between usage and law, between contingent custom and genuine general commandment. In a horizon meant to embrace all the peoples of the earth, as is the case in biblical religion, sooner or later one was bound to make the distinction between mores which fluctuated with the latitude and varied with the meridian, and conduct considered commonly and inherently right.

Some modes of behavior were arbitrary, simply idiosyncrasies of locality. Others were held and shared by all men, were recognized within the borders of Israel and acknowledged beyond them by Israel's foes, the Arameans; they were approved by the people of the covenant and by the uncircumcised Philistines, by fair-skinned Hebrews and dark-skinned Ethiopians, white and black alike. All these peoples and races had a variety of observances and practices which differed with the landscape. But all these peoples and races also were held by the biblical faith to be the children of one God, the father of all men. It would seem inconceivable, if underneath their variety a trace or token of their common origin did not remain. Whatever their differences, the fingerprint of the Creator should be discernible in all His creatures, stamping all as fellow-bearers of the divine image.

Amos found the divine signature in all men in their *sense of justice.* All men have an innate desire for the right, an inborn fear of arbitrary force, an instinctive response to wrong: It is not right! However failing or blundering, legal systems everywhere are but the attempt to articulate this desire for justice and to incarnate it in institutions capable of lifing from the brow of man the fright and curse of brutal force.

Now Amos was not a mandarin, intent upon "rectification of names," nor a professor, immersed in the varieties of anthropology or comparative law. Amos was a seer who beheld God the Lord setting a plumbline to the walls of Israel, and that vision gave him a measure for things human and divine.

Justice has always appeared binding upon men. Therein Amaziah did not differ from Amos. Only, to Amaziah, justice was an obligation like other obligations, a commandment among many commandments of the law. Injustice was improper, of course, but neither more nor less offensive than any other infringement of the rules.

Amos vs. Amaziah makes justice the *supreme command,* overriding every other consideration or obligation, however important to the life of the community. Justice becomes the categorical imperative, transcending all the other requirements of the law. Other ills of society are remediable, but injustice is a stab at the vital center of the communal whole. It instantaneously stops the heartbeat of the social organism. It cuts off the life-giving supply of health and strength that flow through the soul of the community, enabling its members to uphold the harmony, confidence and security of the covenant. The sheer threat and dread of arbitrary force terrorize and brutalize man. They throw him back into the state of nature and its savage standards: *Homo homini lupus.* Arbitrary force shatters the image of God in man.

Justice is the soil in which all the other virtues can prosper. It is the precondition of all social virtue, indeed of all community life. It makes civilized existence, it makes human existence possible. In every society justice must be the paramount concern, for it is the very foundation of all society:

> Let justice roll down like waters,
> And righteousness as a mighty stream.

By making justice the supreme end and the culminating claim, *Amos vs. Amaziah* at once established a clear distinction between duties of worship and duties of righteousness.

Worship in biblical religion could never be an end in itself, for God is not in need of ritual, as in magic religions of antiquity where the performance of the cult replenished the waning energies or dying fires of the divine. In Israel, worship is God's favor to man, an act of His grace intended for the good of man,—not God. These implications of the biblical faith *Amos vs. Amaziah* clearly recognized by making ritual subserve the ends of righteousness.

Ritual is propaedeutic to religion, exercise and training for spiritual life, discipline in the restraints of holiness. Worship is meant to inspirit man with passion for justice, to purify and prepare him for the encounter with God.

Where ritual becomes estranged from its aim and is pursued for its own sake, instead of facilitating an approach, it may clog and clutter it with impediments and importunities of its own; it may even make the very encounter, if possible, impossible. As an end in itself, ritual may become a stumbling block in religion.

Amos vs. Amaziah has served as an impassioned reminder of the ever present danger and disposition to confuse means with ends. Worship and ritual are means, while justice and righteousness are ends. More, even, righteousness and justice are the encounter. God is justice, and His holiness is exalted in righteousness.

Whenever and wherever such claims will be made in the course of history, and they will be numberless, the decision of *Amos vs. Amaziah* will be invariably invoked or inferred. The heirs to prophecy will rehearse and reaffirm this verdict in varied circumstances with varied stress and ever new choice of words, but the soul and substance of the message will remain unchanged. God requires devotion, not devotions. Sacrifice and prayer cannot serve as substitutes for justice. Fasts and penances may be indulged even by the wicked, while the righteous may delight in the merriments of life without detriment to virtue:

> Did not your father eat and drink
> And do justice and righteousness?
> Then it was well with him.
> He judged the cause of the poor and needy . . .
> Is not this to know Me?   (Jeremiah 22: 15f.)

In letter and in spirit it is the lesson and legacy of *Amos vs. Amaziah.*

Religion has never been the same since, for that historic decision made plain and clear what does please God most: not skill in worship but will to justice. That decision, however, reaches beyond the realm of religion and has influenced, also, all subsequent notions of biblical law.

10.

torah and response

ruth f. brin

The study of Torah is not for scholars alone. Every Jew is expected not only to listen to the words of revelation, but also to respond to them. Few are able to respond in such a way as to speak for many. One of those few is Ruth F. Brin, a Jewish mother and a poet in Minneapolis. Mrs. Brin takes as her creative task the writing of a response to each lection of the Torah through the year. We shall read the Scriptures as she reads them and then listen to her response. She allows us to grasp in a very concrete way the shape and substance of Jewish piety in the present age. Later we shall survey the ways in which Torah has been interpreted through the ages, but first we must confront not interpretation but the interpreter herself. The specific Torah-lections are given first; these are among the most exalted moments in the synagogue reading of Scriptures. Then we shall have Mrs. Brin's response to them, always pointed, pithy, and pertinent.

From *Interpretations for the Weekly Torah Reading,* by Ruth F. Brin (Minneapolis: Lerner Publications Co., 1965), pp. 16ff. © 1965 by Ruth F. Brin. Reprinted by permission of the author.

In the Beginning
Genesis 1:1–6, 9, 14, 26; 31 11:7, 8

In the beginning God created the heaven and the earth. Now the earth was unformed and void, and darkness was upon the face of the deep; and the spirit of God hovered over the face of the waters.

And God said, "Let there be light," and there was light.

And God saw the light that it was good, and God divided the light from the darkness.

And God called the light Day and the darkness He called Night, and there was evening and morning, one day.

And God said: "Let there be a firmament in the midst of the waters, and let it divide the waters from the waters."

And God said: "Let the waters under the heaven be gathered together unto one place, and let the dry land appear." And it was so . . .

41

And God said: "Let the earth put forth grass, herb yielding seed, and fruit-tree bearing fruit after its kind, wherein is the seed thereof upon the earth." And it was so.

And God said: "Let there be lights in the firmament of the heaven to divide the day from the night; and let them be for signs, and for seasons, and for days and years;" . . .

And God said: "Let us make man in our image, after our likeness; and let him have dominion over the fish of the sea, and over the fowl of the air, and over the cattle, and over all the earth, and over every creeping thing that creepeth upon the earth."

And God saw everything that He had made, and behold, it was very good.

Then the Lord God formed man of the dust of the ground and breathed into his nostrils the breath of life, and man became a living soul.

And the Lord God planted a garden eastward, in Eden, and there He put the man whom He had formed.

Interpretation

When the divine word ended chaos and nothingness,
when God rolled away the darkness from the light,
that was the first moment of creation.

When Adam opened his eyes and beheld earth and heaven,
that was a moment of creation as real as the first,

For the sun is not bright without an eye to see,
the waves of the sea cannot crash and roar
without an ear to listen,

And unless life marks off the segments,
time is a dimension without measure.

Though we are finite,
God created us both free and conscious,
able to share in His power of creation.

Every moment that we behold anew the work of God,
the jewels of dew on morning grass,
the smile lighting the face of a beloved child,

Every moment that we work for good,
is a moment of creation.

Lord God, renew in us, in every man,
the morning of Adam's awakening;

Let each dawn rise fresh with hope
as it was in the beginning,

Inspire us to create what is good;
quicken our delight in all Thou createst.

Passage of the Red Sea
Exodus XIV:10, 15, 22, XV:8, 13, 18

And when Pharaoh drew nigh, the children of Israel lifted up their eyes, and behold, the Egyptians were marching after them;

And they were sore afraid; and the children of Israel cried out to the Lord
. . .

And the Lord said unto Moses, "Wherefore criest thou unto Me? Speak unto the children of Israel, that they go forward . . ."

And the children of Israel went into the midst of the sea upon the dry ground; and the waters were a wall unto them on their right hand and on their left.

And after they had crossed the Red Sea, Moses sang unto the Lord:

"With the blast of Thy nostrils
the waters were piled up,

"The floods stood upright as a heap;
the deeps were congealed in the heart of the sea . . .

"Thou didst blow with Thy wind, the sea covered them;
They sank as lead in the mighty waters.

"Who is like unto Thee, O Lord, among the mighty?
Who is like unto Thee, glorious in holiness,
fearful in praises, doing wonders?

"Thou in Thy love hast led the people that Thou hast redeemed;
Thou hast guided them in Thy strength to Thy holy habitation . . .

"The Lord shall reign forever and ever."

Interpretation

Here it is written: speak unto the children
of Israel that they go forward . . .

Might we have gone backward into slavery,
had we chosen to forsake Moses?

Who is like unto Thee, O Lord,
Who hast given us the gift of history?

Who is like unto Thee, glorious in holiness,
Who hast delivered our destiny into our own hands?

Of all the wonders Thou hast wrought,
We praise Thy name for this:

That Thou hast created a world whose workings
man can probe with the marvelous tool of his mind,
and alter with the skillful work of his hands,

That Thou in thy love hast given us the gift of
freedom to choose our own ways to seek redemption,
to find for ourselves Thy holy habitation.

The Lord shall reign forever and ever.

The Ten Commandments
Exodus XX:2–14

I am the Lord Thy God who brought thee out of the land of
Egypt, out of the house of bondage.
    It is God Himself who speaks to us, neither
    a legislature, nor a court, nor a ruler,
    but God. And He speaks to each of us singly.

Thou shalt have no other gods before Me.
    Idolatry no longer tempts us, yet we have
    a new sin in our age: to have no God at all.
    We withhold ourselves and our loyalty from
    every good cause, and thus from God Himself.

Thou shalt not take the name of the Lord, thy God, in vain.
    Thoughtlessly and frequently, we profane the
    name of God in common speech, rendering it
    meaningless in prayer.

Remember the Sabbath day to keep it holy.
    We often forget the Sabbath; we seldom meditate
    on the marvels of creation; and we rarely concern
    ourselves with holiness.

Honour thy father and thy mother.
    Children sometimes disobey their parents.
    Adults neglect their aged relatives and debase
    the elderly with disrespect and lack of concern.

Thou shalt not murder.
    Though we do not murder, we glorify war,
    reward aggression, and ignore the sanctity
    of the individual soul.

Thou shalt not commit adultery.
> Can we consider ourselves innocent of
> this sin so long as our society places
> stimulation and temptation in the way of
> youth?

Thou shalt not steal.
> Some of us have stolen property—legally or
> illegally—others have stolen men's hearts
> through deceit and trickery.

Thou shalt not bear false witness
against they neighbour.
> We gossip, we slander, we speak falsely.

Thou shalt not covet.
> We covet the cars, the houses, the trips,
> and the clothes of our friends. We display
> our own wealth to excite the envy of others.

Interpretation

God has spoken, and we have not listened,
He has commanded and we have not obeyed.

Yet return is in the power of man,
and forgiveness is a promise God makes us.

We pray for honesty this day
to measure ourselves against these commandments.

We pray for strength this day
to follow these words of God.

Ordinances
Exodus XXII:20, 21, 22, XXIII:1, 7, 8, 9

And a stranger shalt thou not wrong, neither shalt thou oppress him; for ye were strangers in the land of Egypt.

Ye shall not afflict any widow, or fatherless child.

If thou afflict them and they cry out to Me, I will surely hear their cry . . .

Thou shalt not utter a false report; put not thy hand with the wicked to be an unrighteous witness . . .

Keep thee far from a false matter; and the innocent and righteous slay thou not; for I will not justify the wicked.

And thou shalt take no gift; for a gift blindeth them that have sight, and perverteth the words of the righteous.

And a stranger shalt thou not oppress; for ye know the heart of a stranger, seeing ye were strangers in the land of Egypt.

Interpretation

We were strangers in Egypt and Kiev,
we were foreigners in Babylon and Berlin,

We were outsiders and wanderers
in Spain and Poland and France.

We looked at the citizens of those lands
with the dark pleading eyes of the alien.

Our hearts beat the hesitant beat
of men wihtout rights, fearful and uncertain.

We pray Thee help us to remember
the heart of the stranger
when we walk in freedom,

Help us to be fair and upright
in all our dealings with every man.

Oh, burn and brand the lesson
of all the years and all the lands
on our hearts.

Lord, make us forever strangers
to discrimination and injustice.

Holiness
Leviticus XIX:2, 3, 5, 11, 13–15, 17, 18, 34

Ye shall be holy; for I the Lord your God am holy.

Ye shall fear every man his mother, and his father, and ye shall keep My sabbaths; I am the Lord your God . . .

And when ye offer a sacrifice of peace-offerings unto the Lord, ye shall offer it that ye may be accepted . . .

Ye shall not steal; neither shall ye deal falsely, nor lie to one another.

And ye shall not swear by My name falsely, so that thou profane the name of thy God; I am the Lord.

Thou shalt not oppress thy neighbour, nor rob him; the wages of the hired servant shall not abide with thee all night until the morning.

Thou shalt not curse the deaf, nor put a stumbling-block before the blind, but thou shalt fear Thy God: I am the Lord.

Ye shall do no unrighteousness in judgment; thou shalt not respect the person of the poor, nor favour the person of the mighty; but in righteousness shalt thou judge thy neighbour.

Thou shalt not go up and down as a tale-bearer among thy people; neither shalt thou stand idly by the blood of thy neighbour: I am the Lord.

Thou shalt not hate thy brother in thy heart; thou shalt surely rebuke thy neighbour and not bear sin because of him.

Thou shalt not take vengeance, nor bear any grudge against the children of thy people, but thou shalt love thy neighbour as thyself: I am the Lord . . .

And if a stranger sojourn with thee in your land, ye shall not do him wrong.

The stranger that sojourneth with you shall be unto you as the home born among you, and thou shalt love him as thyself; for ye were strangers in the land of Egypt; I am the Lord your God.

Interpretation

In the center of Torah is the book of Leviticus,
In the middle of Leviticus is the chapter on holiness,

At the core of the chapter or holiness
is the command to love your neighbor as yourself.

In the midst of Israel is the individual Jew,
trying to begin by loving his neighbor,
and finally to become holy, as God Himself is holy.

But before he can love his neighbor,
he must have achieved a certain love of himself;
Before he can revere his parents,
he must have struggled to fulfill the demands
of parenthood himself;

Before he can love the stranger,
he must have been a stranger in a harsh land.

Lord, how can we possibly experience enough
and understand enough
to love as Thou lovest, and so to be holy,
as Thou art holy?

From the deep center of our beings, Lord our God,
we pray to Thee: lead us toward wisdom and humility,
teach us compassion and understanding.

For we long to feel the holiness of Thy presence
at the inmost center of our lives.

II.

torah and interpretation

fritz a. rothschild

Clearly, the interpretation of Torah and response to its message in terms of varied circumstances are not limited to contemporary America. The exegesis of Scripture has gone on for as long as Scripture has existed, and that by definition. For once the words were written down, they had to be made "oral" again, to be removed from their fixed and written condition and made to live in the lives of people. This process of making the Torah's teaching vivid requires the effort to show its message speaks not to a historical time, but to all times, not to a particular culture, but to every mode of human civilization. One recurrent problem is philosophical. The Scriptures reflect a single view of reality, one which rapidly was superseded and made obsolete. The traditionalist will be one who looks back on the meaning of Scripture to some earlier time and regards it as permanent and exhaustive. The modernist in any period is one who claims Scripture is permanently in flux, always changing in its details and effects, but enduring and unchanging as to its fundamental message.

Here Fritz A. Rothschild, a Jewish theologian who is professor at the Jewish Theological Seminary of America, describes the course of biblical interpretation in the history of Judaism. He does so in terms of the issue, Is it appropriate to "interpret" Scriptures at all, or is there some single and abiding meaning which must include the convictions and conceptions of an earlier time?

From "Truth and Metaphor in the Bible. An Essay on Interpretation," by Fritz A. Rothschild, *Conservative Judiasm* XXV, 3, 1971, pp. 3–22. The article is condensed from a version in *The Teachers' Guide to Genesis* (New York: The Melton Research Center of The Jewish Theological Seminary of America, 1966). © 1971 by The Rabbinical Assembly of America. Reprinted by permission of The Rabbinical Assembly.

Both the "modernists" and the "traditionalists" share three assumptions: (1) There is only one meaning of the text that has been authorized by tradition; that meaning was taught in our religious schools until the onset of modern scholarship and secular culture. (2) Attempts to study the Bible in the light of contemporary science and philosophy must lead to a break with the traditional understanding of the text. (3) The present-day confrontation of the tradition and modern scholarship constitutes a new and radical crisis for the contemporary Jew, and presents us with an unprecedented problem in our educational enterprise.

Accepting these common assumptions, modernists and traditionalists draw opposite and often unhappy conclusions. The modernists often feel guilty of having betrayed the age-old legacy of ancestral faith; and the traditionalists realize that the challenges of biblical criticism, science, and philosophy cannot really be met by passing them over in silence. Many a loyal traditionalist must have felt like the two old Victorian ladies who, when first learning of Darwin's theory of evolution, said: "Let's hope it's not true, and if it is, let's hush it up!"

Now it cannot be denied that the modern scientific revolution has created tremendous problems for Jewish religion in general and for the teaching of the Bible in particular. Historical scholarship, the study of comparative religion, the documentary theory of the Pentateuch . . . all these and the implications of modern science present formidable challenges to traditional formulations of Judaism. But it would be wrong to accept without *questioning* the assumptions which we mentioned earlier. We shall try to show in this paper that the idea of a single timelessly valid and authoritative sense of Scripture is a figment of the imagination.

The reasons why such a single meaning cannot exist are both sociological and theological. Sociologically, the meaning of any document depends to some extent on the cultural resources, the linguistic skills, and the particular interests of the reader.[1] The theological assumption that faith in the divine nature of the Torah necessitates a monolithic and unchangeable interpretation of it is a mistaken notion, as is reflected in the history of Jewish Bible interpretation. On the contrary, the view that the Bible contains God's message to man has led to ever new interpretations, since it constantly forced believing readers to reconcile the words of the sacred text with whatever they held to be true on the basis of their own experience, the canons of logic, contemporary science, and their moral insights.

Certainly, the non-believer is under no compulsion to reject older interpretations of the text which contradict the truth of his time and thus denigrate the value of the Bible; while the traditionalist will always feel called upon to interpret the text so that it reflects not ancient error but the highest standards of trustworthy knowledge and insight of his own time. If one believes that the Torah contains eternal truth and valid guidance, it follows that its teachings should be explained and applied to changing situations. Indeed, this is a pre-condition for the sort of appreciation of the Bible that alone can command the loyalty and trust of intelligent people. To freeze a particular understanding of the text and canonize it as the only legitimate one makes its message irrelevant and defeats its very purpose.

Since the traditional study of the Bible adapts itself to changes and advances in knowledge (contrary to the first assumption above), it follows that the study of the Bible in the light of contemporary knowledge, far from leading to a "break with tradition" (the second assumption) is in fact a continuation of traditional practice. Thus the third assumption, that the present-day confrontation of traditional piety and modern scholarship has no parallel in our history, also breaks down. Without denying that the present crisis is more radical and in some ways unique, we ought to realize that basically we face the type of challenge which has confronted our sages and thinkers in every epoch of Judaism.

A Historical Survey

Far from being guilty of having betrayed our heritage, the teacher who expounds the Bible in the light of the best available knowledge stands within the authentic tradition of our faith.

Philo of Alexandria (20 B.C.E.-45 C.E.) was committed to the belief that the highest philosophical knowledge, theology and ethics, or, as he calls them, "the worship of God" and "the regulation of human life," are to be found in the Torah of Moses. Although he emphasized the superiority of Scripture revealed by God over philosophy which represents the imperfect gropings of the human mind, he demanded that we never interpret the Bible in a manner contrary to reason or expectation (common-sense), or unworthy of the dignity of God's inspired words. His opinion on what is worthy of God's dignity reflects the intellectual ideals he had imbibed from the great philosophical schools of Greece. He distinquished the *literal* or *obvious* meaning of a text from the *underlying* or *allegorical* meaning which explains a text in terms of something else. In the case of Philo this something else is his understanding of an inner, deeper, more spiritual meaning and his denial of anthropomorphism. The words "God is not a man" (Num. 23:19) is understood by Philo as enunciating the principle of denying physical attributes to the Deity. While believing that the laws of the Torah are to be observed literally, Philo seems to vary in his opinion on the historical narratives of the Pentateuch, sometimes accepting both the literal and the allegorical meaning, and sometimes denying the literal sense of a passage in favor of an intellectually or morally instructive interpretation.

Although Philo did not have any traceable, direct influence on Jewish exegesis, his indirect effect was immense. The Christian Church Fathers took over his allegorical method, and from them Islamic thinkers borrowed it and thus transmitted it to the great medieval Jewish philosophers. His distinction between the literal and the underlying sense of the Torah, and his conviction that Holy Scripture yields the most profound spiritual and moral truths to the enlightened interpreter, have been influential even where the particular results of allegorical exegesis were rejected by later generations.

Rabbinic literature dealt with the problems not only of scriptural passages which taken at face value were unworthy of the dignity of God, but of statements which seemingly contradicted the moral standards the Rabbis had learned from the Bible, and of others which denigrated the honor and worth of the Jewish people and its heroes.

The statement in the fifth commandment that God "rested on the seventh day" clearly did not seem to agree with the idea of Divine omnipotence and led to the rhetorical question of the *Mekhilta:* "And is He subject to such a thing as weariness?" The solution which is offered proves, by the use of other biblical quotations, that the *peshat* (plain or literal meaning) must be abandoned. We quote it in full to show how the Sages justified their changed interpretation of the text:

Has it not been said: "The Creator of the ends of the earth fainteth not, neither is weary" (Is. 40:28)? And it says: "He gives power to the faint" (ibid. vs. 29). And it also says: "By the word of the Lord were the heavens made," etc. (Ps. 33:6). How then can Scripture say: "And rested on the seventh day?" It is simply this: God let it be written about Him that He created His world in six days and rested, as it were, on the seventh. Now by the method of *qal va-homer* you must reason: If He, for whom there is no weariness, let it be written that He created His world in six days and rested on the seventh, how much more should man, of whom it is written: "but man is born to toil" (Job 5:7), rest on the seventh day.[2]

Changed ideas about the religious factor in social and family behavior also led to significant re-interpretations by the aggadists. Ruth, the Moabitess says to her mother-in-law: "Entreat me not to leave you and to return from following you; for where you go I will go, and where you lodge, I will lodge; your people shall by my people, and your God my God . . ." (Ruth 1:16). The text says nothing about Ruth having made her decision on religious grounds; on the contrary, her resolve not to abandon Naomi and to stick with her through thick and thin is the guiding motive which (since ethnic loyalty could not be separated from religious loyalty) makes her accept even Naomi's God. Now, to the rabbis who saw in Ruth the exemplar of the true proselyte, it was inconceivable that her conversion was merely the by-product of her loyalty to her mother-in-law. Hence they had to re-interpret the passage in the light of their convictions:

> "Entreat me not to leave you" . . . In any case, I had made up my mind to convert to Judaism, and it is best to do so through you and not someone else! When Naomi heard this she began to expound (to Ruth) the laws concerning converts . . .[3]

The popularity and near-canonization of Rashi's commentary on the Torah by generations of Jews can largely be attributed to the fact that he combined a genius for explaining the text according to the *peshat,* with a sensitivity for those passages where the plain meaning led to the kinds of difficulties which we have mentioned. Whenever that happened, he fell back on the fund of "revisionist" aggadic interpretations, of which we have offered some instances, and incorporated them in his work. Thus Rashi supplied what seemed to many readers "the" correct and authoritative interpretation of the Torah. It also explains why his particular reading of the text—reflecting as it does the needs of a particular phase in history—cannot possibly be accepted as the only authentic interpretation in perpetuity.

Saadya Gaon (892–942), in his *Book of Beliefs and Opinions* (*Emunot ve-Deot*), is the first medieval philosopher of religion who supplies a methodological guide for biblical interpretation.

He justifies deviation from the *peshat,* where it is demanded by one of four factors: sense perception, reason, other scriptural statements, and tradition. This approach had a liberating influence on all subsequent exegesis. Since it leaves to the interpreter the task of reconciling the claims of the literal sense with rational and empirical considerations and the oral tradition, it makes reason—namely the interpreter's—the dominant factor in the understanding of Scripture.

Maimonides (1135–1204) developed biblical hermeneutics based on rational considerations to a point where an "inner" speculative meaning beyond the "outer" and common meaning of key terms and narratives was presented as the true and primary meaning of Scripture. The *Moreh Nevukhim (Guide of the Perplexed),* although not written as a commentary on the Bible, is nevertheless devoted to

> biblical exegesis of a particular kind. That kind of exegesis is required because many biblical terms and all biblical similes have an apparent or outer and a hidden or inner meaning; the gravest errors as well as the most tormenting perplexities arise from men's understanding the Bible always according to its apparent or literal meaning.[4]

Maimonides was convinced that fasting and praying were not sufficient to enable men to come close to God; intellectual knowledge is required in addition to the observance of the *mitzvot.* Thus, for example, affirmation of the necessary existence, unity and incorporeality of God is essential for Jewish faith. Physics (*ma'aseh bereshit*) and metaphysics or theology (*ma'aseh merkavah*) are the noblest topics of true religious knowledge.

The need for a novel branch of hermeneutics, philosophical exegesis, follows inevitably if we consider Maimonides' basic presuppositions: 1) The Bible contains God's word and hence theoretical as well as practical guidance. 2) Since it is intended for the instruction of all the people and not only the intellectual elite, it operates on two levels, the exoteric (outer) and the esoteric (inner). 3) It must be possible to extract from the Bible the highest theoretical knowledge, that of nature (*ma'aseh bereshit*) and of the Deity (*ma'aseh merkavah*), as far as these are within the grasp of man. 4) But the Bible does not in its surface meaning contain such speculative information couched in philosophical language. 5) Therefore it must be possible to understand biblical terms and figures of speech in such a way that they can be translated into doctrines of philosophy and theology by the enlightened, while conveying to the uninitiated useful exoteric instruction.

In the *Guide,* where the philosophically competent reader is addressed, thirty-two chapters are "lexicographic," i.e., devoted to a discussion of biblical terms, and the initiated reader is shown how the esoteric truths of Judaism ("the true knowledge of the Torah") can be extracted. In the first book of the *Mishneh Torah,* the indispensable minimum of theology necessary for meaningful and saving faith is rendered in more popular fashion for the benefit of the general reader.

Apart from the intrinsic philosophical merit of Maimonides' work (which is, of course, the most important aspect to the theologian), his emphasis on figurative language, simile, and metaphor focuses on problems of biblical interpretation which will occupy us even though we may not be concerned as he as with the Bible as a textbook of philosophical theology.

The *Kabbalah* as crystallized in the Zoharic corpus[5] uses the form of biblical commentary to expound mystical doctrines which to the critical reader seem to be less interested in what can be found *in* the Torah than to read *into* it the theosophical teachings of its author(s). But we ought to be careful when making such a distinction. David Neumark, historian of Jewish philosophy, once said that "even the critical reader is occasionally plagued by doubts whether the true interpretation of certain passages of the Torah may not after all be found here (i.e. in the *Zohar*) and nowhere else."[6]

The Zohar, like the exegesis of Maimonides and other medieval philosophers, is also driven to a doctrine of inner (*setima*) and outer (*galya*) meaning. If God's word contains the highest knowledge attainable to man, then it simply cannot be limited to stories of mundane happenings as recounted in so many biblical passages.

> Come and behold: there are garments that everyone sees, and when fools see a man in a garment that seems beautiful to them, they do not look more closely. But more important than the garment is the body, and more important than the body is the soul. So likewise the Torah has a body, which consists of the commandments and ordinances of the Torah, which are called *gufey torah,* "bodies of the Torah." Fools see only the garment, which is the narrative part of the Torah; they know no more and fail to see what is under the garment. Those that know more see not only the garment but also the body that is under the garment. But the truly wise, the servants of the Supreme King, those who stood at the foot of Mount Sinai, look only upon the soul, which is the true foundation of the entire Torah, and one day indeed it will be given them to behold the innermost soul of the Torah.[6a]

It is in identifying the nature of the inner meaning that the Zohar diverges from the philosophical exegetes. The aim of mystical enlightenment is not intellectual knowledge of physics and metaphysics, but intuitive understanding of the hidden Divine life which pulsates from its source, the *En Sof,* through the realms of the ten *sefirot* [spheres]. The Torah is at once an organism, a cosmic pattern and a symbolic description of the Divine life process. Functioning on many levels in the ontological realm the Torah is also seen as functioning in the realm of communication (or revelation), as the source of multiple, perhaps even infinite meanings. Thus a distinction is made between the Primordial Torah, the Written Torah and the Oral Torah, corresponding to the *sefirot* of *Hokhmah* (Wisdom), *Tiferet* (Compassion) and *Malkhut* (the last *sefirah* of Divine Judgment). Another distinction among levels of exegesis found in the Zoharic corpus is the fourfold division symbolized by the term *Pardes: peshat,* the literal meaning; *remez,* the allegorical or philosophical meaning; *derash,* the talmudic or aggadic interpretation; and *sod,* the deepest mystical or theosophical meaning.

Strange as the threefold distinction of primordial, written and oral Torah and their assignments to three levels of the "sefiratic" hierarchy may appear to modern readers, it embodies a principle which, when reformulated in less esoteric terms, is a valuable tool in dealing with certain aspects of Torah interpretation. The belief in Divine revelation implies the absolute and infinite nature of the Giver of the Torah and the limited, time-and-language-bound nature of its recipients. The tension implicit in this polarity cannot be avoided by anyone who takes the claim of the Torah as Holy Torah is complemented by the ongoing activity of appropriation and acceptance of the message in every generation. Since the medium of Torah is *language,* and since language is never self-explanatory, acceptance of Torah necessiatates the activity of interpretation. The supernal or primordial Torah may be of infinite potential meaning, but in order to become available to finite man it has to be expressed in a fixed text. This text, combining the allusiveness and depth of its ineffable inspiration with the ordered structure of literary formulation, in turn becomes the source for the oral tradition which allots meanings and allows for their application to specific situations.

The reader who has followed us so far is doubtless aware that our bird's-eye view of a few selected types of exegesis cannot have been intended as a handy guide to the history of Jewish Bible interpretation. Its aim is rather to introduce some of the problems which face the contemporary teacher of the Torah, and which, to some extent, face anyone engaged in the understanding of an important text.

Words by their very nature are not self-centered, immanent and isolated entities; they function as intermediaries ("media"), and their function is the joint result of a variety of factors. A word is spoken (or written) *by* someone and refers *to* something *for* someone else. It stands for something other than itself. If we realize that most words function in multi-stage pointings beyond themselves, it will become even clearer how formidable the basic problem of interpretation is. Apart from (though not independent of) matters of historical, syntactical, and other contexts, the chief problem of interpretation is the relation between primary (first order) meaning and metaphor.

Peshat and Metaphor

The critical reader may feel that, despite our parade of authorities, no convincing case has been made for rejecting the literal sense of Scripture. He might be tempted to quote the talmudic dictum: "A biblical passage never loses its literal meaning" (*Shabbat* 63a). He might point out that the authorities we have cited had recourse to metaphor, allegory or esoteric meanings only when the plain meaning led to difficulties or inconsistencies. Philo and Maimonides were aware that the allegorical method, if applied by radicals to the *mitzvot* of the Torah, could lead to an explaining away rather than an explaining of the obligatory nature of religious law.

Let us deal with this issue by taking a verse which challenges the teacher of Genesis at the very beginning: "God said: 'Let there be light'; and there was light . . ." (Gen. 1:3). Many teachers have pondered the question of its interpretation. Do we really mean to teach the plain sense of this verse, namely, that God did in fact at the outset of His creative work say these words and then light appeared? Or are the fanciful interpretations that reject the *peshat* so many attempts to hide the fact that we have no real faith in the truth of the literal sense of our verse?

We think that the way of meeting this question head-on is by asking a

counterquestion: What *could* the 'literal' meaning of the verse possibly be? Does
the advocate of the *peshat* maintain that God at a certain moment of time (but
there was no time in our sense before Creation) uttered two Hebrew words? (But
to utter words presupposes a vibration of air by a being equipped with physical
organs such a vocal cords, in order to reach the ears of other sentient beings—
and there was no air, and no possible listener, and the idea of God as "speaking"
in the literal sense of that word is anthropomorphism of the crudest kind!) We
do not have to belabor the point. Suffice it to add that if the verse could be
accepted as a plain statement, questions such as "Did God speak with a loud
voice?" or "Did He use the Ashkenazic or Sephardic pronunciation of Hebrew?"
would be legitimate. But to frame such questions is to indicate their absurdity.
It is clear that in this passage (and many others) the real issue is not our acceptance or rejection of the *peshat,* but our inability to ascertain what the *peshat* is
in the first place. Metaphor, simile, analogical language and myth, far from
undermining our ability to take the text seriously, are frequently the only way in
which we can hope to penetrate to its true meaning.

Saadya was trying to convey what he took to be the real meaning of our verse
when he translated it "And God *willed* that there be light." Maimonides was
trying to find the true intention of the passage when he wrote:

> "By the word of the Lord were the heavens made, and all the host of them by the
> breath of His mouth" (Ps. 33:6). In this verse God's acts are likened to those that
> proceed from kings, whose instrument in giving effect to their will is speech. However,
> God, may He be exalted, does not require an instrument by means of which He could
> act, for His acts are accomplished exclusively by means of His will alone; neither is
> there any speech at all. . . .[7]

No wonder that the complier of an anthology on the "plain meaning of Scripture"
from traditional sources comes to the conclusion that perhaps the best definition
of *peshat* is "all those Scriptural interpretations which our sages—early and late
—*thought* to be the *peshat.* . . .[8]

If the reader has learned from the foregoing that a simplistic approach to the
problems of exegesis leads to a *reductio ad absurdum,* he will be in a position to
see the efforts of commentators from Philo to the *Zohar* not as attempts to evade
the true understanding of the Torah, but as attempts to take the text seriously
and to read it in the light of the best methods at their disposal.

When we find it difficult to accept these interpretations of the text, we should
realize that the difficulty results from their having been deduced by a method
which we find unacceptable. This is due to the fact that methodologies change
in the light of available knowledge. If we wish to understand the Bible in the
twentieth century we have an obligation to bring to bear upon its interpretation
the best conceptual tools of our time and the fullest historical and philological
scholarship at our disposal. In other words: we shall need all the knowledge that
the philosophy of language and symbolism can contribute to the analysis of the
text as well as the results of scholarship dealing with ancient Near Eastern
cultures and comparative religion.

To show how that can be done, we shall devote the rest of this essay to the application of this principle to the Creation story. We shall do this in two steps: firstly by using linguistic analysis to clarify some aspects of metaphorical language, and secondly by applying this analysis to selected materials from comparative religion and the Genesis narrative.

Now it is sometimes thought that metaphor or simile is mainly used by poets to relieve the monotony of everyday locutions, to make language more "colorful" and ornate. But where we have to depend on the accuracy of our statements we eschew such poetic trappings and say directly and unambiguously what we want to communicate. According to this view metaphorical language is inaccurate at best and misleading at worst.

But this is a misconception. Metaphor is not a mannerism of poets or rhetoricians; it is inherent in all language. Only the words for the most primitive and obvious physical objects and qualities are non-metaphorical in most languages. As soon as ideas more abstract or subtle are to be expressed, the process of metaphorization sets in. Our language is well equipped to handle spatial reality with "first-order" terms that stand directly for their designata. As soon as "higher-order" experiences are to be described we have a tendency to use spatial terms metaphorically, i.e. as "second-order" similes or pointers.

For example, what has been called the transitive character of words involves the same principle that generates metaphor. The word "Lord" functions as a word precisely because it refers not to itself but to the entity it denotes, a human being who is a master or a commander. But if we push this operation one step further, if we carry the meaning from the area of inter-human relations to the area of human-divine relations, we apply the term "metaphorically" to God (*Adonay*). It is possible to carry this process even further and say that a man obsessed with worldly success recognizes money as his true Lord (in which case we use a religious term metaphorically to point to the absolute and demonic power which the pursuit of money exerts over its devotees). This is what we mean by the "multi-stage pointings-beyond-themselves" of certain words.

At this point it is necessary to introduce the term "myth" into our discussion. Since it is used in a bewildering variety of senses by various writers, we want to stipulate that we shall use it almost interchangeably with the term "metaphor" in religious contexts. Wherever a metaphor is elaborated in the form of a coherent story we shall feel free to call it a myth. It indicates that the story, although couched in terms of concrete empirical happenings, is metaphorical and refers to the Divine reality which by its ineffable nature cannot be described in direct first-order language.

Metaphors function in two different ways: they *explain* and they *enlarge* our experience. Explanation usually involves making the strange "plain" or by use of the more familiar. Molecules or atoms are strange entities to most of us; picturing them as miniature billiard balls and "explaining" their behavior in terms of analogous movements and collisions supplies an acceptable elucidation (until the analogy breaks down and another theory has to be developed).

The functions of explaining and enlarging our experience by means of metaphors or models overlap frequently. To describe the behavior or gases in a container we use the model of billiard balls moving around in random fashion at various speeds ("faster" corresponding to higher, and "slower" to lower, temperatures). By extrapolating from this model we can arrive at Boyle's Law which enables us to predict the pressure and volume of the gas corresponding to changes in temperature. Thus the metaphor enlarges our knowledge by letting us predict behavior which we could not possibly expect without the help of the model.

Using the model of the organism to describe the various individuals and groups that make up society not only helps us to understand their mutual interdependence, but also adds a new dimension to life by helping us experience our role in society as that of an organic part that stands in a dynamic and intimate relationship to all the others. In order to see this we have only to observe people who do not experience their relationship to society in this manner: the rebel, the anarchist, or the hippie who looks upon "Them" or "the Establishment" as enemies, exploiters or tools of a "conspiracy." As a result he acts and feels differently, although he is aware of the same "facts" as the person who has a sense of "belonging" to the community.

By accepting a metaphor we may not add new facts to our experience, but we see the old disjointed facts in a new and meaningful way. "It is possible to have before one's eyes all the items of a pattern and still to miss the pattern."[9]

One risk in using metaphors is that of deploying our model (or analogue) too far, for the model is never completely isomorphic with the domain that is to be interpreted. Thus the model of light as travelling in straight lines (the principle of the rectilinear propagation of light) has made possible certain advances in geometrical optics. The metaphor "travelling" can be used, for instance, to ask the question: At what speed does light travel?—and the answer: at 300,000 kilometers per second, is an important piece of scientific information. But is we stretch the metaphor and ask: Does light "travel" by road, by rail or by rocket? we have overextended its range and have fallen into absurdity. The Torah uses the "travelling" and "light" metaphor of God:

> The Lord came from Sinai;
> He shone upon them from Seir;
> He appeared from Mount Paran,
> And approached from Ribeboth-kodesh . . . (Deut. 33:2)

Here, however, we can neither inquire about the Lord's speed nor His mode of transportation.

It is in these last two examples (light shining forth, and God shining forth) that a fundamental difference emerges between religious and other kinds of metaphor. In science and poetry, metaphor illuminates one domain of finite reality through another domain of finite reality. In discourse about God (myth) we use metaphors taken from an area of finite experience to illuminate the Infinite Source of all reality, which by its very nature cannot be reduced to categories of human knowledge. Since all our models and metaphors are taken from ordinary experience we are always in danger of either distorting the Divine by representing it in anthropomorphic or physicomorphic ways, or of abandoning all efforts to speak about God—except in negations—and thus isolating ourselves from any relationship with Him.

It is against this twofold danger of reducing God to human scale or resigning ourselves to utter ignorance, that we must understand the biblical approach. It tells us in the form of myth and metaphor something significant and true about God, but warns us at the same time that the myth and metaphor are not literal or scientific descriptions of the ultimate truth.

Since metaphors are not literally true, but allusive and evocative, we might think that we do not have to employ them with unchanging rigidity. Mixed metaphors make for poor style, but they do not necessarily frustrate the communication of the intended meaning. The British Lion who roams the Canadian mountains and African jungles and who will never pull in his horns or withdraw into his shell may be an odd creature; but nevertheless, we get the message! In the Song of Songs the girl is called a mare, a rose, a dove, a sister and a palm tree, but there is no danger that we misunderstand the poet's intention.

It might seem, therefore, that although we cannot do without *some* metaphor where literal descriptions fail us, it does not matter *which* particular metaphor we use. God and His relationship to the world cannot be described in empirical terms, but does it really matter whether we allude to Him as the Begetter, the Engineer, the Arranger or the Creator of the Universe? This view, however, is erroneous, and so fraught with dangerous consequences that we have to expose it decisively. The *raison d'être* for teaching the story of Genesis, and not Babylonian or modern "scientific" myths, as fundamental truth lies at the foundation of Jewish thought and conduct. We shall not be able to teach the Creation story as an important doctrine of our faith unless we have clarified the question of the metaphorical conception of God.

The relationship between God and the world is of crucial importance to one's way of thinking and acting. The way we conceive of the Ultimate and its connection with the here-and-now—nature and mankind—must inevitably influence our views about the potentialities and purposes of life. Our metaphors about particular domains of reality, such as the nature of society, determine our modes of conduct and the quality of our interpersonal experiences. Now, the more comprehensive the scope of a metaphor, the more pervasive is its influence on the lives of those who accept it.

A root metaphor extracted from an area of common-sense fact is extended into a "world hypothesis" or a philosophical system.[9a] A root metaphor embedded in a religious myth gives rise to a system of values and a way of life. We shall briefly discuss three root metaphors used to describe the relationship of God to the world: God as the Begetter, God as the Stranger, and God as the Creator. . . .

Notes

1. Rashi (1040–1105), for example, who was not acquainted with all the research of grammarians using Arabic philology could not utilize knowledge which was readily available to Abraham Ibn Ezra. Modern recovery of Mesopotamian languages and literatures has given contemporary scholars knowledge of the Bible that was unavailable to the Babylonian rabbis who lived in Mesopotamia fifteen hundred years ago.

2. *Mekhilta de-rabbi Ishmael,* Yitro ch. 7; Lauterbach ed. Vol. II pp. 255f.

3. *Ruth Rabba,* 2, para. 22.

4. Leo Strauss, "Introductory Essay," *The Guide of the Perplexed,* tr. Shlomo Pines, Chicago, 1963, p. xiv.

5. *Zohar, Tiqqune Zohar, Zohar Ḥadash* in the printed editions.

6. Quoted in G. Scholem, *Major Trends in Jewish Mysticism,* p. 158.

6a. *Zohar* III, 152a.

7. *Moreh Nevukhim* I, ch. 23.

8. Shimon Kasher, *Peshuto shel Mikra,* Vol. I, Jerusalem, 1963, p. 9.

9. John Wisdom, "Gods," *Logic and Language,* First Series, ed. A. G. N. Flew, Oxford, 1951, p. 191.

9a. Cf. Stephen Pepper, *World Hypotheses,* Berkeley, 1942.

part four

rabbis: the men of torah

Torah as it is now understood and interpreted consists of much more than the *Tanakh,* the Hebrew Scriptures. The "Old Testament" and Judaism are not one and the same thing. From the early centuries of the common era onward, Judaism has consisted of the Hebrew Scriptures as interpreted, understood, applied, and augmented by the rabbis, the Jewish sages of the first seven centuries of the common era. The rabbis' teachings are contained in a great document, the Babylonian Talmud, as well as in several lesser collections, which reached their final form before the seventh century of the common era. From their time to the present, Judaism has meant *rabbinic* Judaism. The Scriptures together with the Talmud as interpreted by the rabbi were authoritative and definitive.

The rabbis are important as legal and moral interpreters of the Torah. But they are also influential by their ideals and teachings. These are conveyed in two ways. First of all, Talmudic and later rabbinic tradition contains numerous wise sayings. These are learned and memorized, so that, as occasion arises in ordinary life, they may be recalled and applied. Second, stories about the lives and deeds of the rabbis are told, and these too had a powerful formative influence on the doings of ordinary folk.

Here we shall consider three of the early rabbis: Hillel, who stands at the beginning of rabbinic Judaism, and lived at the beginning of the common era; Yohanan ben Zakkai, who survived the destruction of the Second Temple in 70 and showed the people how to overcome the disaster and achieve reconciliation with God; and Akiba, an early second-century master who devoted his life to the study of Torah and was martyred.

12.

hillel and the study of torah

nahum n. glatzer

Hillel was the founder of classical Judaism, that is, that form of Judaism known to us in the pages of the Mishnah and the Talmud and regarded from the first century of the Common Era onward as normative (C.E. = A.D.). We know very little about his life, and most of the sayings attributed to him and stories told about him come to us from a much later time than that in which he lived. So we cannot claim to know much about the "historical" Hillel. But we know a great deal about the ideals attributed to him, and in fact, those ideals and teachings characterized the Pharisaic group from his time onward, thus becoming dominant in classical Judaism during his own day. So whether or not Hillel said exactly what is attributed to him hardly matters, in that people from that time not only believed he did, but, of far greater importance, followed those teachings and made them normative.

What is central in classical Judaism is by now going to be familiar to you: *study of Torah.* That central ideal has already predominated in the prayers about the unity of God, in arguments about why one should be a Jew, in interpretations of the meaning and purpose of Torah itself. What is important in Professor Nahum Glatzer's account, therefore, is his reliable exposition of both the ideal of study and the place of study in the time in which Hillel lived, as well as of the nature of Torah-study as the formative force in Jewish law and ethics, morality and theology.

Professor Glatzer teaches at Brandeis University and is known for his mastery of both classical Judaism and its modern expositors.

From *Hillel the Elder: The Emergence of Classical Judaism,* by Nahum N. Glatzer (Washington, D.C.: Bnai Brith Hillel Foundations, 1959), pp. 46–55. © 1959 by Bnai Brith Hillel Foundations. Reprinted by permission of the author and Bnai Brith Hillel Foundations.

Hillel introduced a new note into the house of study. We say introduced, not invented. We do find traces of this new type of learning in Judea before Hillel; we find a strong emphasis on, and a cultivation of, this learning in the sectarian movements of the time. Through Hillel, it seems, this emphasis and culture were transplanted from the isolation of the sectarian associations into the schools of Jerusalem.

We will first turn our attention to the place of study in the sectarian movements, then come back to Hillel.

Learning in the Sectarian Movements

In the Essene community we encounter special meetings for the study of sacred writings. Philo tells us that the Essenes at all times "study industriously the ethical part (of philosophy)," particularly on the Sabbath. The group follows the discourse of the master. Study enables a husband "to transmit knowledge of the laws" to his wife, the father to his children, the master to his servant.[1]

The *Manual of Discipline* tells us that the men of the Community of the Covenant gave a third of all the nights of the year to the study of the Torah. In any given group of ten men there should always be one "who expounds the Law day and night, continually.[2]

The *Manual* quotes Isaiah 40.3, "Clear ye in the wilderness the way of the Lord." This "way" is defined as "the study of the law" [midrash ha-torah].[3] The community, led by an "interpreter (or searcher) of the Torah" [doresh ha-torah],[4] studied the teachings in common, in a process in which the mind and the heart, the intellectual, spiritual and emotional faculties took part. Study here was a sacred action; a connection was perceived between knowledge and piety. Through study, the Torah revealed something of the "way of the Lord" in the affairs of the world and of man. Study though pursued in community is a highly individual affair; it is one of man's links with the divine and thus a mystery. Our *Manual* speaks of the "true knowledge" which will be gained by those who have chosen the Way.[5]

To the Community of the Covenant this pursuit of knowledge and piety cannot take place in the midst of the people who have made peace with the corrupt world around them. "This is the time of clearing the way to go to the wilderness," the *Manual* states.[6]

Hillel: The Ignorant Cannot be a Hasid

The culture of the Dead Sea sects was, we assume, known to Hillel. But he did not think that this culture should flourish only in the wilderness. True, few were left in Jerusalem to do the work. But "in a place where a man is needed and there is none, try to be a man." Here Hillel voiced his wish to reestablish the deserted center of learning in Judea. "The ignorant cannot be a Hasid"; the sectarians knew this and acted accordingly in their retreats. Hillel wanted to battle ignorance—in Jerusalem.

Even before his time it had been taught: "Raise up many disciples," "Let your house be a meeting house for the wise"; the masters' responsibilities towards their disciples had been recognized.[7] But studies mainly meant studies of the established traditions. Now, however, a new form of learning was needed and a new kind of relationship between master and disciple. Only in the School of Hillel do we find this true community of disciples and the communion of learning.

Some of Hillel's sayings, though touching also on other motifs, mainly emphasize the theme of study.

First let us consider the entire saying, parts of which we have quoted before:

> The uneducated knows not fear of sin;
> the ignorant cannot be a Hasid.
> The timid is not apt to learn,
> the impatient is not fit to teach.
> He whose whole time is absorbed in business will
> not attain wisdom.
> In a place where (a man is needed and) there are no
> men, try to be a man.[8]

There is an intimate relationship between learning, personal ethics, and the attitude toward one's fellowman:

> Do not separate yourself from the community.
> Trust not yourself until the day of your death.
> Judge not your fellow-man before you have come
> into his situation.
> Say not a thing that cannot be understood at once in
> the assumption that sometime in the future it will
> be understood.
> Say not: "When I shall have leisure I shall study";
> perhaps you will not have leisure.

The warning against absorption in business is followed by a warning against yielding to temptations of material achievement at the expense of study:

Hillel used to say:

> The more flesh, the more worms;
> the more possessions, the more worry;
> the more women, the more witchcraft;
> the more maid-servants, the more immorality;
> the more men-servants, the more thieving.

But:

> The more Torah, the more life;
> the more study and contemplation, the more wisdom;
> the more counsel, the more discernment;
> the more charity, the more peace.

And:

> A good name, once acquired, is your own possession;
> he who has knowledge of the Torah has life in the
> world to come.

Learning requires selflessness and constant care:

> A name made famous is a name lost.
> Knowledge that does not grow will shrink.
> He who refuses to teach faces death.
> He who uses the crown of learning for material gain
>   vanishes.

In explaining the first line of this saying, the sages remark: "If a man makes himself great, he is not really great, unless one greater than he has made him great."[9]

The man of learning will attempt to gain disciples from among the simple and the humble:

> How did Hillel bring his fellow-man near to the
>   Torah?
> One day Hillel stood in the gate of Jerusalem and
>   met people going out to work.
> He asked: "How much will you earn to-day?"
> One said, A denarius; the other said, Two denarii.
> He asked them: "What will you do with the
>   money?"
> They gave answer: "We will pay for the necessities
>   of life."
> Then he said to them:
> "Why don't you rather come with me and gain
>   knowledge of the Torah,
> that you may gain life in this world
> and life in the world-to-come?"
> Thus Hillel was wont to do all his days and has
>   brought many under the wings of Heaven.[10]

Hillel's method of starting a conversation reminds us of the Stoics and the Cynics and, of course, of Socrates. He refers to the occupation of the one spoken to; it is this person's terminology and mode of thinking which Hillel uses in order to let him discover for himself what the right thing is.

Learning is worship, indeed. And as worship is not confined to special times and occasions but pervades the whole of man's conscious life, so learning has to be continual. The prophet Malachi speaks of the distinction "between him that serveth God and him that serveth Him not." "He that serveth Him not," Hillel explained, is the one who had studied but had ceased to do so; only he who studies without cessation is the one "that serveth God."[11]

Nomos in Hellenism

Our analysis of learning would not be complete without an attempt to describe the scope of Torah, or Law.

The Septuagint, the Greek translation of the Hebrew Bible, renders the word

Torah usually by the Greek word *nomos,* which means law. To later users "Law" suggested a collection of statutes, commandments and injunctions. The importance of laws for the welfare of a society was readily recognized, but beyond that the term yielded no deeper significance.

Yet when the Greek-speaking world used the word *nomos,* the term meant a great deal. To the Stoics, Law suggested primarily a cosmic, universal law. The Hellenist thinker found the true law only in the cosmos.[12] The law which governed the universe was valid also for the community of men and for the gods. The *nomos,* being the highest reason (*logos*), ruled both in nature and in man's moral action. This universal law was divine. What law, in the narrow sense, meant for the state, God was to the world; some identified God with the universal order.

Man follows his inborn reason in making his commitment for *nomos* and for a life according to *nomos.* It is man's nature and his destiny to fulfill the law; thus, man reaches true freedom. In obeying the law, man lives according to nature, which is a Stoic ideal; he becomes happy and beloved of God; in following the law, man follows God.

In the Hellenist world the term *nomos* in its broad application roughly carried the range of meaning that the term Torah conveyed to the Jew. In translating *nomos* as law we are philologically correct, but in applying the term law to Torah, we are considerably narrowing down its meaning.

Torah in Judaism

Reminiscent of the position of *nomos* in the Stoa, the Jew sees in the Torah a cosmic, universal force. Tradition has it that the creation of the Torah preceded the creation of the world;[13] before creating the world, God looked into the Torah. The meaning which it established was valid not only for man but also for nature and for the universe. God Himself is described as studying the Torah. In principle, the validity of the Torah is not limited to Israel. It was not given in the Land of Israel but on Sinai, in the wilderness between Egypt and the Land of Israel, thus "in public, for all to see, in the open, and everyone who wishes to receive it, let him come and receive it." To emphasize the universal character of the Torah, the revelation took place in the seventy languages of mankind, but the nations of the world were not ready to accept it. In accepting the Torah, Israel has made peace between God and His world. The Torah charges man with many responsibilities; in fulfilling them he becomes free.

These views upheld by the Palestinian masters are paralleled by Philo of Alexandria. Philo sees a basic harmony between Torah and reason, cosmos and nature, all rooted in the oneness of God. To the perfect man the Torah is the expression of divine reason and wisdom which a man will choose to follow—in freedom.[14]

Halakhah

In a more definite sense Torah, law, represents to classical Judaism the expression of God's will. Once declared on Sinai, this will is now recorded in the

Torah in human language. Since God is not primarily law-giver but father, creator, lover of His creatures and of His people, the pronouncement of His will inspires ready acceptance. By living according to Halakhah—the classical Jewish term for the law—the Jew overcomes the chaos which threatens human life; he emerges victorious over anarchy and establishes order in himself. There is no sphere which can be considered irrelevant. Everything in life, big and small, is given form and significance by Halakhah.

The examination of the written law—the Torah—is pursued along logical, rational lines. Hillel is known to have promulgated the so-called "seven rules" or norms of interpretation which were expanded by later sages.

As an example we may mention the rule of "generalization of a special law" (*binyan av,* literally, the formation of a leading regulation). The law states: "No man shall take the mill or the upper millstone to pledge; for he taketh a man's life to pledge."[15] The law clearly states that only these objects were not to be used as security for debts. However, confiscation of other objects could equally jeopardize a man's life. Therefore, Hillel's rule provides that the special law may be generalized. It implies "everything which is used for the preparation of food." Unless a biblical law appears directed to a particular case, it is examined as to its general validity.

This system of exposition made it possible to apply the law liberally to new conditions of time and society. Thus, everything could be found in the Torah; a tradition in law or custom did not have to rest on a school regulation or on legal enactment but could be traced back to its origin in the Torah. In this point Hillel's activity was decisive.[16]

The Aim of Learning

The term "learning," or study of the Torah, is so frequently used that our ears are dulled to its meaning. We must attempt to redefine it. True, there had been instruction in Israel since biblical days and there were occasions when the Torah was read and explained in public. But it was only in the last generations before Hillel that the learning of the Torah became a principal force in Judaism: First, in the sectarian movements and in the Diaspora, then, through Hillel, in Jerusalem and in classical Judaism.

Learning is more than the sum of the portions studied. The very process of immersion into the biblical word is more than a quest for information. Learning ultimately aims not at "practical," usable knowledge. The study of the Torah is only outwardly the study of a book; actually it is the study of the divine thought. There is no "new" revelation; there are no longer prophets in Israel who would utter a new divine word; but through dedicated learning, the learner will understand anew the word spoken on Sinai. This understanding is the aim of learning.

Notes

1. *Hypothetica* 7.13. See also *Quod Deus Sit Immutabilis* 24; on the contemplative life of study, see *De Specialibus Legibus* IV. 26; II. 15: *De Fuge et Inventione* 6. Cicero,

on the other hand, prefers the *vita civilis* of the statesman to the *vita quieta* of the sage. *De Re Publica* II. 3.

2. *Manual of Discipline,* VI. 6–8.

3. *Ibid.,* VIII. 12–16.

4. *Zadokite Documents,* VII. 18.

5. *Manual of Discipline,* IX. 16–21.

6. *Ibid.,* VIII. 13; IX. 20–21.

7. Abot I. 1, 4, 11.

8. This and the following quotations: Abot II. 5; II 4; II 7; I. 13.

9. Abot de Rabbi Nathan II, ch. I, beginning.

10. *Ibid.,* ch. XXVI.

11. *Hagigah 9b,* quoting Malachi 3.18.

12. This and the following quotations: Platarch, *de Exilio* 5; *De Stoicorum Repugnantiis* I; Epictetus, *Dissertationes* IV. 3.9–12.

13. Sources for this section: Pesahim 54ᵃ; Sifre on Deuteronomy 11:10; Genesis Rabbah I.2; I.6; Abodah Zarah. 3b; Mekhilta on Exodus 19.2; Shabbat 88b; Sifre on Deuteronomy 33.2; Abot VI. 2; Mekhilta on Exodus 13.3; Deuteronomy Rabbah IV. 4; Genesis Rabbah LXVI.2.

14. *Legum Allegoria* I, 93f. See H. A. Wolfson, *Philo,* 1947, II, Ch. XII.

15. Deuteronomy 24.6; the following interpretation, Mishnah Baba Metzia IX.13.

16. Hillel is the first teacher to whom the use of the term "oral law" is found ascribed. See I. H. Weiss, *Dor Dor ve-Doreshav,* III, 24b.

13.

torah in a time of crisis

jacob neusner

The ideal of study of Torah must seem static and one-dimensional. It must seem appropriate for people who live in times of peace, who have the leisure and the intelligence to learn. But clearly that is a false impression, for the history of the Jewish people has been anything but peaceful, and the Jews have scarcely ever enjoyed long periods of tranquility and leisure. To be appropriate to the condition of a small, harried, and sometimes persecuted group, the ideal of study of Torah has to exhibit dynamism and the capacity to help people confront great challenges and even overwhelming crises.

Certainly one exceedingly difficult moment was the destruction of the Second Temple of Jerusalem in the year 70 C.E. If the ideal of Hillel was to endure, it had to show people how to respond to the catastrophe represented by the destruction of the center of Jewish cult and piety, the place made holy by God and believed to enjoy his special blessing; by the cessation of sacrifices by which God was served; and by the devastation of the city seen as sacred. Yohanan ben Zakkai is alleged in rabbinic tradition to have been the disciple of Hillel, and whether or not this is true, in the reality of the history of Judaism Yohanan is Hillel's continuator and true student. For Yohanan, who survived the disaster and founded at the village of Yavneh, in the southern part of the land of Israel, a center for the study and application of Torah in the aftermath of the destruction, taught that what was needed for the present hour indeed was found in the Torah. And what he found in the Torah was the message that God is served not through cult and sacrifice but through service to one's fellow man and sacrifice of one's own selfish inclinations. Yohanan showed that the Torah "really" insists that true service is service to the men and women of one's own time and place. The opposite of war, aggression, self-aggrandizement—that is the demand of Torah: peace and loyalty and acts of loving kindness.

Yohanan's Torah-center, at Yavneh, was only one choice facing the surviving people. Another was the last fortress of the Jewish patriots, at Masada. That represents an entirely different interpretation of the message of Torah. Here is an account of Yohanan's view of the crisis of the destruction of the Temple and of Jerusalem and how it was to be turned into a spiritual opportunity of unending significance.

It should be noted that the Hebrew name *Yohanan* translates as *John* in English, and *ben Zakkai* may be understood to mean "the righteous." The sages of another culture seem alien, in part, because they bear names difficult for us to grasp and remember. Let him be John the Righteous, if that makes matters more familiar. The message is the thing—and that, in a century of total war, will always be alien.

From *A Life of Yohanan ben Zakkai,* by Jacob Neusner (Leiden, Holland: E. J. Brill, 1969), pp. 174–177, 188–192. © 1969 by E. J. Brill, and reprinted with their permission.

Two roads led out of Jerusalem, one to Yavneh, the other to Masada. Zealots fled to the Dead Sea and barricaded themselves in a massive old fortress of Herod. There they held out for three more years, fighting a hopeless fight rather than surrender. With their wives and children, perhaps a thousand people in all, they withstood advancing siegeworks, engineering marvels, until with the walls breached, they saw at best another day of resistance. That night, the fathers slew their wives and children, and the soldiers one another, until the last Zealot, seeing none alive, slit his own throat. So all was deathly quiet at last.

Rome was surely right, the soldiers must have thought as they entered the smoking ruins of a mighty fortress. She had achieved final victory. Nothing at all remained. The Zealots left no legacy, no vision for the future. They offered no ideal but a military, Spartan one: better suicide than subjugation. If the warriors of Masada represented the only option for the Jews, then and there Judaism would have ended for all time, as the Zealots of Masada supposed it had. The Jewish group may have lingered on, but not for very long.

The road to Yavneh, to the vineyard and the abundant fields and the open port—that was the other way. It was the way taken by the Jews who did not commit suicide and did not regard the disaster as the last drama in a tragic history. They did not suppose that the failure of the sword marked the final catastrophe. These Jews had a better memory of the message of Isaiah, that trust in the sword is arrogance against God. They kept alive the hope that God, and not the sword, would eventually bring salvation. Yohanan ben Zakkai led the way to Yavneh. Because he did, he fathered another generation, and they another. Judaism endured as a living faith and the Jews as an enduring people from that day to this one. Masada and its battlefield bravado was a dead end. Through Yavneh and its tentative, hopeful faith led the way to the future. Masada left behind a few fragments of cloth, some coins, smashed rocks and bones, a monument to futile, barren courage. Yavneh left behind twenty centuries of life, and, I think, many more to come.

But for Yohanan the question was, Where to begin? Much was lost, much was even now slipping away. With the Temple gone, who was to give practical decisions which formerly came from the high priests' court? With the city in ruins, what was to become of the great pilgrim festivals? What indeed was to happen to the corpus of law by which the people had lived their lives in former times, now that those who had administered it were no longer able? And what was to be done about the sacred calendar which had been proclaimed in Jerusalem? These were the questions of detail. They presupposed only one thing: the Jews and their ancient tradition would continue to flourish for time to come. But that very conviction met challenge from every side. Few really believed that "Torah" in any form could sustain Israel after so complete a rout of its zealous exponents. Whatever the claims of Yohanan and the other Pharisees, it is quite clear that the Torah they exposited and that which the people earlier had wanted to obey and heard from the competing groups were by no means identical. And those whom the people followed to war now had little more to tell them.

The next decade, from 70 to approximately 80, marked Yohanan's effective years. Before then, he had sought the power to realize his associates' understanding of God's will for Israel. Now he held that power, but in the most dreadful circumstance imaginable. He wanted to supervise the Temple, not to preside over its ruins. He hoped to direct the lives of Jews toward the will of their father in heaven, not to mediate between them and their conquerors, to exert authority as collaborator with the enemy. He sought to convince his Saducean and other opponents of the rightness of his viewpoint, not to inherit their wreckage in the hour of universal disaster. And above all, he intended to instruct his students in the right path, not to send them forth as agents of a foreign army of occupation. So the irony of Yohanan's life must now have yielded bitter reflection, for he had gotten just what he wanted, but not in the way he had envisaged.

What indeed were his alternatives at Yavneh? He could have chosen to live as before, master of a circle of disciples, leader of one party in a bitterly divided population. If others had taken up the daily task, perhaps Yohanan would have chosen such a life. Passing his seventieth year, where was he to find the energy and vigor for another active career? He could, alternatively, have addressed to the people one final bitter sermon: "You were forewarned, and now bear the disagreeable consequence of your indifference." And he could thereupon have turned his back upon the country and its leaderless, heartbroken masses. How tempting it must have been to say to the world, "I who share your fate bid you a last farewell," and to retire to some foreign exile or to a barren wilderness, there to start a commune, the "new Israel" of the future. Scripture prevented it. Moses, tempted to create of his own seed a new Israel, reminded God that all He had, and all He ever would have, was the old one. Jeremiah, weeping for the destruction of his people, purchased land to signify that once again in the Land of Israel would be heard the voice of rejoicing and of laughter, the voice of the bridegroom and the bride. He chose to stay at home and to bind up the broken spirit of the remnant left behind.

How could Yohanan ben Zakkai do otherwise than give his last, best years to the surviving Jews and their government? Now he must have understood the ultimate meaning of the years of preparation, deep isolation and then conflict, and rigorous study. The Galilee he left behind so long ago had now become the country's chief resource. If it hated the sages' Torah, today it needed the instruction which only expositors of Torah such as Yohanan could offer. Jerusalem, so long ago destined for destruction, now lay in ruins. Nothing was left to purify. Only Torah could speak for her. "Forty years in business, forty years in study"

—and now? He knew he had little time. Even of that, the tired old man could hardly be certain. Jeremiah was left a few years, perhaps five at most, and achieved nothing after the destruction of the First Temple. Perhaps, however he might will it, Yohanan could not carry through the task he even now dreamed of doing. We today know otherwise, but then how could he have been sure? With hindsight, we doubt the Yohanan could have done other than take up the duties of a dreadful hour. He would in a few critical years insure the continued prosperity of the ancient tradition in the *very* form he gave to it. But faced with the same grave crisis, others may not have had the audacity to try.

Here we perceive another unexpected consequence of the years of fruitless strife. Yohanan was not used to success and was therefore quite prepared to struggle tenaciously without its slightest prospect. Eighteen years in the Galilee produced little result, but he stayed there all those eighteen years. A lesser man would have gone away after one or two. Twenty-five years in Jerusalem left him an exhausted old man, without much influence over public opinion and with practically none at all at the Temple. And still he struggled that quarter of a century. The years hardened him and taught him to accept defeat and to fight again. He now no longer had even to expect success in order to justify the effort. He needed only to think the effort necessary, whatever the outcome. Even when he died, he did not claim he had done much to merit great reward. He prevailed not only against what seemed inexorable history, but against the natural inclinations of the heart. So too Jeremiah, who knew his own frailty and perceived the heart's inconstancy, nonetheless spoke the words that burned within him, while almost certain he would be repaid by assassination. But to Jeremiah came the reassuring word of God. Yohanan depended only upon faith, the echo of that word in Scripture and tradition.

Yohanan had earlier taught, in commenting on the words of Qohelet, *Let your garments always be white, and let not oil be lacking on your head* (Qoh. 9:8), that Jews should clothe themselves in Torah, commandments, and acts of kindness. Each of these categories represented a fundamental concern of the pious man. Through the study of Torah man learned what the God wanted of him. Through doing the commandments he carried out that will. Through acts of lovingkindness he freely honored God who gave the Torah. These elements were probably a transformation of the teachings of Simeon the Righteous two centuries earlier: "On three things does the age stand: on the Torah, on the Temple service, and on acts of piety." By "Torah" Simeon had meant the books of the Torah; by "Temple service" the sacrificial cult in Jerusalem; by "acts of piety," acts of loyalty and obedience to God. Yohanan survived the destruction of the Temple. He came at the end of a long struggle for the Torah, both written and oral, as interpreted by the Pharisees. Acts of obedience to God seemed to him to comprehend a broader obligation than piety. He therefore infused these categories with new content. We here see his thought:

> Once as Rabban Yohanan ben Zakkai was coming out of Jerusalem, Rabbi Joshua followed him, and beheld the Temple in ruins.

> "Woe unto us," Rabbi Joshua cried, "that this place, the place where the iniquities of Israel were atoned for, is laid waste."
>
> "My son," Rabban Yohanan said to him, "be not grieved. We have another atonement as effective as this. And what is it? It is acts of lovingkindness, as it is said, *For I desire mercy, not sacrifice* (Hos. 6:6)."

Yohanan's treatment of the verse, *For I desire mercy, not sacrifice,* was consistent with the contemporary hermeneutic. In biblical times, *hesed* had meant (in part) the mutual liability of those who are friends and relatives, master and servant, or any relationship of joint responsibility. In relationship to God *hesed* meant acts in conformity to the covenant between man and God. Hosea meant that God demanded loyal adherence to His covenant, rather than sacrifice. By Yohanan's time, however, the word had acquired a different connotation. It meant mercy, or an act of compassion and lovingkindness. Thus to Jesus of Nazareth was attributed the saying,

> Those who are well have no need of a physician, but those who are sick. Go and learn what this means, I desire mercy (eleon) and not sacrifice. For I came not to call the righteous, but sinners (Matt. 9:13).

Later rabbinic sources likewise preserved this connotation in commenting on the verse. . . . Yohanan thought that through *hesed* the Jews might make atonement, and that the sacrifices now demanded of them were love and mercy. His choice of the verse in Hosea gave stress to the ethical element of his earlier trilogy of study of Torah, doing the commandments, and acts of lovingkindness. Yohanan emphasized the primacy of hesed itself in the redemptive process: *Just as the Jews needed a redemptive act of compassion from God, so must they now act compassionately in order to make themselves worthy of it.* This primary emphasis on personal moral quality rather than specific external action, either ritual or legal, is in accordance with the increasing concern for the inner aspect of religion characteristic of the age. The act of compassionate fellowship, which in Yohanan's opinion was the foundation of true religion, became the central focus of his consoling message for the new and troubled age.

Yohanan shared the common sense of grief, and taught, like others, that the sins of the nation had brought the disaster. But he added, its virtues might bring redemption. He differed from others in rejecting the eschatological focus of consolation. He offered the ideal of *hesed,* a means by which Jews might change their own hearts. He provided an interim-ethic by which the people might live while they awaited the coming redemption. The earlier age had stood on the books of the Torah, the Temple rites, and acts of piety. The new age would endure on the foundation of studying the Torah, doing the commandments, and especially performing acts of compassion. Compassion strikingly embodied that very quality which the brutality of war must paradoxically have accentuated in his mind: man's capacity to act kindly and decently to his fellow man.

The consequence of Yohanan's lesson may have been embodied in a later encounter between his disciple Joshua and a group of apocalyptists. One recalls that II Baruch had lamented:

Blessed is he who was not born, or he who having been born has died,
But as for us who live, woe unto us. Because we see the afflictions of Zion, and
    what has befallen Jerusalem . . .
You husbandmen, sow not again.
And earth, who do you give your harvest fruits?
Keep within yourself the sweets of your sustenance.
And you, vine, why do you continue to give your wine?
For an offering will not again be made therefrom in Zion,
Nor will first-fruits again be offered.
And do you, O heavens, withhold your dew,
And open not the treasuries of rain.
And do you, sun, withhold the light of your rays,
And you moon, extinguish the multitude of your light.
For why should light rise again
Where the light of Zion is darkened?
Would that you had ears, O earth,
And that you had a heart, O dust,
That you might go and announce in Sheol,
And say to the dead,
"Blessed are you more than we who live."

(II Baruch, 10.6–7, 9–12, 11.6–7)

Yohanan's student Joshua met such people. It was reported that when the Temple
was destroyed, ascetics multiplied in Israel, who would not eat flesh nor drink
wine. Rabbi Joshua dealt with them:

> He said to them, "My children, On what account do you not eat flesh and drink
> wine?"
> They said to him, "Shall we eat meat, from which they used to offer a sacrifice on
> the altar, and now it is no more? And shall we drink wine, which was poured out on
> the altar, and now it is no more?"
> He said to them, "If so, we ought not to eat bread, for there are no meal offerings
> any more. Perhaps we ought not to drink water, for the water-offerings are not
> brought anymore."
> They were silent.
> He said to them, "My children, come and I shall teach you. Not to mourn at all
> is impossible, for the evil decree has already come upon us. But to mourn too much
> is also impossible, for one may not promulgate a decree for the community unless
> most of the community can endure it . . . But thus have the sages taught: 'A man
> plasters his house, but leaves a little piece untouched. A man prepares all the needs
> of the meal, but leaves out some morsel. A woman prepares all her cosmetics, but
> leaves off some small item . . .'"

I do not believe that Yohanan's words to Joshua—"My son, be not grieved;
we have another atonement as effective as this. And what is it? It is acts of
lovingkindness, as it is said, *For I desire mercy, not sacrifice* (Hosea 6:6)"—have
been more penetratingly elucidated than by Judah Goldin:

> This anecdote . . . reports a revolutionary discovery—that, unlike what all the historic
> religions display, unlike even the natural impulse of every pious creature to bring

something to, do something for, his God—as any lover is frustrated if he is reduced to words only—it *is* possible to worship God and to show one's love for and to Him, without giving Him a material gift. In at least this respect He is unique. If we cannot win His good opinion by means of holocausts, we can win it by acts of lovingkindness to our fellowman. An idea like this takes a long time to sink in, and in reality it never entirely displaces the primary impulse. If only there were the Temple: what a busyness could go on, what a tangible reassurance it would be to see the High Priest change from one set of garments to another . . .

The change spoken of here took place not formally, but in the heart. What Yohanan demanded was that Israel now see in its humble, day-to-day conduct, deeds of so grand a dimension as to rival the sacred actions, rites, and gestures of the Temple.

If we appreciate the force of powerful emotions aroused by the Temple cult, we may understand how grand a revolution was effected in the simple declaration, so long in coming, that with the destruction of the Temple the realm of the sacred had finally overspread the world. Man must now see in himself, in his selfish motives to be immolated, the noblest sacrifice of all. So Rabban Gamaliel son of Rabbi Judah the Patriarch said, "Do His will as if it was your will, so that He may do your will as if it was His will. Make your will of no effect before His will, the He may make the will of others of no effect before your will." His will is that men love their neighbors as themselves. Just as willingly as men would contribute bricks and mortar for the building of a sanctuary, so willingly ought they to contribute love, renunciation, self-sacrifice, for the building of a sacred community. If one wants to do something for God in a time when the Temple is no more, the offering must be the gift of selfless compassion. The holy altar must be the streets and marketplaces of the world.

14.

torah and martyrdom

louis finkelstein

Torah-study is not only a communal ideal. It is the obligation of every individual. The founding rabbis of classical Judaism taught that the Torah is worth living for and that, if need be, one must accept martyrdom for its sake. That is a very personal thing, for, after all, one gives one's own private life on behalf of a very public and, therefore, impersonal idea. The message of Hillel is that study of Torah is central. Yohanan ben Zakkai teaches that Torah guides the people through difficult times. Akiba, the third in the trilogy of the founders of classical Judaism, adds that Torah is for each individual to do, and that Torah demands all of life, even unto death.

Akiba was a rabbi educated at Yavneh by Yohanan ben Zakkai's disciples. He himself taught the most important rabbis of the second century C.E. His dominance in the legal traditions ultimately promulgated as *The Mishnah,* or law-code, by Judah the Patriarch of the Jewish community of the land of Israel at the end of the second century, is axiomatic. But Akiba's importance for us is not as a great legislator and formative mind in the development of the religious-legal heritage of Judaism. His importance is as the embodiment of the third component in the ideal of Torah: Torah is to be understood as the source of life for each individual, as for the community as a whole. It is, as I said, not only of social and historical importance, but vital for the existence of each and every person.

Akiba was a leader in the war led against Rome by Bar Kokhba, a general who inspired the people to try to retake Jerusalem and reestablish the Temple. That war, fought from 132 to 135 C.E., failed despite extraordinary bravery and self-sacrifice. Afterward, for a time, the Romans saw the masters of Torah, implicated in the war, as subversive, and they sought to suppress the teaching of Torah and its practice. Akiba, the greatest rabbi of his day, taught by his example that life without Torah was worthless. Faced with the choice of giving up the study and practice of Torah or facing martyrdom, he chose martyrdom.

Louis Finkelstein, historian and scholar of rabbinic texts, was chancellor of the Jewish Theological Seminary of America and is today one of the acknowledged masters of Talmudic studies. This is his account of the martyrdom of Akiba.

From *Akiba, Scholar, Saint, and Martyr,* by Louis Finkelstein (Cleveland and New York: The World Publishing Co. and Meridian Books; Philadelphia: The Jewish Publication Society of America, 1962), pp. 272–277. © 1936 by Louis Finkelstein. Reprinted by permission of the author and Jewish Publication Society of America.

It was not long before the loyalty of Akiba and his colleagues to the principle of study was to be put to the ultimate test. The savagery of the repressions grew from month to month. It was probably in the year 134, just before the capitulation of Betar, that the Romans issued their drastic decree, forbidding not only the practice, but also the study of the Torah. Now Akiba knew that he had reached the end of compromise. He had counseled the people to accept the Roman gift of a Temple when that had been offered; he had warned them not to be disappointed when the offer was withdrawn; he had asked them to sacrifice the right to observe the Law, in order that its study might be perpetuated. But the last stronghold, the innermost shrine of all was to be defended at all costs. If the study of the Torah was abolished, there was no further purpose in living. And so, at the age of ninety-five, the compromising pacifist once more took up the weapons of non-resistant war. Calmly he gathered his students, gave his decisions, delivered his lectures. Gatherings in secret, he both disdained and feared. They were unworthy of the dignity of the Torah; and were certain to raise the suspicion of political activity. He had always taught in the open, in the shade of a tree; and he would continue to do so. He made only one compromise with necessity. He invited his disciples to dine with him; and they discussed the Law during their meal.

A casual remark which he made at one of these gatherings reveals his serenity, his intellectual youthfulness and his enduring faith, in this last period of his life. He disregarded the havoc of the moment, and thought only of the future. The Romans were a passing phenomenon, about which he could do nothing. Palestine's farms, her trees and her children, were his primary concern. "Those who raise crop-destroying cattle, those who chop down good trees, and those who teach children dishonestly, will never see a blessing," he said.

When his old antagonist, Pappias, warned him that he was courting death by continuing to teach so publicly, Akiba replied with the parable of the fishes and the fox. The fox, coming to the river's bank, suggested to the fishes that they might find safety from the fishermen by coming on the dry land. But the fishes replied, "If in the water which is our element, we are in danger, what will happen to us on the dry land which is not our element?"

"So, too," continued Akiba, "If there is no safety for us in the Torah which is our home, how can we find safety elsewhere?"

Akiba could not have expected to continue teaching for long. Soon he was seized by the soldiers and carried off to prison. The Romans, still respecting his learning, his reputation and his distinguished personality, perhaps also remembering his pacifist and conciliatory teachings, hesitated to put him to death. They kept him in confinement for three years, treating him with consideration, even with courtesy. He was allowed the attendance of his disciple, Joshua ha-Garsi, who waited on him; and was permitted to enjoy the visits of Simeon ben Yohai, who had returned from Zidon to be near the Master in his affliction. "Continue to instruct me," Simeon begged of him.

At first reluctant, out of fear that he might endanger his pupil's freedom and even his life, Akiba finally yielded to his importunities, "My son," he said, "more than the calf wants to suck, the cow wants to suckle!" And he taught him. Convinced at last that there was no point in trying to conciliate the oppressor, Akiba decided to bring the calendar, which had been neglected for a decade, into order. He added an intercalary month to each of three successive years—an unprecedented procedure—until Passover, which had been thrown back into January, once more occurred in its appropriate season. He gave his visitors secret instructions, intended to mitigate the rigors of the Law for the harassed survivors of the persecution. In one decision, he rejected a tradition which had developed naturally in plebeian Jerusalem but was entirely unsuited to the new conditions of Jewish life. This tradition required persons who had been authorized by a husband to arrange his divorce to write the necessary document in person. It was not sufficient for them to supervise the writing. The provincial sages, living in communities where the ability to write was far from universal, had always objected to this rule. Now, when the government had declared the practice of Jewish ceremonies a state offense, it was frequently necessary to obtain the sanction of the husband for divorce and to postpone the writing for some more convenient time. Hence, Akiba felt compelled to accept, perhaps as an emergency measure, the provincial view to which he had always objected.

Although he pursued these audacious activities secretly, Akiba must have known that the Romans would soon learn of them. When this happened, he was merely transferred to a prison in distant Caesârea, where no one but his servant-pupil, Joshua ha-Garsi, was permitted to attend him.

And still he carried on. The impoverished and leaderless community made unheard-of sacrifices to obtain decisions from Akiba during these days. When one difficult question arose, they hired a man at a cost of four hundred *zuz* to make his way into the prison and get Akiba's opinion. On another occasion stratagem had to be used. Since the Romans had forbidden the Jews to observe any of their ceremonies, the rite of *halizah* had been carried out in private, and the scholars wondered whether under those circumstances it was valid. One of them took a peddler's basket and daringly went up and down before the jail, crying, "Needles for sale! Needles for sale! What is the Law regarding a private *halizah?* Needles for sale; needles for sale!"

Akiba, hearing the noise, replied from his jail, "Have you any spindles? It is permitted."

Even in his new prison, Akiba continued to observe every detail of the Law. His pupil-servant, Joshua ha-Garsi, brought him daily a small quantity of water, half of which he would drink keeping the remainder for his ritual washing. One day the guard, meeting Joshua, inspected his pitcher, and cried: "You have too much water. Are you trying to wash away the walls of the jail?" With these words, he seized the vessel and poured out half of its contents.

When Joshua at last came to his master and presented what was left of the precious liquid, Akiba's face fell. "Joshua," he said, "you know that I am an old man, and my life depends on you!" Joshua then told him what had happened. "Let me have the water, so that I may wash," said Akiba.

"There is not enough left for your drink," Joshua cried, "and how can any be spared for washing?"

"What can be done?" Akiba said. "The Law requires that we wash when we awake and before we eat. It is better that I should die than that I should transgress the words of my colleagues." And he declined to taste a morsel until he was given sufficient water to wash his hands.

Finally Akiba was brought to trial; his judge was to be his former friend, Rufus. There was no possible defense against the charges; Akiba had violated the Law by offering instruction to his disciples. Yet Joshua ha-Garsi, standing in the open Court, at a little distance from the prisoner, and in front of the grim Roman general, prayed that somehow the aged scholar might be saved. But even as the half-smothered words came from his mouth, he noticed a cloud covering the sun and the sky. "I knew then that our prayer was useless," he said, "for it is written, 'Thou hast covered Thyself with a cloud, so that no prayer can pass through' " (Lam. 3:44).

Akiba was found guilty and condemned to death. Still attended by his faithful Joshua, he retained his courage and his strength of mind until the very end. The popular story tells that the Romans killed him by tearing his flesh from his living body. As he lay in unspeakable agony, he suddenly noticed the first streaks of dawn breaking over the eastern hills. It was the hour when the Law requires each Jew to pronounce the *Shema*. Oblivious to his surroundings, Akiba intoned in a loud, steady voice, the forbidden words of his faith, "Hear, O Israel, the Lord is our God, the Lord is One. And thou shalt love the Lord thy God with all thine heart, and with all thy soul, and with all thy might."

Rufus, the Roman general, who superintended the horrible execution, cried out: "Are you a wizard or are you utterly insensible to pain?"

"I am neither," replied the martyr, "but all my life I have been waiting for the moment when I might truly fulfill this commandment. I have always loved the Lord with all my might, and with all my heart; now I know that I love him with all my life." And, repeating the verse again, he died as he reached the words, "The Lord is One."

The scene, indelibly impressed on the eyes of Joshua ha-Garsi, became part of Jewish tradition. The association of the *Shema* with the great martyr's death made its recitation a death-bed affirmation of the faith, instead of a repetition of select verses; and to this day the pious Jew hopes that when his time comes he may be sufficiently conscious to declare the Unity of his God, echoing with his last breath the words which found their supreme illustration in Akiba's martyrdom.

part five

torah as a way of life: the joy of the commandments

It is time to ask, What is the life of Torah actually like? How do people understand their situation? Do they feel, when confronted by a myriad of religious deeds to be done, that they are burdened by an endless set of requirements? If they do the commandments, what is the effect for their spirit? You might suppose that having done one's duty, a person will feel self-satisfied and self-righteous, so that life within the Torah produces a sense that one is, so to speak, able to "do things for God."

We therefore turn to the question, What is the attitude of the pious Jew toward his own life of piety? We want to know how he sees himself, his life with God, and his relationship to the Torah. What we shall find is that the way of Torah leads to a life of perpetual awareness of the presence of God and love for his commandments and his Torah. All day long, in all sorts of situations, the Jew is reminded of his context. That context is to be described as follows: "I am a child of Abraham, Isaac, and Jacob, whom you loved. I am responsible to you because, in your love, you have revealed your will—your Torah—to me, and have asked of me many sorts of religious deeds, or *mitzvot* (translated, commandments). In doing these deeds I fulfill my true being and in achieving a sense of oneness and wholeness with you, I am made glad. But that is not a joy of pride or self-righteousness. It is rather the joy of thankfulness that one may fully carry out the ultimate purpose for which a person is created."

This viewpoint will come to us from two sorts of writings. First, as usual, we look into the *Siddur,* the order of prayers, seeking those prayers which tell us about the Jew's conception of himself and his relationship to God. Second, in the more abstract writings of a scholar, we shall review important sayings in rabbinic literature which, put together into a coherent account, explain the exaltation and fulfillment contained within the commandments.

15.

standing before god

The morning worship, said either in the synagogue or at home, begins with private prayers and blessings. These are the opening words, the way in which a Jew, upon rising from his sleep, addresses God.

From *Weekday Prayer Book,* edited by Jules Harlow (New York: The Rabbinical Assembly of America, 1962), pp. 10–13, 28–29. © 1961 by The Rabbinical Assembly of America. Reprinted by permission of The Rabbinical Assembly.

Our Soul in His Keeping

My God, the soul You have given me is pure. You created it and You formed it. You breathed it into me and You keep it within me. A time will come when You will take it from me, but You will return it to me in the life to come.

So long as the soul is within me I acknowledge You, O Lord my God and God of my fathers, Master of all creation, Lord of all souls. Praised are You, O Lord, who restores the soul to the body.

Daily Renewal of Life

Praised are You, O Lord our God, King of the universe, who enables man to distinguish between night and day.

Praised are You, O Lord our God, King of the universe, who fashioned man in Your image.

Praised are You, O Lord our God, King of the universe, who has placed upon me the responsibilities of a Jew.

Praised are You, O Lord our God, King of the universe, who gives sight to the blind.

Praised are You, O Lord our God, King of the universe, who clothes the naked.

Praised are You, O Lord our God, King of the universe, who sets captives free.

Praised are You, O Lord our God, King of the universe, who raises those who are bowed down.

Praised are You, O Lord our God, King of the universe,
who created heaven and earth.

Praised are You, O Lord our God, King of the universe,
who provides for all my needs.

Praised are You, O Lord our God, King of the universe,
who guides man to a sure footing.

Praised are You, O Lord our God, King of the universe,
who girds Israel with courage.

Praised are You, O Lord our God, King of the universe,
who crowns Israel with glory.

Praised are You, O Lord our God, King of the universe,
who restores vigor to the weary.

Praised are You, O Lord our God, King of the universe,
who removes sleep from my eyes and slumber from my eyelids.

With Torah as our Guide

May it be Your will, O Lord our God and God of our fathers, that we walk
in the way of Your Torah and hold fast to Your commandments.

Keep us from falling into sin, transgression, or iniquity. Bring us not to trial
or disgrace. Let no evil impulse gain mastery over us.

Keep us far from wicked men and corrupt companions; strengthen our desire
to perform good deeds, and bend our will to Your service.

May we, this day and every day, find grace, love, and compassion in Your
eyes and in the eyes of all who look upon us. May You grant us a full measure
of kindness. Praised are You. O Lord, who bestows blessings upon His people
Israel.

Sons of the Covenant

Man should always revere God, in thought as in deed, acknowledge truth, and speak the truth even
in his heart. On arising he shall declare:

O Lord of all worlds! Not upon our righteousness do we rely when we bow
in supplication before You, but upon Your great compassion.

What are we? What our lives? What is our piety? What is our righteousness?
What is our attainment, our strength, our might? What can we say before
You?

Before You, O Lord our God and God of our fathers, the mighty are as nothing, the famous as if they had never been; the wise as if without wisdom, the clever as if with no reason.

Their doings are without meaning, their days are as a breath. Man's superiority over the animal is but a vain illusion; all life is but a fleeting breath.

We are Your people, the sons of Your covenant, children of Your beloved Abraham, with whom You made a pledge on Mount Moriah. We are the seed of Isaac, Abraham's only son, who was bound upon the altar. We are Your firstborn people, the congregation of Jacob, whom You named Israel and Jeshurun because You loved him, and delighted in him.

Therefore, it is our duty to thank and to praise, to glorify and to sanctify You:

How great is our joy! How good is our portion!
How pleasant our lot! How beautiful our heritage!

What great joy is ours that twice each day,
Morning and evening, we are privileged to declare:

HEAR, O ISRAEL: THE LORD OUR GOD, THE LORD IS ONE!
Praised be His sovereign glory for ever and ever.

You are the Lord everlasting before creation and since creation, in this world and in the world to come.

May Your holiness be made manifest through those who suffer martyrdom in Your name. May Your holiness be made manifest through our redemption to dignity and to strength.

Praised are You, O Lord, whose holiness is manifest before all mankind.

16.

mitzvah

solomon schechter

What is the meaning of *mitzvah*—commandment? Why does classical Judaism lay so much stress on concrete religious actions? The answer is, Judaism holds that a person is what he does. The actions speak for the individual; they not only express, but also shape his ideals. Schechter here answers those scholars who have exaggerated the burdens of "life under the law" and have held it to be a burden and not a joy. Schechter was the President of the Jewish Theological Seminary of America until his death in 1915. His essays are generally regarded as classics of the accurate and informed exposition of the beliefs of rabbinic Judaism.

It should be understood that not every religious requirement applies to every person at all times. Some are more important than others. Schechter points out that the Talmudic rabbis saw the purpose behind the commandments and said what it was. They did not want the Jews to be robots, who would mindlessly do whatever they were told. Different circumstances will make different commandments more important. The main thing is that one must, through his deeds, express his awareness of the transcedent God, creator of heaven and earth, revealer of the Torah, redeemer of mankind.

From *Some Aspects of Rabbinic Theology,* by Solomon Schechter. (New York: Behrman House, 1936, and Schocken Books, 1961), pp. 138–147 (Behrman House edition). © 1961 by Schocken Books, Inc., and reprinted with their permission.

R. Simlai, a well-known Agadic teacher and controversialist of the third century, said as follows: "Six hundred and thirteen commandments were delivered unto Moses on Mount Sinai; three hundred and sixty-five of which are prohibitive laws, corresponding to the number of days of the solar year, whilst the remaining two hundred and forty-eight are affirmative injunctions, being as numerous as the limbs constituting the human body." This is one of the earlier comments on the number of the six hundred and thirteen laws, which are brought forward in many of our theological works, with the purpose of proving under what burden the scrupulous Jew must have laboured, who considered himself under the duty of performing all these enactments. The number is, by its very strangeness, bewildering; and the Pharisee, unable to rise to the heights above the Law, lay under the curse of its mere quantity. A few words as to the real value of these statistics are therefore necessary, before we pass to other questions connected with our subject.

The words with which the saying of R. Simlai is introduced are, "He preached," or "he interpreted," and they somewhat suggest that these numbers were in some way a subject for edification, deriving from them some moral lesson. The lesson these numbers were intended to convey was, first, that each day brings its new temptation only to be resisted by a firm Do not; and, on the other hand, that the whole man stands in the service of God, each limb or member of his body being entrusted with the execution of its respective functions. This was probably the sentiment which the preacher wished to impress upon his congregation, without troubling himself much about the accuracy of his numbers. How little, indeed, we are justified in urging these numbers too seriously is clear from the sequel of R. Simlai's homily. It runs thus: "David came (after Moses) and reduced them (the six hundred and thirteen commandments) to eleven, as it is said: Lord, who shall abide in thy tabernacle? who shall dwell in thy holy hill? He that walketh uprightly, etc. Then Isaiah came and reduced them to six, as it is said: He that walketh righteously, etc. Them Micah came and reduced them to three: He hath shewed thee, O man, what is good; and what doth the Lord require of thee, but to do justly, etc. Then Isaiah came again, and reduced them to two, as it is said: Thus saith the Lord, Keep my judgements, and do justice. Then Amos came and reduced them to one, as it is said: Seek the Lord and live. Whilst Habakkuk (also) reduced them to one, as it is said: But the just shall live by his faith." The drift of this whole passage shows that the homily was not so much intended to urge the necessity of carrying out all the commandments with their numerous details, as to emphasise the importance of the moral laws, which themselves, nevertheless, may be compressed into the principle of seeking God, or of faith in God.

Granted, however, that R. Simlai took it seriously with him number of six hundred and thirteen: granted, again, that his enumeration rested on some old authority which may be regarded as a guarantee for its exactness, this would prove nothing for the "burden theory," The only possible explanations of our Rabbi's saying are the lists of R. Simon Kiara and of Maimonides. But even a superficial analysis will discover that in the times of the Rabbis many of these commandments were already obsolete, as, for instance, those relating to the arrangements of the tabernacle, and to the conquest of Palestine; whilst others concerned only certain classes, as, for instance, the priests, the judges, the soldiers and their commanders, the Nazirites, the representatives of the community, or even one or two individuals in the whole population, as, for example, the king and the high priest. Others, again, provided for contingencies which could occur only to a few, as, for instance, the laws concerning divorce or levirate-marriages. The laws, again, relating to idolatry, incest, and the sacrifices of children to Moloch, could hardly be considered as coming within the province of the practical life even of the pre-Christian Jew; just as little as we can speak of Englishmen being under the burden of the law when prohibited from burning their widows or marrying their grandmothers, though these acts would certainly be considered as crimes. A careful examination of the six hundred and thirteen laws will prove that barely a hundred laws are to be found which concerned the everyday life of the bulk of the people. Thus the law in its totality, which by the number of its precepts is so terrifying, is in its greater part nothing else than a collection of statutes relating to different sections of the community and to its multifarious institutions, ecclesiastical as well as civil, which constituted, as I have already said, the kingdom of God.

And here lay the strength of Judaism. The modern man is an eclectic being. He takes his religion from the Bible, his laws from the Romans, his culture from the classics, and his politics from his party. He is certainly broader in his sympathies than the Jew of old; but as a composite being, he must necessarily be lacking in harmony and unity. His sympathies are divided between the different sources of his inspiration,—sources which do not, as we know, always go well together. In order to avoid collision, he has at last to draw the line between the ecclesiastical and the civil, leaving the former, which in fact was forced upon him by a foreign religious conqueror, to a separate body of men whose business it is to look after the welfare of his invisible soul, whilst reserving the charge of the body and the world to himself.

The Rabbinic notion seems to have been that "if religion is anything, it is everything," The Rabbi gloried in the thought of being, as the Agadic expression runs, "a member of a city (or community) which included the priest as well as the prophet, the king as well as the scribe and the teacher," all appointed and established by God. To consider the administration of justice with all its details as something lying without the sphere of Torah would have been a terrible thought to the ancient Jew. Some Rabbis are anxious to show that the appointment of judges was commanded to Moses, even before Jethro gave him the well-known advice. The Torah, they point out, is a combination of mercy and justice. That the ways of the Torah "are ways of sweetness, and all her paths are peace" (Prov. 3:17, 18), was a generally accepted axiom, and went without saying; what had to be particularly urged was that even such laws and institutions as appear to be a consequence of uncompromising right and of rigid truth, rather than of sweetness and peace, were also part and parcel of the Torah, with her God-like universality of attributes. Hence the assertion of the Rabbis that God threatens Israel with taking back his treasure from them should they be slow in carrying out the principle of justice *(dinim)*. "To the nations of the earth he gave some few laws; but his love to Israel was particularly manifested by the fulness and completeness of the Torah, which is wholly theirs." And in it they find everything. "If thou wantest advice," the Rabbis say (even in matters secular, or in questions regarding behaviour and good manners), "take it from the Torah, even as David said, From thy precepts I get understanding" (Ps. 119:104). . . .

R. Judah Hallevi, with the instinct of a poet, hit the right strain when he said, in him famous Dialogue *Kusari,* "Know that our Torah is constituted of the three psychological states: Fear, love, and joy" (that is to say, all the principal emotions of man are enlisted in the service of God). "By each of these thou mayest be brought into communion with thy God. Thy contriteness in the days of fasting does not bring thee nearer to God than thy joy on the Sabbath days and on festivals, provided thy joy emanates from a devotional and perfect heart. And just as prayer requires devotion and thought, so does joy, namely, that thou wilt rejoice in his commandments for their own sake, (the only reasons for this rejoicing being) the love of him who commanded it, and the desire of recognising God's goodness towards thee. Consider these feasts as if thou wert the guest of God invited to his table and his bounty, and thank him for it inwardly and outwardly. And if thy joy in God excites thee even to the degree of singing and dancing, it is a service to God, keeping thee attached to him. But the Torah did not leave these things to our arbitrary will, but put them all under control. For man lacks the power to make use of the functions of body and soul in their proper proportions."

The law thus conceived as submitting all the faculties and passions of man to the control of the divine, whilst suppressing none, was a source of joy and blessing to the Rabbis. Whatever meaning the words of the Apostle may have, when he speaks of the curse of the Law, it is certain that those who lived and died for it considered it as a blessing. To them it was an effluence of God's mercy and love. In the daily prayer of the Jews the same sentiment is expressed in most glowing words: "With everlasting love thou hast loved the house of Israel, thy people; Torah, commandments, statutes, and judgements hast thou taught us. . . . Yea, we will rejoice in the words of thy Torah and thy commandments forever. . . . And mayest thou never take away thy love from us. Blessed art thou, O Lord, who lovest thy people Israel." Beloved are Israel, whom the Holy One, blessed be he, surrounded with commandments, (bidding them) to have phylacteries on their heads and arms, a mezuzah on their door-posts, fringes on the four corners of their garments. . . . "Be distinguished," said the Holy One, blessed be he, to Israel, "by the commandments in order that ye may be pleasing unto me. Thou (Israel) art beautiful when thou art pleasing." Indeed, there is not a single thing which is not connected with a commandment, be it the farm, or the home, or the garments of the man, or his flocks. And it is on account of this fact that Israel considered themselves blessed in the city and in the field. It is the very light sown for the righteous, God not having loved anything in the world which is not connected with a law.

17.

the joy of the torah

solomon schechter

What is the right motive for doing the *mitzvot?* Is the pious Jew under the bondage to the letter of the law? The opposite is the case. The Jew constantly speaks of his pleasure in the commandments, of his sense of being sanctified by keeping them, of his expressing his love of God through them. We have already seen that worship is both intensely private and very public, and the same is so for the practice of the commandments. They are done by the individual, yet he does them in consonance with the procedures of the entire community of Israel and in order to participate in the consecrated life of the community. Religion is a wholly private affair which also is entirely public. Joy is very personal, yet it means more when it is shared with others—and the same is true for sorrow.

Again you will perceive in Schechter's writings a polemical purpose, and you are right. In Schechter's time people distinguished between the "law"—that is, the commandments, which were "external" and forced on people against their natural impulses—and "love" or "the spirit," which was inward and beautiful. Schechter therefore felt he had to meet the polemical attacks on the Judaism of his day. Yet that polemic is natural for people whose religious orientation begins in stress on the private person and on his individual "conversion" to religion. For such people, everything beings now, with me and my turning toward God. But Judaism does not begin with the individual. A person is born a Jew (or, to be sure, may convert to Judaism) and there never is a time in which he or she is not subject to the commandments, until death. The way of Torah is not explored afresh from generation to generation, in the sense that people have to seek inspiration or make things up as they go along. It is a way that is well-trodden, just as the Jewish people continue from age to age. The creative tension in Judaism is not going to be between the individual and "organized religion" or between "the law" and "the spirit." As we have seen, the way in which the religious deeds are carried out preserves a place for both the private expression of the individual and communal expressing and preserves continuing discipline of the group. Prayers are said by people together. Yet each person prays by himself. That is a different, and fruitful sort of tension.

From *Some Aspects of Rabbinic Theology,* by Solomon Schechter (New York: Behrman House, 1936, and Schocken Books, 1961), pp. 148–169 (Behrman House edition). © 1961 by Schocken Books, Inc., and reprinted with their permission.

Law and commandments, or as the Rabbinic expression is, *Torah and Mitzvot,* have a harsh sound and are suggestive to the outsider of something external, forced upon men by authority from the outside, sinister and burdensome. The citations just given show that Israel did not consider them in that light. They were their very love and their very life. This will become clearer when we consider both the sentiment accompanying the performance of the Law and the motives urging them.

The joy experienced by the Rabbinic Jew in being commanded to fulfil the Law, and the enthusiasm which he felt at accomplishing that which he considered to be the will of God, is a point hardly touched upon by most theological writers, and if touched upon at all, is hardly ever understood. Yet this "joy of the Law" is so essential an element in the understanding of the Law, that it "forms that originality of sentiment more or less delicate" which can never be conceived by those who have experienced it neither from life nor from literature. . . .

This joy of the *Mizwah* constituted the essence of the action. Israel, we are told, receives especial praise for the fact that when they stood on Mount Sinai to receive the Torah, they all combined with one heart to accept the kingdom of heaven in joy. The sons of Aaron, again, were glad and rejoicing when they heard words (of commandment) from the mouth of Moses. Again, "let man fulfil the commandments of the Torah with joy," exclaimed a Rabbi, "and then they will be counted to him as righteousness." The words, "Moses did as the Lord commanded him" (Num. 27:22), are explained to mean that he fulfilled the Law with joy. In a similar manner the words, "I have done according to all that thou hast commanded me" (Deut. 26:14), are interpreted to signify, I have rejoiced and caused others to rejoice. Naturally, it is the religionist of high standard, or as the Rabbis express it, "the man who deserves it," who realises this joy in the discharge of all religious functions, whilst to him "who deserves it not" it may become a trial of purification. But the ideal is to obtain this quality of joy, or "to deserve it." The truly righteous rejoice almost unconsciously, joy being a gift from heaven to them, as it is said, "Thou (God) hast put gladness in my heart."

This principle of joy in connection with the Mizwah is maintained both in the Talmud and in the devotional literature of the Middle Ages. The general rule is: Tremble with joy when thou art about to fulfil a commandment. God, his Salvation, and his Law, are the three things in which Israel rejoices. Indeed, as R. Bachye Ibn Bakudah declares, to mention one of the later moralists, it is this joy experienced by the sweetness of the service of God which forms a part of the reward of the religionist, even as the prophet said, "Thy words were found, and I did eat them; and thy word was unto me the joy and rejoicing of mine heart" (Jer. 15:16). R. Bachye Ibn Chalwah, again, declares that the joy accompanying the carrying out of a religious performance is even more acceptable to God than the *Mizwah* itself. The righteous, he points out, feel this ineffable delight in performing God's will in the same way as the spheres and planets (whose various revolutions are a perpetual song to God) rejoice in their going forth and are glad in their returning; whilst R. Joseph Askari of Safed (sixteenth century) makes joy one of the necessary conditions without which a law cannot be perfectly carried out. And I may perhaps remark that this joy of the *Mizwah* was a living reality even in modern times. I myself had once the good fortune to observe one of those old type Jews, who, as the first morning of the Feast of Tabernacles drew near, used to wake and rise soon after the middle of the night. There he sat, with trembling joy, awaiting impatiently the break of dawn, when he would be able to fulfil the law of the palm branches and the willows! . . .

And let it be noticed that the notion of *Lishmah* [doing a deed for its own sake] excluded even the intention of fulfilling a law with the hope of getting such rewards as are promised by the Scriptures. Though the Rabbis never tired of urging the belief in reward and punishment, and strove to make of it a living conviction, they yet displayed a constant tendency to disregard it as a motive for action. The saying of Antigonos of Socho, "Be not like servants that serve their master with the view to receive reward," is well known. All the commentators on the sayings of the Fathers explain this sentence as meaning that love pure and simple is the only worthy motive of the worshipper. But we must not look upon this saying of Antigonos as on one of those theological paradoxes in which divines of all creeds occasionally indulge. It is a sentiment running through the Rabbinic literature of almost every age. Thus the words in Deut. 11:13, "To love the Lord your God," are explained to mean: "Say not, I will study the Torah with the purpose of being called sage or Rabbi, or to acquire fortune, or to be rewarded for it in the world to come; but do it for the sake of thy love to God, though the glory will come in the end." The words in Ps. 112:1, "Blessed is the man who delighteth greatly in his commandments," are interpreted to mean, that he is blessed who delighteth in God's commandments, but not in the reward promised for his commandments. This proves, by the way, that the Rabbis could depart from the letter of the Scripture for the sake of the spirit, the succeeding verses in this very Psalm being nothing else than a description of the reward awaiting the pious man who fulfils God's commandments. In another place, those who, in view of Prov. 3:16, look out for the good things which are on the left side of wisdom, namely, riches and honours, are branded as wicked and base. And when David said, "I hate them that are of a double mind, but thy law do I love," he indicated by it, according to the Rabbis, his contempt for mixed motives in the service of God, as the Law should not be fulfilled either under compulsion or through fear, but only from the motive of love. Indeed, God bears evidence to him unselfishness of Israel and their full confidence in him, saying, "I gave them affirmative commands and they received them; I gave them negative commands and they received them; and though I did not explain their reward, they said nothing" (making no objection). In the devotional literature of the Middle Ages there is hardly a single work in which man is not warned against serving God with any intention of receiving reward, though, of course, the religionist is strongly urged to believe that God does reward goodness and does punish wickedness.

The real motive of this enthusiasm for the Law must be sought in other sources than the hope of reward. Those who keep the commandments of God are his lovers. And when the lover is asked, Why art thou carried away to be burned, stoned, or crucified? he answers, Because I have studied the Torah, or, Because I have circumcised my son, or, Because I have kept the Sabbath; but he considers the suffering as wounds afflicted upon him for the sake of his beloved one, and his love is returned by the love of God. The Law is thus a means of strengthening the mutual relations of love between God and his people. The fulfilment of the Law was, in the eyes of the rabbis, a witnessing on the part of the Jews to God's relationship to the world. "Why does this man," they say, "refrain from work on the Sabbath? who does he close his business on the seventh day? He does so in order to bear witness on the fact of God's creation of the world, and to his providence over it." The Law, according to the Rabbis, was a source of holiness. Each new commandment with which God blesses Israel adds holiness to his people; but it is holiness which makes Israel to be God's own. They deduce this doctrine from Exod. 20:30, which verse they explain to mean that it is the fact of Israel being holy men which gives them the privilege of belonging to God. Hence the formula in many benedictions: "Blessed art thou, O Lord our God, ... who hast sanctified us by thy commandments, and found delight in us." Another version of the same sort is, "Beloved are the commandments by which the Holy One, blessed be he, exalted the seed of his friend Abraham and gave them unto Israel with the purpose of beautifying and glorifying them; whilst Israel, his holy people, and his inheritance, glorify his name for the commandments and statutes he gave them. And it is because of these commandments that Israel are called holy. These reasons, namely, the motive of love, the privilege of bearing witness to God's relationship to the world, the attainment of holiness in which the Law educated Israel, as well as the other spiritual motives which I have already pointed out, such as the joy felt by the Rabbis in the performance of the Law and the harmony which the Rabbis perceived in the life lived according to the Torah, were the true sources of Israel's enthusiasm for the Law. At least they were powerful enough with the more refined and nobler minds in Israel to enable them to dispense utterly with the motives of reward and punishment; though, as in every other religion, these lower motives may have served as concurrent incentives to a majority of believers.

part six

torah as a way of life: some specific commandments

Abstract discussion of the joy of the commandments can mean little until we examine some of the concrete deeds—things one actually does, or refrains from doing—which are regarded as divinely-ordained commandments. Only then are we able to put together the theory of the commandments with the actual practices. As we have already seen, the best testimonies come either from people who actually act by and believe in the commandments, or from the prayers said in connection with carrying them out. We shall listen in the next two selections to an Orthodox Jew on dietary and other practical laws, and on the rites of passage connected with birth, puberty, and death. These are important because, in contemporary Judaism, however unobservant a Jew may be, he very likely will resort to the tradition at the crucial turnings in life; his son is apt to be circumcised on the eighth day, in accord with the law and to be called to the Torah at age thirteen; his daughter is going to be married under the *huppah,* the wedding canopy; and he will be buried in accord with Jewish law and mourned with the *Kaddish,* the sanctification of God's name. Though the unobservant Jew may not keep the dietary laws, moreover, he knows about them and at least at some points in his life is apt to come into contact with their requirements. These, therefore, are the most commonplace aspects of the practical life under the Torah.

18.

the dietary laws and their meaning

herman wouk

The commandments focus upon things people do in normal, everyday life. They are meant, as we have seen, to impose a sacred discipline upon the secular world, to sanctify the profane. It is therefore natural that one expression of living within the way of Torah is going to concern what you eat and how you eat. After all, eating is something you do every day. The Pentateuch contains various laws about food, which are understood to apply to everyone in ordinary circumstances, not merely to a certain class of holy people, such as the priests, or to a certain particularly sacred place, such as the Temple. These laws were developed and articulated over the centuries. Nowadays the word "kosher" is applied to those foods Jews are permitted to eat. "Kosher" simply means "fitting" or "appropriate." In addition, great stress is laid within the dietary disciplines upon the appropriately humane slaughter of those animals one is permitted to eat, and the laws of "ritual slaughter," or *shehitah,* have to be kept if meat is to be regarded as *kosher.* Herman Wouk, a novelist and also an Orthodox Jew, here explains the meaning of the dietary laws.

From *This Is My God,* by Herman Wouk (New York: Doubleday & Co., 1959), pp. 126–135. Copyright 1959 by The Abe Wouk Foundation. Reprinted by permission of Harold Matson Company, Inc.

A Touchy Topic

The Jewish diet discipline cuts sharply across general manners and ideas. It is one of the stress points where observance tends first to break down, and so it is a sore subject. A detached picture is not likely to please anybody. The nonobservant dig in their heels at the whole idea. The devout, on the other hand, who have to work pretty hard at keeping up the diet, expect to be praised, and they want to see the non-observant excoriated. The purpose here is only to tell what the dietary laws are. The reader will have to supply the moral judgments; from his emotional bias if he approaches the topic with one, otherwise from his common sense.

We are looking at a detail of a symbol system that stamps all the customary acts of life. This is the stamp on eating: an act that all people perform several times a day, given the choice. People may neglect work, play, prayer, and love-making, but they seldom forget to eat. All religions include grace over food. Many religions go farther and set a mark on what one eats and how one eats. Often such austerities are reserved for the monk, the nun, the priest, the ascetic, the lama. Judaism's disciplines are relatively mild, but they are for everybody.

The Torah gives only one brief reason for the laws: they will help discipline Israel to holiness. My agnostic friend . . . thought that declining to eat lobsters was no answer to the threat of hydrogen war. I think he has something there; but neither is getting married, or building a home, or having children, or doing a day's work. There is nothing I can think of that does not look pitifully absurd under the threat of a hydrogen holocaust, except possibly the quest for God. If the diet laws have some structural purpose in a major religion, we ought to try to find what that may be.

We will get into guesswork. The sages of Jewry have offered varying opinions on the laws. The great trap is to notice a visible effect of the diet in one's own time, and to assume that that was the whole cause of the laws when they were given in the Sinai desert. But let us see what the laws are and how they operate.

The Diet

There is no limit on food that grows from the ground; the disciplines deal only with sentient life. The Bible gives us physical tokens of the creatures that may be eaten.

For animals, the two marks are a split hoof and cud-chewing. In effect this admits a small class of beasts that live on grass and leaves, and shuts out the rest of animal life: beasts of prey, rodents, reptiles, swine, horses, pachyderms, and primates, most of which have been eaten at one time or another by various peoples. It is sometimes argued that the ban on pigs was meant only for hot countries in olden days. Obviously the range of excluded animals puts that argument out of court. We cannot eat polar bears either. The pattern has nothing to do with climate. It seems to be formal; in logic it almost has to be. If the diet were only an advanced health notion of the brilliant Moses, the world would have in time caught up with his wisdom, and the Jewish forms would have vanished in universal observance.

Of the creatures in the sea, Jews eat those with fins and scales. This rule eliminates the shellfish so popular in America—shrimps, oysters, and lobsters; also a number of French delicacies—sea urchins, snails, mussels, frogs, octopuses, squids, and the like. I have read attempts to defend this discipline on the ground that octopuses and lobsters are revolting, while fish are not, but I think this resembles the debater's point about pork in hot countries. To anyone who eats octopuses, I am sure that a well-cooked one is an attractive sight, tentacles, suckers, and all. The fact is that within the Hebrew formal diet lie many excellent fish, and outside it—as in the case of animals—lie creatures which some folks esteem as delicacies.

There are no specific marks for birds. The Torah lists a large number of proscribed ones, all birds of prey or carrion eaters. In general Jews and non-Jews eat the same fowl. The difference is in the kosher slaughtering. Insects are wholly out. Few insects show up as food in America, but now and then at a cocktail party one has to forgo such tidbits as chocolate-covered ants.

Kosher Rules

"Kosher means pure," runs the slogan of a major manufacturer of such products.

It is pleasant to see the advertising mind strike such a round blow for Judaism, but as usual it speaks to simple intelligences, at some sacrifice of exactness. The concept is in all truth a hard one to pin down. "Kosher" is a late Hebrew word that does not occur in the books of Moses. Perhaps the nearest English word is "fit," in the sense of proper or suitable. But the fitness, it must be clear, is mostly ceremonial. Kosher preparation of food does result in a high degree of hygienic fitness. But a hog could be raised in an incubator on antibiotics, bathed daily, slaughtered in a hospital operating room, and its carcass sterilized by ultra-violet rays, without rendering kosher the pork chops that it yields. "Unclean" in Leviticus is a ceremonial word. That is why the Torah says of camels and rabbits, "They are unclean *for you,"* limiting the definition and the discipline to Israel. Chickens and goats, which we can eat, are scarcely cleaner by nature than eagles and lions, but the latter are in the class of the unclean.

All this being understood, "kosher means pure" may perhaps stand as a statement of fact. There is a general ban against eating carrion: defined as the flesh of an animal that dies of old age or of disease, or that is torn to death by beasts of prey, or that meets any other violent death. The assurance that no such meat can be sold as kosher is certainly of hygienic value, even today. In less civilized times and places it has given the Jewish diet a vast margin of sanitary excellence. This law supplies a word that Jews extend to all unfit food: *trefe,* or torn.

The Torah has four main rules for preparing meat. Commentators variously take them as humane regulations and as sanitary laws. Without forcing logic, one can perhaps find both aims in the rules. At any rate, breaking any one of the four renders the meat "torn" and inedible under Hebrew law.

The first rule, the only law of diet in the Bible for all mankind, is clearly humane in intent. It bars the eating of flesh cut from a live creature—"the limb of the living." If the reader shrinks with horror at the thought, he is not familiar with ancient killing and cooking practices that still survive in primitive communities, and in some not considered primitive.

The second law forbids the drinking of blood, on the ground that "the blood is the life." The use of blood in sophisticated cookery is common, especially for sauces. Jewish law not only bans this, but it excludes the meat itself unless most of the circulatory blood is removed. The impression is widespread that for this reason one cannot get a decent kosher steak. Since we barbecue pretty good rare steak in my home—sometimes to the stunned surprise of Jewish guests—I can testify otherwise. Enough juice remains in the tissues to make perfect steaks. But in the old country, Jewish housewives fried steaks gray-brown. They brought the style with them. The so-called Jewish steak is therefore done to death by the standards of American cookery, but it need not be. Out West on the farm one usually encounters the Jewish-style steak fried clear through. It is a matter of regional taste, nothing more.

The third rule stems from the bizarre prohibition repeated three times in the Torah in identical words: "You shall not boil a kid in the milk of its mother." The repetition suggested to Maimonides that in Mosiac times this was a common rite of idolatry. However that may be, the strong emphasis led long ago to complete separation of flesh and dairy food in the Hebrew diet. Food from the ground or from the sea is eaten with meat meals or dairy meals. Meat and milk, or their products, never appear together on the table. In observant homes, there are separate utensils and crockery for the two types of meals. In Israeli army kitchens and navy galleys, this dual equipment is standard.

The fourth rule bans suet, the hard fat formed below the diaphragm. The regulations separating suet from edible fat are complex and help make butchery of kosher meat a work for skilled and learned men. Prohibited fats are identical with those specified for the altar in the Book of Leviticus.

The Genesis tale of Jacob's wrestling with a mysterious stranger [Gen. 32:22ff.] accounts for another ban in Jewish diets: the sciatic nerve of the hind-quarter. Jacob was injured in the nerve of his thigh, we are told, and left the battle with a limp. The story has all the marks of a mystic vision. The encounter occurs the night before he meets his vengeful brother Esau after a separation of twenty-years; it goes on till dawn; and Jacob's successful struggle against the stranger results in the change of his name from Jacob to Israel, "because you have contended with God and with men and have prevailed." The Torah adds, at the end of the tale, that in memory of the event the children of Israel do not eat the sciatic nerve.

It seems like a small deprivation. It could be small, but today it is not. The complete removal of the nerve from the hindquarters of an animal is a difficult point of butchery. It is simpler, and evidently less costly, to sell the hindquarters of kosher-slaughtered cattle to the general packers. Observant Jews therefore forgo some excellent cuts of meat. This is a remediable situation, and with a rise in demand it may be remedied.

Slaughter

The bans against drinking blood and against "the limb of the living" determine the rigid, indeed sacred, method of taking animal life under Hebrew law. There is only one way: a single instantaneous severance of the carotid arteries in the neck. The blood pours out; the supply to the brain is at once cut off; the animal's consciousness vanishes. The rest is muscular reflexes, to which the beast is as oblivious as a man in a coma, and swift death. This is what the animal physiologists tell us. Scientific testimony, gathered when this mode of slaughter has been under attack, shows that it is a death as merciful as any that humans can visit on animals, and far more merciful than most.

Stringent conditions to ensure a painless death are part of our law. If one of these precautions is omitted, the meat is called torn, and we cannot eat it. The death stroke must be a single slash. Even one sawing motion disqualifies, let alone a second stroke, a stunning blow, or any other inflicting of pain. The edge of the knife must be ground razor-sharp and smooth; one detectable nick causes rejection of the meat. The animal must be motionless at the instant of the death stroke, so that the knife may cut true. Skilled professional slaughterers, who undergo qualifying examinations for dexterity and technical knowledge, do this work. Equally knowledgeable insepctors watch each move. The guilds of slaughterer and inspector (the Hebrew terms are *shohet* and *mashgiah*) are ancient and strong. Often the office, with the complete training, passes from father to son.

The inspectors study the carcass for certain traces of disease which for thousands of years rendered meat non-kosher. This part of our procedure is unquestionably sanitary, centuries in advance of its time. Over the generations it has helped create the exceptional health statistics of Jewish communities. As the meat passes to the consumer, there are further procedures for draining the residue of blood. These were once the province of the housewife, and mothers handed the knowledge to their daughters, but more and more today the mass distributor of kosher food performs these last steps and sells meat ready for the pot. He assumes the responsibility for getting a rabbinic opinion on doubtful symptoms.

Degrees of Observance

In former times this was not so. The housewife did most of her own inspection, especially of poultry. She bought a chicken slaughtered before her eyes, took it home, and in cleaning it checked the viscera for signs of disease and internal injury known to her since childhood. In doubtful cases she brought the meat to her rabbi. Friday morning was always the businest time of the week for my grandfather, in his twenty-three years of ministry on the Bronx. The stream of housewives with *shailas,* religious queries, on bloody new-killed fowl was almost continuous. If he and I were studying together that morning we did not get far.

Nowadays answering shailas on fowl does not loom large in the Jewish ministry; not nearly so large as raising funds, making amusing speeches, writing persuasive brochures, and so forth. New times, new tasks. Old-fashioned people look askance at the change and hint that young rabbis today are mere affable ignoramuses. The fact is that the orthodox seminarists still get an exhaustive training, and have to pass a searching test, in the laws of meat inspection. Nineteen out of twenty seldom use the knowledge. They hardly can, unless they go into the kosher-meat-packing industry. The main task of a rabbi today is elementary education; not for the learned few, naturally, but for the disoriented general community. I for one would like to see the young divines speak, and write, and raise funds, even better than they do, since that is the task in hand. I joined the faculty of Yeshiva University to make available to them my scraps of knowledge about English usage. Once my grandfather said to me, "What do you have to teach them English for? They're American-born. They know English." This comment can stand as a summary of the distance, for better or worse, between the old and the new.

In the old country a pious man either did his own slaughtering or he worshipped side by side with the town shohet and knew his piety, skill, and intelligence at first hand. In the United States we must rely on seals of eminent rabbis, guaranteeing proper slaughter, inspection, and handling. There are devout people who cannot bring themselves to trust the guarantees. Such control of industrial processing seems too loose, too liable to error. To them the most remote risk of eating defiled meat—let alone the flesh of banned creatures or a fragment of their products—is unacceptable. My grandfather during his twenty-three years in the United States did not eat the flesh of cattle. His Sabbath meat was a fowl killed under his own supervision. He did not ask the rest of the family to follow his example. He ate in my mother's home and in mine, but he would not eat our meat. Yet even he had to rely to some extent on seals and signatures. The milk and butter he used bore guarantees of rabbinic supervision. He did not see the milking and the churning himself because he could not.

My grandfather was such a cheerful and jovial man that it never occurred to us that he was an ascetic; as indeed he was, a rather extreme one. Few people are able to forgo beef and lamb for half an adult lifetime as he did, on a point of ritual. The exceptionally pious today eat flesh called *glat kosher,* carrying special guarantees. Some members of Hasidic sects eat only meat which has been canned by other members of their sect under the seal of their own chief rabbi. If they travel, they carry enough of such provisions to last them the journey. If they run out, they subsist on raw vegetables and fruit. They will not use the utensils of public dining places. So the degrees of observance shade upward, or leftward if you will, to strictness, scruples, and self-denial, which some consider extravagant and which others regard as minimum compliance with the law.

An important point in this matter of shades of observance, it seems to me, is to avoid calling one's own practice the only true Judaism; to lable anything stricter mere fanaticism, and anything less strict mere pork-eating. One can fall into such an attitude because the old stability and uniformity of practice do not at the moment exist. People who eat ham or shrimps, or steaks from electrocuted or poleaxed cattle, are clearly not following the law of Moses. People who never eat or drink in public restaurants surely run less risk of accidental deviation from the diet than those who do. The exigencies of an active life may make this strictness difficult. The observant follow conscience under guidance of teachers they trust. They all hold to the same disciplines; the variations are in detail.

19.

birth and beginnings

herman wouk

From *This Is My God,* by Herman Wouk (New York: Doubleday & Co., 1959), pp. 140–147. Copyright 1959 by The Abe Wouk Foundation. Reprinted by permission of Harold Matson Company, Inc.

Circumcision

Voltaire spoke with scorn of a God who could care whether or not people cut off their children's foreskins; thus summing up in one entertaining image the whole skeptical reaction to religious form. Spinoza, an equally severe skeptic, was not as funny as Voltaire; in fact there was little fun in him; but he was the profounder of the two. "So great importance do I attach to this sign," said he, "I am persuaded that it is sufficient by itself to maintain the separate existence of the nation for ever."

Circumcision has lately become respectable, after serving as a joke about Jews for centuries. It turns out to be sound hygiene. On the recommendation of medical science, informed people everywhere are now cutting off their children's foreskins. If Voltaire were alive he would probably have his own cut off. He might even find himself wishing, the day after the operation, that his parents had had it done for him when he was an infant.

But for Jews circumcision today, as in the past four thousand years, is not a detail of hygiene. It is the old seal of the pledge between Abraham and his Creator, a sign in the flesh, a mark at the source of life. It makes a man look different naked, all his life long, than the natural man looks. The levellers like to say that when you strip off men's clothes, nobody can tell the beggar from the king. But naked or dead, the Jew is recognizable for what he is. True, in the twentieth century this sign turns out to be not a comic mutilation, but wise prophylaxis, and so the critics of Judaism lose their old foreskin jokes. But the disclosure should hardly be a surprise. We expect the symbols of a lasting faith, where they touch the body, to be safe and intelligent in themselves, not to kill the faithful off. The Jews have followed the Mosaic law with a confidence which modern medicine progressively ratifies. The medical endorsement is not, however, the glory of Judaism. It is a footnote.

We circumcise our sons on the eighth day after birth, as Abraham did Isaac, except when a doctor puts off the day for a delicate child. The ordinary infant of eight days passes through the operation easily, sleeping most of the time. Done with skill, the cut causes little pain, and it heals in a couple of days.

The event is what we call a *bris,* the Hebrew word for covenant. When lying-in was a part of home life, a bris always meant a family feast, with crowds of friends and kinfolk, learned discourses, and merrymaking. Each step of the ceremony was an honor, remembered for life, conferred solemnly by the parents on a relative or distinguished guest. Babies arrive today in hushed, coldly tiled hospitals, in the odor of antiseptic, with illness above and death below. Regulations often bar any trace of gaiety. But in large cities, in hospitals where Jewish mothers go in numbers, there is sometimes a remote chamber set aside for the purpose, enigmatically labelled the Bris Room; and from this room now and then there still escape muted echoes of an ancient joy.

The father pronounces this blessing at the ceremony:

> Blessed are you, Lord our God, Master of the Universe, who have made us holy with your commands, and have commanded us to bring this boy into the covenant of Abraham our father.

Ideally the father should do the circumcision himself, as Abraham did. In universal practice he appoints a highly skilled *mohel,* or circumciser, to do it. Performing hundreds of such ceremonies every year, the mohel attains experience in this operation which many surgeons will candidly admit they cannot match. Mohels use, of course, all existing medical safeguards and antisepsis.

Some Jewish parents allow a hospital surgeon to circumcise their sons, believing that he can perform the act more safely, or perhaps that it makes no difference who does it. They are in error for several reasons.

First, the mohel's familiarity with the surgical problem and its possible complications makes him the proper man for it. Accidents can occur under the most skilled hands on earth, but the parents can do no more to ensure the infant's safety than to get a qualified mohel.

Second, the circumciser takes the place of the father in a dedication rite going back four millennia. It stands to reason that he should be familiar with our religion and given to it.

Third, and perhaps decisive, Jewish circumcision differs from routine hospital practice. There is no margin of extra safety or painlessness in the hospital way, but it may be incorrectly done.

Bar-Mitzva

Bar-mitzva means "son of the commandment." The ceremony is the next milestone in a Jewish child's days; his entrance into a responsible religious life.

In my novel, *Marjorie Morningstar,* I did my best to portray a bar-mitzva with accuracy and with affection. I thought I succeeded pretty well, but for my pains I encountered the most bitter and violent objections from some fellow Jews. I had, they asserted, made a sacred occasion seem comical. There were comic touches in the picture, of course, but I believe these lay in the folkway as it exists, not in the imagination of the writer.

It is a sad people that does not have humorous excess as part of its life on

one occasion or another. The Dickensian Christmas is the nearest thing in literature I know to an American bar-mitzva. It has in much the same degree the
fantastic preparations, the incredible eating, the enormous wassailing, the swirl
of emotions and of family mixups, all superimposed with only partial relevance
on a religious solemnity. Christmas in the books of Dickens bursts with extravagant vitality, and so does our bar-mitzva. We Jews are a folk of great natural
gusto. In the freedom of the United States, where for the first time in centuries
we have known equality of opportunity, we have made of the bar-mitzva a blazing
costly jubilee. I do not see that there is anything wrong with that. The American
coming-out party is not too different. If the religious occasion really held its own,
and retained its meaning, all would be well. My reservation about the American
bar-mitzva is much the same as the doubts of some Christian clergymen about
the department-store Yuletide. The risk exists that the mere machinery of pleasure can work to obliterate the meaning of the event, leaving the celebration a
tuneful and colorful hurricane whirling about an empty center.

The event itself is both moving and important.

Like any other way of life, Judaism requires training, beginning when intelligence appears in the infant. A child does not develop the mind to grasp the
concepts, nor the stability to hold to the disciplines, until the age of thirteen. The
father then formally gives up the burden of his son's religious duties. The boy
takes them on himself. He begins to pray in phylacteries, and on the Sabbath
nearest his birthday he receives an *aliya,* a call to the Torah, to speak the blessing
over a part of the weekly reading, a privilege of male adults. This call marks his
new status.

The most honorific call in the popular view is the last, the *maftir,* because
it includes reading the weekly piece from the Prophets. The custom long ago arose
in the European communities to give the maftir to a boy on his bar-mitzva
Sabbath. That is what we do still.

But of course this custom took hold in a time of general compulsory Hebrew
education. For the ordinary European Jewish boy, chanting a maftir in its special
melody was no harder than for an American boy of thirteen to pick up a newspa-
per and read it aloud. All this changed completely when the main body of Jewry
shifted to the United States, with a catastrophic drop in Hebrew culture. The
American Jewish boy who could read a page of Hebrew prophecy aloud without
stumbling was exceptional. One who could translate it at sight, or could chant
it without long painful practice, was almost a freak.

Nevertheless the existing custom was to give the boy a maftir. And so during
two generations in the United States countless boys who barely knew the Hebrew
alphabet were schooled to parrot foreign words in a strange musical mode, by dint
of coaching stretched over a year or more. This uninforming and disagreeable
process was, for the majority of them, the sum total of their exposure to Judaism.

The damage was great. The boys could see—and the sages were quite right
in turning over religious responsibility to boys of thirteen, for they can perceive
and evaluate very sharply—the phoniness of what they were doing. The bored

coaches who for pay drove them through dreary chanting sessions every night for a year, the crutches of transliterated Hebrew and recordings, did not escape their satiric eyes. They judged that they were being drilled to palm themselves off as something they were not—properly trained young Hebrew scholars.

And yet how inevitable it all was, and is! Which parents would be the first to admit that their children were unskilled in Hebrew, when the custom was to go through a pretense that they were skilled? Human nature being what it is, the choice for the parents of ill-educated boys was to give them the customary bar-mitzva or none at all. For a long time the American rabbis were overborne by the momentum of the custom. The rationale was, "Better this than nothing," At last the evil results became too evident to ignore. Now a new and long-overdue procedure is gaining ground.

What is happening is that educators are harnessing the custom instead of being stampeded and trampled by it. Since parents and children alike have been regarding the bar-mitzva as a graduation, the rabbis have begun to treat it as such; and to require, as in any graduation, satisfying evidence of knowledge before conferring the diploma. The rote maftir under this rule no longer answers. The lad has to pass serious examinations in Hebrew, in the classics, in the laws of the faith, and in the history of Jewry. If he cannot, the rabbis do not permit the family to take over the synagogue for an empty ceremony. This means serious training has to start, at the latest, by the age of eight or nine. Judaism cannot be crammed into a boy in a year, though a maftir can be.

This policy takes courage in the rabbi and firm backing by his trustees. But since it is the obvious alternative to a continuing disaster in education, it is emerging year by year into more general use. As it takes hold, the Jewish faith stands some chance of being judged by the new generation—even if on the very simplest terms—for what it truly is. Our religion has its hard points, but it is colorful and powerful, and for four thousand years it has been interesting. It is not a chant of gibberish, which is all that the most sublime chapter in Isaiah can be to an insufficiently trained boy.

Some people of late, in a reaction to the extravagance of the American bar-mitzva, have dropped the public gala, appropriating the cost of it either as a gift to charity or as a fund to send the boy in later years on a trip to the Holy Land. This austerity seems commendable, but I wonder if it will become the rule. There is a time for everything. To provide a grand feast at such a turning point in life is an old and strong human impulse. Fireworks in season are always welcome, though they blaze and die at high cost in a short time.

When the overburdened bar-mitzva boy used to say in his memorized speech (a vestigial gesture at a scholarly discourse, now on the wane), "Today I am a man," he was of course speaking metaphorically, as his small stature, pink smooth cheeks, and breaking voice usually indicated. The manhood conferred by this event is ceremonial. The father does not expect him to start earning a living, or go to sleep at night without being ordered to, or do his schoolwork with enthusiasm, or begin reading the *Wall Street Journal.* Judaism simply holds that the boy is bright enough and advanced enough now to start operating as a Jew. He is out of his intellectual infancy. As soon as he is, the traditional masculine duties fall on him.

Bas-Mitzva

As sometimes happens with hurricanes, the whirling tempest of the American bar-mitzva has spun off a minor whirlwind called a bas-mitzva. The rationale is that girls no less than boys enter into religious obligations when they reach early adolescence, and that therefore there is no real reason why a fuss should not mark the event for girls as well as for boys.

It is easy enough to understand why there was no "bas-mitzva" for thousands of years and why it has sprung up now. Traditionally girls are exempt from most of Jewish ritual. Our faith put the formal structure on the men to uphold, leaving the women free for their family tasks; probably the only way the system could work. The bar-mitzva when it came was a minor synagogue formality, not a family Fourth of July. A girl would have been out of her head to agitate for the burdens of scholarship that engrossed her brothers from the age of five onward for the sake of that formality; and parents would have been fools to impose them on her. But when the intensive training of boys dwindled; when the bar-mitzva became a huge festival, earned at the price of some mechanical drilling which a girl could do as well as a boy; when there were no other visible burdens or consequences; when the boy, after the fun was over, dropped all Hebrew study and most observance, the girls and the parents sensibly saw no reason why they should not have a "bas-mitzva."

The difficulty of course has been to provide the proper synagogue solemnity for girls where none has existed since Judaism began. Since there is no custom, improvisation has come into play. The bas-mitzva is often a sort of graduation from Sunday-school training, or at least the completion of one stage. In traditional synagogues the bas-mitzva does not exist. Among the other denominations it has not taken on the pomp and circumstance of the bar-mitzva. In the nature of things it hardly can.

20.

the last confession

From the midst of life we turn to the end and read the words of the last confession, to be pronounced, if possible, before a person dies.

From *A Rabbi's Manual,* edited by Jules Harlow (New York.: The Rabbinical Assembly of America 1965), pp. 96–97. © 1965 by The Rabbinical Assembly of America. Reprinted by permission of the Rabbinical Assembly.

My God and God of my fathers, accept my prayer; do not ignore my supplication. Forgive me for all the sins which I have committed in my lifetime. I am abashed and ashamed of the wicked deeds and sins which I committed. Please accept my pain and suffering as atonement and forgive my wrongdoing, for against You alone have I sinned.

May it be Your will, O Lord my God and God of my fathers, that I sin no more. With Your great mercy cleanse me of my sins, but not through suffering and disease. Send a perfect healing to me and to all who are stricken.

Unto You, O Lord my God and God of my fathers, I acknowledge that my life and recovery depend upon You. May it be Your will to heal me. Yet if You have decreed that I shall die of this affliction, may my death atone for all sins and transgressions which I have committed before You. Shelter me in the shadow of Your wings; grant me a share in the world to come.

Father of orphans and Guardian of widows, protect my beloved family, with whose soul my own soul is bound.

Into Your hand I commit my soul. You have redeemed me, O Lord God of truth.

Hear O Israel: the Lord is our God, the Lord alone.

The Lord, He is God. The Lord, He is God.

21.

funeral prayers

Funeral rites in Judaism are very simple. The body is returned to the earth on a tablet or in a plain and unadorned box, as rapidly as possible after death. It is customary for burial to take place within twenty-four hours. The burial service itself is equally stark. It consists primarily of psalms, and these should be read not as biblical "literature" but as expressive of the meaning of the present occasion. The service is full of reflection on the nature and condition of humankind and provides little occasion for the glorification of this or that specific individual, except for a normally brief eulogy.

From *A Rabbi's Manual,* edited by Jules Harlow (New York.: The Rabbinical Assembly of America, 1965), pp. 104–107. © 1965 by The Rabbinical Assembly of America. Reprinted by permission of The Rabbinical Assembly.

O Lord, who shall dwell in Your sanctuary? Who shall abide upon Your holy mountain? He who lives with integrity, does what is right, and speaks the truth in his heart; who has no slander upon his tongue, who does no evil to his fellow man, who does not reproach his neighbor. In his eyes, a vile person is despised, but he honors those who revere the Lord. He takes an oath, even to his own harm, and does not change. He does not lend money at usurious interest; he does not take a bribe against the innocent. Whoever does these things shall stand firm forever.

Psalm 15

The Lord is my shepherd; I shall not want. He has me lie down in green pastures. He leads me beside the still waters. He guides me on paths of righteousness, He revives my soul for the sake of His glory. Though I walk in the valley of the shadow of death, I fear no harm, for You are with me. Your staff and Your rod do comfort me. You set a table in sight of my enemies; You anoint my head with oil; my cup overflows. Surely goodness and mercy shall follow me all the days of my life, and I shall abide in the house of the Lord forever.

Psalm 23

O Lord, You have been our refuge
From generation to generation.
Before the mountains were born,
Before the earth was fashioned,
From eternity to eternity
You are everlastingly God.

But man You crumble to dust;
You say: Return, O mortals.
A thousand years are in Your sight
As a passing day, an hour of night.
You sweep men away and they sleep;
Like grass they flourish for a day.
In the morning they sprout afresh;
By nightfall they fade and wither.

In Your anger, we are consumed;
In Your wrath, we are overcome.
You set out our sins before You,
Our secrets before Your Presence.
Your wrath darkens our days;
Our lives expire like a sight.

Three score and ten our years may number,
Four score years if granted the vigor.
Laden with trouble and travail,
Life quickly passes and flies away.
Who can know the power of Your anger?
Who can measure the reverence due You?
Teach us to use all of our days
That we may attain a heart of wisdom.

Relent, O Lord. How long must we suffer?
Have compassion upon Your servants.
Grant us of Your love in the morning
That we may joyously sing all our days.

Match days of sorrow with days of joy
Equal to the years we have suffered.
Then Your servants will see Your power;
Then their children will know Your glory.

The favor of the Lord our God be upon us;
He will establish the work of our hands.
The work of our hands He will surely establish.

Psalm 90

part seven

torah as a way of life: the sanctification of time

The cycle of life—birth, puberty, marriage, death—has its counterpart in the rhythm of the seasons—spring, summer, fall, and winter. These times too are celebrated through sanctification; they are marked off from one another and endowed with meaning and transcendent significance in the life of the Jew. Each is made into a moment of the commemoration of three aspects of sacred history: creation, revelation, and redemption.

The Sabbath is the celebration of the creation of the world: "For in six days God created the heaven and the earth, and on the seventh day he rested." At the same time the Sabbath is marked by the reading of the Torah in the synagogue. And the Sabbath is represented as the foretaste of redemption, the Sabbath of the world.

Similarly, there are three great festivals: *Pesah,* Passover, the festival of freedom; *Shavuot,* or the feast of weeks, the festival of revelation; and *Sukkot,* or the feast of tabernacles, the festival of rejoicing and of harvest. They all commemorate events in both creation and sacred history.

Passover, marking the spring and the end of the winter rains, celebrates the exodus of the Israelites from Egypt.

Shavuot, the time of the gathering of the first fruits, commemorates the giving of the Torah at Mount Sinai.

Sukkot, the celebration of the harvest and the advent of the fructifying rains of the winter in the land of Israel, commemorates the Israelites' dwelling in frail huts during the sojourn in the wilderness. The dominant theme of *Sukkot,* too, is God's protection, blessing, and ultimate redemption of Israel.

22.

the sabbath as the bride

samuel h. dresner

The Sabbath is called many things: a crown, a queen, a glory. But chief among the images by which Sabbath-holiness is conveyed is the comparison of the Sabbath to a bride. Here we have an exposition of that religious symbol.

From *The Sabbath,* by Samuel H. Dresner (New York.: The Burning Bush Press, 1970) pp. 14–15, 16–20. © 1970 by the National Academy for Adult Jewish Studies of the United Synagogue of America, and reprinted with their permission.

The Sabbath holds within its bounds one of the surest means of finding peace in the war-torn realm of the soul. It is one of the basic institutions of humanity —an idea with infinite potentiality, infinite power, infinite hope, perhaps, as some claim, the single most significant contribution of Judaism to world culture. Through the Sabbath, Judaism has succeeded in turning its greatest teachings into a day. Out of a remote world of profound thoughts, grand dreams and fond hopes —all of which seem so distant, so intangible and so unrealizable—the Sabbath has forged a living reality which can be seen and tasted and felt at least once a week. "The Sabbath is the hub of the Jew's universe," wrote Israel Zangwill; "to protract it is a virtue; to love it a liberal education." Among the Ten Commandments only one observance, one holiday, is mentioned—not Passover or the Day of Atonement, but the Sabbath: "Remember the Sabbath day, to keep it holy" (Exodus 20:8). It is the supreme symbol of Judaism, a recurring sign and reminder of creation and redemption.

Even the Festivals cannot compare to the Sabbath. The Festivals, said Rabbi Moshe of Kobrin, are like a poor man who is visited by a great king. Though the honor of the visit brings him joy, he is still aware of his own poverty. On the Sabbath, however, the pauper is invited into the king's palace where all awareness of his humble station vanishes.

The Rabbi of Ger gave a different reason. He said that the Festivals are bound by time, while the Sabbath is an aspect of eternity. Thus the Festivals come at fixed seasons of the year—the spring, the early harvest and the late harvest—and bring blessings to each season. But the Sabbath, because it partakes of the timeless, is the source of all blessings. It is, as Abraham Heschel has said, "eternity uttering a day."*

The Sabbath has taught us how to sanctify time and bring a dimension of

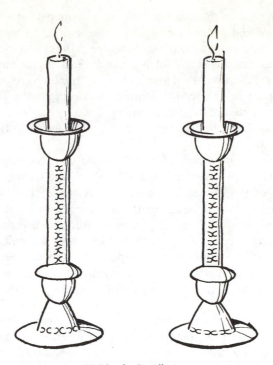

Sabbath Candles

holiness into the profane rhythm of life; how to unite a way of thinking with a way of living and join body and soul, heart and mind to the service of God; how to be worthy of having been created in His image and touch the hem of the world-to-come in this world; how to find a foretaste of heaven on earth and sense the eternal within the temporal. If Israel had done nothing more than give the Sabbath to mankind, it would deserve to be called "the chosen people."

But glorious though the Sabbath may be in theory and nostalgic though it may be in memory, in actual practice today it has all but been forfeited. Only scattered diehards still continue to maintain it in its dignity and grandeur. More and more it is defiled by the indifference of the majority and the ignorance of the mob who rumble over the sanctity of the day with neither understanding nor concern. The tendency of the Jew to attempt to conform to the prevailing pattern of the Gentile majority is powerful. . . .

The Sabbath is often referred to in Jewish literature as the Sabbath Bride, *Shabbat HaKallah*. Why? How can a day become a person? This strange transformation is precisely what happened in the course of the centuries through which Israel's observance of the Seventh Day grew and deepened and overflowed its former bounds. The Sabbath came to be considered not simply a day like any other day—abstract, opaque, comprised of so many hours and minutes and seconds—but it took on the characteristics of a living person whose presence one became aware of and whom one looked upon with affection and yearning. So much richness and meaning did the day acquire in the course of the centuries that it was treated not as a day at all, but as a wondrous and gracious personality who poured forth an endless stream of love and peace which was received and returned in joy by all those who awaited her coming. According to the Talmud, God gave each day a mate. Thus Sunday had Monday, Tuesday had Wednesday, Thursday had Friday. Only the Sabbath day was alone. So God gave it to the people of Israel as its mate, as its bride.

Why is the Sabbath called a "bride?" What does the term symbolize? The symbol of a bride is love, devotion and joy—an inward feeling. It is this peculiar inward feeling of the Jew which characterizes the Sabbath day. To him the Sabbath is a bride. Just as one prepares for a bride with the utmost care and meticulous detail, so the Sabbath is preceded by careful preparation. Just as one yearns for the arrival of a bride, so is the Sabbath met and welcomed. Just as the presence of the bride elicits tender concern, so does the Sabbath evoke love and devotion. Just as the departure of a bride occasions sadness, so is the departure of the Sabbath in darkness and regret. In all ways she is *Shabbat HaKallah,* the Sabbath Bride.

What is the difference between the Christian Sunday and the Jewish Sabbath? One way to distinguish them is to ask yourself whether Sunday, now or in the past, could be transformed into a person, a bride? Sunday is followed by Monday, Tuesday, and so forth, each day having a special name and standing by itself. But to Jews only the seventh day—the Sabbath—has a name, the others but a number. Thus: the "first day," the "second day," or the "third day," in accordance with how near or far they are to the "seventh day." Sunday is a day of commencement, the beginning of a week of toil. The Sabbath is a day of completion, the end of a week of yearning. Sunday arrives at midnight when the world sleeps; it is received passively, automatically. But Jews must "make" Sabbath; they must prepare for it, for the bride will not show her face unless she is invited and loved.

According to the Talmud, the world was created only for the Sabbath Bride. " 'And on the seventh day God finished His work which He had made' (Genesis 2:2). Genibah and the Sages discussed the passage. Genibah explained it thus: It may be compared to a king who made a bridal chamber, which he plastered, painted and adorned. What did the chamber lack? The bride. Likewise, what did the world still lack after six days of creation? The Sabbath."

> The Sabbath is a bride, and its celebration is like a wedding. . . .
> "There is a hint of this in the Sabbath prayers. In the Friday evening service we say *Thou hast sanctified the seventh day,* referring to the marriage of the bride to the groom (sanctification is the Hebrew word for marriage). In the morning prayer we say *Moses rejoiced in the gift* [of the Sabbath] bestowed upon him which corresponds to the groom's rejoicing with the bride. In the additional prayer we make mention of *the two lambs, the fine flour for a meal offering mingled with oil and the drink thereof,* referring to the meat, the bread, the wine and the oil used in the wedding

banquet. [In the last hour of the day we say] *Thou art One,* to parallel the consummation of the marriage by which the bride and groom are united."

A beautiful song was composed to welcome the Sabbath Bride—*L'khah Dodi:*

Bridegroom come to meet the bride.
Let us welcome the presence of the Sabbath.

The overflowing love of the people of Israel for their Bride-Sabbath led them over the centuries to set this poem to more melodies than any other prayer we possess. To the mystics of sixteenth-century Safed, where this poem was written, the synagogue was not grand enough to receive the Sabbath: its walls were too limiting, its presence too confining. So they would go out into the open fields, dressed in white, the color of the wedding garment, and there chant psalms and sing *L'khah Dodi,* accompanying the Sabbath Bride into their synagogues. Still today, when the last verse of the prayer is sung:

Come in peace, and come in joy,
Thou who art thy bridegroom's pride;
    Come, O bride, and shed thy grace
    O'er the faithful chosen race;
Come, O bride! Come, O bride!

the congregation turns from the Ark, faces the entrance and bows to the Bride who is about to enter.

The Bride comes not only into the synagogue, but into the home and into the hearts as well, bringing love and joy and song. A new tenderness is nurtured between mother and father, a new devotion between parents and children; and throughout the house a spirit of radiant joy permeates. No sadness is permitted on the Sabbath. Even the seven days of *shivah,* the mourning period, are interrupted for the Sabbath. The famous story from the Talmud of how Beruriah, the wife of Rabbi Meir, delayed telling her husband the terrible news of the death of their two sons until the Sabbath had passed and night had fallen, became a living example in countless Jewish homes through the ages, that one must take every precaution to preserve the sweet peace and joy of the day. Jews have always explained the special mood of exaltation they felt on the Sabbath, the inner tranquility and outer calm, the light that was said to shine from their faces, by claiming that with the arrival of each Seventh Day, God gives them an added soul, a *neshamah yeterah.* That is why we inhale from the spice box during the *Havdalah* ceremony when the Sabbath is ushered out on Saturday night: to revive us at the departure of *neshamah yeterah.*

Notes

* I am indebted to Dr. Heschel's profound study, *The Sabbath: Its Meaning for Modern Man,* for the basic concept out of which this book has developed.

23.

between the sacred and the profane

The Sabbath-liturgy is rich and wide-ranging. Here we consider the prayer said to mark the conclusion of the Sabbath and to make a distinction between the holy time just ending and the profane week just beginning. The moment is the advent of darkness on Saturday night. The sun has set, the week of work awaits. These are the prayers of the *Havdalah*-ceremony of making a distinction between the sacred and the profane.

From *Weekday Prayer Book,* edited by Jules Harlow. (New York: The *Rabbinical Assembly of America,* 1962), pp. 167–172. © 1961 by The Rabbinical Assembly of America. Reprinted by permission of The Rabbinical Assembly.

God is my deliverance; confident is my trust in Him;
The Lord is my strength, my song, my deliverance.

Joyfully shall you drink from the fountains of deliverance;
The Lord will rescue; the Lord will bless His people. Selah.

The Lord of hosts is with us, the God of Jacob is our fortress.
O Lord of hosts, happy is the man who trusts in You.
O Lord and King, answer us when we call, and rescue us.

Grant us the blessings of light, of gladness and of honor,
Which the miracle of Your deliverance brought to our fathers.

I lift up the cup of deliverance;
I call upon the Lord.

Praised are You, O Lord our God, King of the universe,
who creates the fruit of the vine.

Praised are You, O Lord our God, King of the universe,
who creates fragrant spices.

Praised are You, O Lord our God, King of the universe,
who creates the light of fire.

Praised are You, O Lord our God, King of the universe, who has endowed all creation with distinctive qualities and differentiated between light and darkness, between sacred and profane, between Israel and the nations, and between the seventh day and the other days of the week. Praised are You, O Lord, who differentiates between the sacred and the profane.

A Spice-Box for *Havdalah*

24.

passover: the festival of our freedom

theodor h. gaster

Passover is the first of the three great pilgrim festivals, coming in April. The second is *Shavuot,* the festival of weeks, and the third, *Sukkot,* the festival of tabernacles. Passover is celebrated in the home with a formal meal, or *Seder,* marked by the recitation of the Passover Narrative, or *Haggadah.*

We shall first ask about the meaning of the festivals, as expounded by Professor Theodor Gaster, Columbia University historian of religion and an important scholar of Judaism, and then survey some of the practices connected with the Seder. Finally, we shall read the main, and dramatic, liturgy of the Passover *Haggadah.*

From *Festivals of the Jewish Year. A Modern Interpretation and Guide,* by Theodor H. Gaster (New York: William Sloane Associates, 1952), pp. 31–33. Copyright © 1952, 1953 by Theodor H. Gaster. Reprinted by permission of the author and William Morrow & Co., Inc.

The festival of Passover is known in Jewish tradition as the "Season of Our Freedom." Its central theme is Release. On the seasonal plane, it marks the release of the earth from the grip of winter. On the historical plane, it commemorates the exodus of the Children of Israel from Egypt. On the broad human plane, it celebrates the emergence from bondage and idolatry.

In each case, the release is accompanied by a positive achievement; it is not simply an escape. It is also a cooperative act between God and man. On the seasonal plane, Passover inaugurates the reaping of the new grain; man sows the seed, but God—or the cosmic power—provides the rainfall and sunshine which quickens it. On the historical plane, it commemorates the birth of the Jewish nation: Israel was prepared to face the hazards of the wilderness, so God, in His providence, brought it to Sinai, gave it the Law, and concluded the Covenant. On the broad human plane, it celebrates the attainment of freedom and of the vision of God: man casts aside his idols and repudiates his ignorance and obscurantism, and in that very act God reveals His presence and imparts knowledge.

The three aspects of the festival run parallel to one another: the dark and dreary winter corresponds at once to the dark era of bondage and to the black night of ignorance, while the burst of new life in spring corresponds, in turn, to the flowering of Israel and the burgeoning of freedom.

Yet the freedom which is celebrated in the Passover festival is freedom of a special kind. Our own modern concept of freedom has developed through diverse channels and is today a fusion—or, perhaps, a confusion—of several originally distinct categories of thought. It is mixed up, for instance, with ideas of sovereign independence, personal liberty and democratic government; yet none of these ideas—however fervently Jews may today adhere to them—enters significantly into the Passover ideal. In Jewish tradition, freedom, in the modern sense, is scarcely a virtue; at best, it is an opportunity. What matters is *volitional dedication,* and it is this and this alone that forms the theme of the Passover story. If Israel had gone forth out of Egypt, but not accepted the Covenant at Sinai, it would have achieved liberation—that is, mere release from bondage—but it would not have achieved *freedom,* in the Jewish sense of the term. For the only freedom, says Judaism, is the yoke of the Torah; the only true independence is the apprehension of God.

The complex of ideas which today make up the Passover festival is the result of a long process of development and, more especially, of Judaism's inspired transformation of a primitive seasonal ceremony.

The nature of that ceremony is described in detail in the twelfth chapter of the Biblical Book of Exodus. At full moon in the first month of spring, we read, it was customary for every family to slaughter a lamb or goat at twilight and then, in the middle of the night, to eat it in common, along with unleavened bread and bitter herbs. The eating had to be done "in haste," and whatever portion of the meat remained unconsumed had to be burned ere break of dawn. Moreover, as soon as the slaughtering had been effected, a bunch of hyssop was dipped into the victim's blood, and a few drops were sprinkled with it on the doorposts and lintels of each house. The ceremony was known as *pesah,* and was followed immediately by a six-day festival, called the Feast of Unleavened Bread, during which no fermented food was allowed to be eaten, and the first and last days of which were regarded as especially sacred and marked by a total abstention from work.

25.

seder customs and practices

isaac levy

Here Rabbi Levy, Senior Jewish Chaplain in the British Army and former minister of the Hampstead Synagogue, London, reviews some of the practices in connection with the Passover Seder. The table is decorated with symbols of the festival; he tells us what they are and what they are supposed to mean.

From *A Guide to Passover*, by Isaac Levy (London: Jewish Chronicle Publications, 1958), pp. 49–60. © 1958 by Isaac Levy. Reprinted by permission of Jewish Chronicle Publications.

The Three Matzoth

The generally accepted practice is to display three *matzoth* on the *Seder* table. The middle *matzah* is broken during the early part of the recital of the *Haggadah,* one half being left on the table and the other set aside for the *Aphikoman*. At various times these three *matzoth* have been given descriptive names such as *Kohen, Levi, Israel,* representing the three sections of the House of Israel, or simply *Aleph, Beth, Gimmel* [the first three letters of the Hebrew alphabet]. In some oriental communities these *matzoth* were marked prior to the baking with one, two and three strokes respectively. The first recorded reference to the use of three *matzoth* is to be found in the Siddur of R. Amram (died 875), the first scholar to produce a systematic order of the liturgy for use in the communities of North Africa. The custom, however, was not universally accepted, for such leading scholars as Saadiah Gaon (882–942), Isaac ben Jacob of Fez (1013–1103), Maimonides (1135–1204) and even the Gaon of Vilna used only *two matzoth.* Their view was based on the fact that on Sabbaths and Festivals only two loaves are used and since this *matzah* is the "bread of affliction" and the poor could only afford an incomplete loaf, one of the two *matzoth* was to be broken at the appointed place in the *Seder.* The use of the three *matzoth* was based on the principle that the symbolic bread of affliction applied to an additional loaf and not to those normally used on the Sabbaths and Festivals.

The Seder Plate

Prominently displayed on the *Seder* table is the plate containing all the symbols of the ceremony to which reference is made during the recital of the

Haggadah. The order in which these items are to be arranged has varied from time to time. In Talmudic times, when the whole family reclined on couches or cushions, each item was brought in on a separate table when required for the exposition of the *Haggadah.* With the introduction of the family table the items were placed on a centre plate but no order of arrangement was fixed and the officiant placed them in whichever pattern he desired. Some scholars insisted that the order should be chronological following the order of each item's requirement during the *Seder,* those needed first to be placed nearest to the officiant thus avoiding any disrespect being shown to the items by stretching across them.

A Seder Plate

As in early Rabbinic times when the tables were brought in for the display of the special items referred to in the *Haggadah,* so to this day it is customary to raise the *Seder* plate and point to the item concerned whenever the recital requires it thus stimulating the children's interest. The Jews of Morocco preserve the custom of waving the plate three times over the head of each person present.

They claim that this serves to protect them against evil and symbolises the passing of the angel of death over the houses of the Israelites in Egypt. In other communities in North Africa it is customary to preserve the shank bone for the whole year and to suspend it over the door as a protection for the household.

The Four Cups of Wine

The universal practice to drink four cups of wine during the *Seder* ceremony is directly traceable to Temple times. It is generally accepted that these cups celebrate the four expressions of redemption contained in *Exodus*, vi: 6–7: "I will bring you out . . . I will deliver you . . . I will redeem you . . . I will take you." Other suggestions are that they recall the four cups of wine mentioned in the narrative of Pharaoh and his cupbearer (*Gen.* xl), or that they call to mind Israel's oppressors of old, the Chaldeans, the Medes, the Greeks and the Romans. M. Friedmann endeavoured to trace the practice to Roman times when it was the general practice to partake of three cups at every banquet; the first as an *apéritif* before the meal, the second during the meal and the third after the meal. In order to manifest the difference between this meal and the normal banquet, he suggests, the fourth cup was introduced over which the *Hallel* was recited. It was therefore ordained by the Rabbis that additional wine may be drunk between the second and third cups, but not between the third and the fourth so that the recital of the *Hallel* should not be impaired by intoxication.

The Fifth Cup

The reason for the practice to fill a fifth cup, which is placed on the table but not drunk, has produced suggestions similar to those concerning the four cups. The passage in *Exodus* cited above contains a fifth expression of deliverance: "I will bring you in unto the land." This gave rise to some uncertainty whether five cups should be drunk and not four. In some early Rabbinic works such as that of Isaac ben Jacob of Fez and R. Amram this fifth cup is prescribed for the specific purpose of accompanying the recital of the *Great Hallel.* Maimonides in his code states that the fifth cup should be placed on the table but makes no reference to its being distributed to each participant. It is generally accepted that since Elijah alone will solve all unanswered religious questions, the use of this cup awaits his decision. Hence it bears the expressive name of "Elijah's cup."

This cup is filled at the commencement of the second half of the *Haggadah.* Since this section is mainly devoted to songs of praise and expressions of hopefulness for future redemption, the association of the harbinger of the messianic era with this part of the ceremony is most appropriate. In some communities it is customary to encourage the children to watch this cup closely in order to see whether the invisible prophetic visitor has sipped from his cup. When the wine fails to diminish the children are asked to wait patiently for the coming year. This serves as a gentle reminder to the chidren of the article in the Creed: "Though he tarry, I will wait daily for his coming."

Red Wine

The colour of the wine to be used at the *Seder* table has, at different times, given cause for concern. The *Shulchan Aruch* prescribes the use of red wine, but permits white wine if the latter is superior in quality. The author of the *Ture Zahav,* David ben Samuel Halevi (1586–1667), however, advised against it because of the consequences of the blood libel and the fear that the sight of red wine might excite undue attention from the non-Jewish community. This scholar had good reason to adopt this view for he was himself a victim of the Chmielnicki pogroms (1648–9). The infamous blood libel forms a tragic chapter in the history of Jewish-Christian relations. It is closely associated with the Easter celebrations and the commemoration of the crucifixion, a period in the Christian calendar which aroused the baser elements to mob violence. The Beilis trial of 1912 inspired David Frishman to write on "Pesach and Easter" and to describe the stark terror which every Jew in Eastern Europe felt during "Passion Week." It offers but a modicum of comfort to know that the Blood Libel called forth the great apologetic work, *The Jew and Human Sacrifice* by the Christian divine, Hermann Strack. Even in our own generation the Nazis did not fail to realise the potentialities for evil in the Libel.

The Spilling of Wine

The custom to spill drops of wine when the ten plagues are recounted is first found in the *Rokeach,* by Eleazar of Worms (1176–1238). The finger is dipped into the cup and the wine is dropped into the saucer. It is suggested that thereby one recalls the "Finger of God" which wrought the plagues. Another reason offered is that the decreasing wine in the cup symbolises the diminished strength of the Egyptians. Some have suggested that this is a relic of an ancient belief that no food may be eaten over which unpleasant things have been recited. The custom may, however, call to mind the delightful Midrash which states that on the day the Egyptians were drowned the angels were forbidden to chant their daily song of praise. "My creatures are drowning in the sea," said God, "and ye desire to sing praises!" In the midst of Israel's jubilance a poignant moral lesson is imparted —some pleasure must be sacrificed in memory of fallen former enemies.

Leaning at Table

The practice to lean at table during the recital of the *Haggadah* and the partaking of the meal is referred to in the Mishnah. Even the poor man was expected to adopt this posture. The practice, which is doubtless of Babylonian origin, derives from the custom of the rich to recline on couches during meals. It was adopted on this occasion to indicate that every Jew, rich and poor alike, is free and independent. With the adoption of western customs several scholars urged that the practice be discontinued since neither the garb nor the furniture were suitable for such a practice. But the custom remained firmly entrenched and the cushions supporting the participants are still a recognised feature of the celebration.

The question whether leaning is obligatory *throughout* the *Seder* ritual did arouse some difference of opinion. It was generally agreed that one should lean when *matzah* is eaten because it recalls the redemption, and not when the bitter herbs are taken because they recall the bondage. But should one lean when the wine is drunk? Some held the view that since the first two cups accompany the narration of the Exodus and the deliverance, they alone require this posture; others held that one should lean at the second two cups too, because they are associated with the hope for future redemption. All agreed, however, that one should lean on one's left side to avoid any discomfort while eating.

Aphikoman

In Temple times the Passover meal was concluded when the company partook of the paschal lamb. Since *matzah* was eaten together with the lamb, the practice prevailed to commemorate the original procedure by distributing a piece of the broken middle *matzah* to each participant at the termination of the *Seder* meal. As the taste of the lamb was to linger with the celebrants in those days so the taste of *matzah* should remain during the remainder of the *Haggadah's* recital. The prescription stated in the Mishnah, "We do not partake of the *Aphikoman* after the Passover," was variously interpreted by the scholars of Bablyon. Rab regarded the expression as an abbreviation of *aphiku manaihu,* "remove your vessels," i.e. let us proceed to another family group and join them in the celebration. Such conduct was forbidden, for groups were not permitted to mingle, but each had to celebrate the Passover separately. Samuel, on the other hand, derived the expression from *aphiku man,* "remove the food," i.e. let us proceed to the delicacies. It was customary in those days to serve nuts, mushrooms and sweetmeats after the main meal. This, too, was forbidden for no dessert may be taken after the paschal lamb. Some, however, seek to derive the word *Aphikoman* from the Greek meaning "entertainment." This being a serious occasion no revelry is permitted to follow the celebration.

A number of customs are associated with the use of the *Aphikoman.* The most familiar is for the father to hide the broken *matzah* and to offer a reward to the children for its discovery. This custom probably arose out of the practice to conceal the *matzah* until the end of the meal in order not to confuse it with the rest of the *matzah* eaten during the meal. This concealment was responsible for the word *zafun,* "conceal," being included in the rubric of the *Haggadah.* Some moralists, however, have read into this word a delightful association with the verse "How great is thy goodness which thou hast laid up (literally, *concealed*) for them that fear thee," (*Psalm* xxxi: 20), which gives fervent expression to the confidence in future redemption. In some oriental communities the custom prevails to bore a hole in that part of the *Aphikoman* which is left after the *Seder* and to hang it near the door of the house. There it remained until the following Passover as a symbol of protection for the members of the household.

Eggs

In addition to the roasted egg displayed on the *Seder* plate which serves as a reminder of the original festival offering, it has become the popular practice, particularly in western Europe, to commence the main meal with eggs in salt water. The origin of this custom has been traced to a variety of sources. Some regard it as a relic of the typical *hors d'œuvre* of Roman times, others consider that it was a freeman's dish in antiquity. A more prosaic view is that the popularity of eggs is purely seasonal, due to their being in plentiful supply at this time of the year. Another view allies the custom with the hope of future redemption and associates the egg with the symbol of resurrection. In view of the fact that the first day of the Passover falls on the same day of the week as the fast of the 9th of Ab some trace the custom to the mourner's practice to eat eggs after the funeral. Abudarham (fourteenth century), a great medieval authority on the liturgy, has suggested that the custom derives from the interpretation of the Aramaic word for egg, *be'ah,* which is closely related to *ba'a* meaning "desire." The egg symbolises God's *desire* to redeem Israel.

In western communities the roasted egg is used for ceremonial purposes only, but in some oriental communities the custom prevails for the firstborn son to eat it at the termination of the *Seder* as a symbol of the protection of the firstborn of Israel. In other communities young maidens were encouraged to eat it as the egg was regarded as efficacious for happy and fruitful matrimony.

Dramatization of the Seder

Since the primary purpose of the *Seder* is the exposition of the Exodus story to children, it has long been considered essential to enlist the art of visual aid. The display of the symbols on the *Seder* plate is directed to this end, but the exposition is heightened by the dramatic presentation of the theme. The oriental communities are known to specialise in this practice. In order to lend emphasis to the passage "in every generation each man should regard himself as though he came forth from Egypt," the father places a girdle on his loins, carries a staff in his hand, wraps the three *matzoth* in a bundle which he places on his back and paces up and down the room or walks round the table. The children ask him "Whence do you come?" and he replies, "From the land of Egypt." "And whither are you going?" they ask, and he replies, "To the land of Israel." "And where is the food for your journey?" they ask, and he shows them the *matzoth* wrapped in the bundle slung across his back. In some communities a young member of the family dresses himself in tattered clothes, knocks on the door and begs admission to the *Seder.* When questioned as to his identity he explains that he is a messenger who has travelled far from the Holy City bringing tidings of the redemption which is at hand.

The wearing of the white robe, called the *kittel,* by the officiating head of the household was a common practice in eastern Europe. This robe is worn on the High Festivals and because of its association with shrouds served to engender the spirit of humility essential for these solemn days. Some associate a similar thought with the Passover because of the similarity of the day of the week with the 9th of Ab. The white robe, however, is symbolic of purity and is probably worn at the *Seder* because no one was permitted to participate in the paschal celebrations unless he was in a state of levitical purity. The Midrash on the Book of Esther associates the word *hur,* meaning "white" with *horin* which means "freedom" and states "white garments are those which are worn by freemen."

In some communities the passage in the *Haggadah* describing the crossing of the Red Sea was also given dramatic presentation. As soon as that passage was reached a bowl of live fish was placed on the table to remind the celebrants of the fate which befell the Egyptians.

26.

the passover haggadah

From *The Passover Haggadah, with Explanatory Notes and Contemporary Readings,* edited by Morris Silverman, (Revised Edition), © 1972 by Prayer Book Press, Bridgeport, Conn. Reprinted by permission of Media Judaica Inc.

The Leader uncovers the matzah, lifts up the ceremonial plate, and says:

Behold the Matzah, bread of poverty, which our ancestors ate in the land of Egypt.

Let all who are hungry come and eat; all who are needy, come and celebrate the Passover with us.

Now we are here; next year may we observe the Passover in the Land of Israel.

Now many are still enslaved; next year may all men be free.

The Four Questions

Why is this night different from all other nights?

(1) On all other nights we may eat either leavened or unleavened bread, but on this night, only unleavened bread.

(2) On all other nights we eat all kinds of herbs, but on this night we eat especially bitter herbs.

(3) On all other nights, we need not even once dip our herbs in any condiment, but on this night we dip herbs twice: one herb in salt water, and the bitter herbs in *haroset.*

(4) On all other nights we eat either sitting or reclining, but on this night we recline.

The Answer

In the beginning (before the days of Abraham), our forefathers were idol worshipers. God, however, called us to His service. For so we read in the Torah: "And Joshua said unto all the people, 'Thus said the Lord, God of Israel: In the days of old, your fathers, even Terah, the father of Abraham and Nahor, lived beyond the River Euphrates, and they worshiped idols. But I took your father, Abraham, from beyond the River Euphrates and I led him

125

through the entire land of Canaan. I multiplied his offspring and gave him Isaac. To Isaac I gave Jacob and Esau. To Esau I gave Mount Seir as an inheritance; but Jacob and his sons went down into Egypt.' " (Josh. 24:2–4)

Praised be God who keeps His promise to Israel; praised be He! For the Holy One, praised be He, determined the end of our bondage in order to fulfill His word, pledged in a solemn covenant to our father Abraham: "And God said to Abram, 'Know this for certain: your descendants shall be strangers in a land not their own, where they shall be enslaved and oppressed for four hundred years. But I will also bring judgment on the nation that held them in slavery; and in the end they shall go free with great substance.' " (Gen. 15:13, 14)

Raise The Cup of Wine and Cover the Matzot.

God's unfailing help has sustained our fathers and us. For not only one enemy has risen up to destroy us, but in every generation do men rise up against us seeking to destroy us; but the Holy One, praised be He, delivers us from their hands.

The Symbols

Rabbi Gamaliel (grandson of the great Sage Hillel) said: "He who has not explained the following symbols of the Seder has not fulfilled his duty:

> Pesah, the Paschal Lamb;
> Matzah, the Unleavened Bread;
> Maror, the Bitter Herb.

One of the Participants Asks:

What is the meaning of the Paschal Lamb which our forefathers used to eat at the time when the Temple was still in existence?

The Leader Points to the Shank Bone of the Lamb and Answers:

The Paschal Lamb is to remind us that the Holy One, praised be He, passed over the houses of our forefathers in Egypt, as it is written in the Bible: "You shall say that it is the sacrifice of the Lord's passover, for He passed over the houses of the Children of Israel in Egypt when He smote the Egyptians, but spared our houses. The people bowed their heads and worshiped." (Ex. 12:27)

One of the Participants Asks:

What is the meaning of the Matzah that we eat?

The Leader Raises the Matzah and Answers:

The Matzah is to remind us that before the dough which our forefathers prepared for bread had time to ferment, the supreme King of Kings, the Holy One, praised be He, revealed Himself to them and redeemed them. We read in the Bible: "They baked matzah of the unleavened dough which they had brought out of Egypt, for it had not leavened because they were thrust out of Egypt and could not linger, nor had they prepared any food for the journey." (Ex. 12:39)

One of the Participants Asks:

What is the meaning of the Bitter Herbs which we eat?

The Leader Points to the Maror and Answers:

The Maror is to remind us that the Egyptians embittered the lives of our forefathers in Egypt, as the Bible explains: "They made their lives bitter with hard labor, with mortar and brick, and with every kind of work in the field. All the labor which the Egyptians forced upon them was harsh." (Ex. 1:14)

In every generation each Jew should regard himself as though he personally went forth from Egypt. That is what the Bible means when it says: "And you shall tell your son on that day, saying, 'It is because of what the Lord did for *me* when I went forth from Egypt.' " (Ex. 13:8) It was not only our forefathers whom the Holy One, praised be He, redeemed from slavery, but us also did He redeem together with them, as we read: "He brought *us* out from there so that He might bring us into the land, and give us this land which He promised to our forefathers." (Deut. 6:23)

Therefore, we should thank and praise, laud and glorify, exalt and honor, extol and adore God who performed all these miracles for our fathers and for us. He brought us from slavery to freedom, from sorrow to joy, from mourning to festivity, from darkness to great light, and from bondage to redemption. Let us, then, sing unto Him a new song: Halleluyah, praise the Lord!

Praised be Thou, O Lord our God, King of the universe, who redeemed us, and redeemed our fathers from Egypt, and enabled us to reach this night on which we eat Matzah and Maror. Even so, O Lord our God and God of our fathers, do Thou enable us to reach in peace other holy days and festivals when we may rejoice in the restoration of Zion, Thy city, and find delight in serving Thee. There we shall partake of the Paschal meal and bring Thee the offerings which shall be acceptable unto Thee. And there we shall sing unto Thee a new song of praise for our freedom and redemption. Praised be Thou, O Lord, Redeemer of Israel.

27.

shavuot and its observance

chaim pearl

Shavuot follows Passover by seven weeks, and the intervening days are carefully counted. It is taken to commemorate the revelation of the Torah on Mount Sinai and frequently is celebrated by religious school graduations in Conservative and Orthodox synagogues and by Confirmation ceremonies in Reform and some Conservative ones. Chaim Pearl, a leading contemporary rabbi of British origin, explains the fundamental meaning of the festival.

From *A Guide to Shavuoth,* by Chaim Pearl (London: Jewish Chronicle Publications, 1959), pp. vii, 55–60. © 1959 by Chaim Pearl. Reprinted by permission of Jewish Chronicle Publications.

Shavuot, the Feast of Weeks, is one of the shortest of our biblical festivals, yet its message and the event it commemorates make it among the most important of our religious celebrations.

The Bible concentrates on the agricultural aspects of the day with its impressive and joyous ceremonies. Throughout centuries of exile the Jew treasured the record of those harvest festivities and now is lovingly re-introducing something of its spirit into the new State of Israel.

But important as this is, *Shavuot* has been chiefly associated with *Zeman Matan Toratenu*—the time of the giving of our Torah. It is this aspect of *Shavuot* which has made it of permanent importance and it is no exaggeration to say that Judaism, and consequently the Jewish people, exists or falls by the lessons underlined by this festival. Our sages always fully understood this truth and consequently cast *Shavuot* into a very special role in the historic development of our people. In their typically figurative language they suggested that *Shavuot* was the time of God's marriage to Israel, the day on which the contract of God's covenant with His people was formally completed and handed over. . . .

The Days Preceding the Festival

The three days immediately preceding *Shavuot* are known as *Shloshet Yemai Hagbalah,* the three days of setting bounds. This description is derived from the Bible where we read that for three days the people were kept off Sinai around which Moses set bounds to discourage any attempt to climb the mount until after the Revelation. At the same time the people were instructed to subject themselves to a strict physical and spiritual preparation for the great event.

Shavuot Night

This period of preparation finds its symbolic culmination on the first night of *Shavuot* when the devout stay up all night in order to study Torah.

For the festival of the Torah this is a particularly appropriate custom and in order to cover, if only in spirit, the whole of the Bible and the Talmud a special lectionary was compiled containing the first and last verses of each *Sidra* in the Pentateuch, the opening verses of the rest of the biblical chapters and the beginning of each of the 63 tractates of the *Mishnah.*

Notwithstanding the obvious and practical reasons for an anthology of just the chapter beginnings, the poetic thought has been suggested that the chapter headings represent the jewels with which the bride (Israel) is bedecked before her marriage on *Shavuot.*

Some lectionaries contain also chapters of the mystical work the Zohar as well as poetic exhortations on the theme of the 613 commandments known as *Azharot.* The entire anthology is called *Tikkun Lel Shavuot* (a compendium of perfection for *Shavuot* Eve) although, strictly speaking, this name relates to the observance as a whole.

Those taking part usually assemble after the evening meal. The reading of the anthology is customarily interrupted during the night with light refreshments of a kind appropriate to the festival. Morning Service is read very early—at the break of dawn—after which those taking part return home for sleep.

The custom is also associated with the mystical idea that on *Shavuot* night the heavens open at midnight and receive with favour the prayers and studious meditations of those assembled to observe the night long vigil on the eve of the festival of Revelation.

Although this observance is assumed to be fairly old, going back perhaps as far as five hundred years, there is no historical record of it prior to the sixteenth-century cabbalists. It is thought that it was a *Shavuot* night gathering in Salonica that Joseph Caro, Solomon Alkabetz and others were inspired to leave for the Holy Land. Soon after the festival they made their way to Palestine where they settled in Safed, a city which became famous as a centre of Cabbalah.

Although the *Shavuot* night anthology would be regarded as "prescribed reading," there is nevertheless absolutely nothing to prevent anyone from reading and studying any section of sacred literature. Indeed, today it is probably true that in many communities the study of a passage in the Talmud has taken the place of the lectionary. The story is told of the Maggid of Dubnow (Jacob Kranz, eighteenth-century Poland) who visited the famous Elijah, Gaon of Vilna, on *Shavuot.* On the first night they both observed the custom, but while the Gaon read the anthology the Maggid studied Talmud. On being asked his reason, the

Maggid replied, "For you, the great Gaon, it is good that you read the *Tikkun* which comprises only samples of the great stock you have. But I have no stock, so why should I parade samples?"

Floral Decorations

Most synagogues today are decorated with flowers and other plants in honour of the festival, but it is not out of place to observe that the distinguished Gaon of Vilna, referred to in the previous section, strongly opposed the custom on the grounds that it came close to copying from non-Jewish practice. That the custom survived in spite of his opposition is a further illustration of the power and place of *minhag* in Jewish life.

Several reasons are suggested for this practice and we can note the following. The decorations are simply indicative of the main summer harvest; they remind us of Mount Sinai, which was covered with vegetation in honour of the great event of the Revelation; judgment day for fruit trees is thought to be on *Shavuot;* they are symbolic of the beautifully decorated *Bikkurim* offerings brought in Temple days.

The Synagogue was not the only place honoured in this way. In an earlier generation, in a period when ghetto life was restricted, urbanised and very far from the fresh atmosphere of the countryside, the Jew would make a special effort to decorate his home for *Shavuot* in the customary manner. Often, it could amount to no more than fresh grass strewn on the floor, but it was sufficient to bring its fragrant and joyous message to the household.

Dairy Food

For a home-loving and family-centered people like the Jews and with a religion which is so largely lived in the home, it is not at all surprising to find that the festivals have left their impression upon the dietary traditions of the Jewish household. What, however, is especially worth noting in this connection is that the special foods prominent at each festive occasion have their place of distinction, very often, as a result of some religious symbolism. This is certainly the case with *Shavuot* foods.

The characteristic food for *Shavuot* is dairy food. If we wish to be very matter of fact about this we can say simply that the reason is, because *Shavuot* is a summer festival and in hot climates light dairy dishes would in any case be usual at that time of the year. But less prosaic reasons have often been suggested. The connection has been made with the milk and honey, symbolic of the Torah which is as nourishing as milk, as sweet as honey, and which finds poetic reference in the *Song of Songs* in the words, "Honey and milk are under thy tongue." The land of Israel is also biblically described as "a land flowing with milk and honey" so that on the festival of the summer harvest of crops it would be fittingly symbolic to partake of such food. For those who can accept a little homiletic play with words a further indication has been suggested in the text "And on the day of the first ripe fruits when ye bring a new offering unto the Lord on the Feast of Weeks." . . . The initial letters of the last three words spell the word [for] milk. . . .

A Beginning in Jewish Education

Since *Shavuot* is the season of the Torah it was natural to introduce certain practices which would impress the young with the importance of the occasion, and what more meaningful custom than to introduce him to Jewish studies at *Shavuot* time itself. These days the practice would have no place in a school year with an entirely different organisation, but in previous ages it was customary to take the child to Hebrew class for the first time a few days before *Shavuot*. We read of the picturesque practice whereby the child was given a small slate with Hebrew lettering representing his first lesson. After this, and presumably to indicate that Hebrew knowledge was to be sweet, the slate became a plate for honey and thereafter he always associated his first Hebrew lesson with things enjoyable. Our predecessors had a sounder understanding of pedagogics than we are prepared to grant.

28.

the feast of weeks: the festival of the covenant

theodor h. gaster

In this selection, Theodor Gaster provides an account of the history, development, and significance of *Shavuot,* the Feast of Weeks.

From *Festivals of the Jewish Year. A Modern Interpretation and Guide,* by Theodor H. Gaster (New York: William Sloane Associates, 1952, pp. 59–63. Copyright © 1952, 1953 by Theodor H. Gaster. Reprinted by permission of the author and William Morrow & Co., Inc.

In the Bible, the Feast of Weeks plays a somewhat minor role beside the major seasonal festivals of Passover on the one hand and Booths (or Ingathering) on the other. It is simply the end of the barley harvest, and its distinctive feature is the presentation to Jehovah (apart from special sacrifices) of an offering consisting, according to one version of the Law (Deut. 16:10), of whatever one feels prompted to give, or according to another (Lev. 23:17), of two loaves made out of the new corn. The festival, we are told, is to take place a full seven weeks after the sickle has been first applied to the standing grain (Deut. 16:9).

It is easy to dismiss this early phase of the festival as nothing but the product of a crude, unsophisticated age, and to think one has explained the presentation of firstfruits by collecting parallels from other parts of the world, without stopping to penetrate to their significance. The truth is, however, that even at this primary stage, though the form of expression may be primitive, the underlying meaning of the festival is at once subtle and profound. Two ideas are combined, and each is capable of an extension and development of far-reaching import. . . .

Translated into broader terms, what is here proclaimed is that the relation between God and man is not one of master and servant but of mutually dependent partners in a joint enterprise of continuous creation. This idea gives new validity to human existence and at the same time provides a signal and momentous alternative to that more common conception which, projecting the image of God from the model of kings and magicians, regards Him merely as a supernal lord and benefactor of mankind. For the conventional attitude of subservience, worship and adoration there is substituted a concept of God which is at once more robust and more mystical and which, indeed, modern religion might do well to recapture.

The second idea which underlies this early phase of the festival stems from the fact that primitive man regards anything new and unused as being fraught with potential peril, much as an infant might regard a new toy. The firstfruits of the harvest (and likewise the firstborn both of men and beasts) are therefore consigned to the gods or spirits so that the newness may be taken away and the rest thereby rendered "safe." The important thing, however, is not so much the *why* as the *how* of the ritual; the danger of a new thing is removed by bringing it into contact with some eternal being to whom it is *not* new, inasmuch as he transcends the limitations of our own temporal existence. Behind the symbolism of the primitive procedure, therefore, there lies once again a permanent, universal message: the only immunity against the terror of new things is to try to see them in the light of eternity, and the only protection against the perils of human existence is to dedicate the prime portion of it to God.

Thus, even in its rudimentary stage, the Feast of Weeks possessed its own spiritual values. For Judaism, however—especially after it had outgrown its Palestinian origins—these alone were not sufficient. The presence and activity of God had to be recognized at this season not only in the phenomena of nature but also, and on parallel lines, in some crucial event of history. Accordingly, in the first centuries of the Common Era, inspiration and ingenuity combined to produce the necessary development.

The Scriptural narrative states clearly (Exod. 19:1) that the children of Israel reached Mount Sinai in the third month, to the day, after their departure from Egypt. This, it was now argued, does not mean that a full three months elapsed, but only that the event took place *in the third month of the year,* and in that case the giving of the Ten Commandments might (with a little latitude and fancy) be made to coincide with the Feast of Weeks. The festival thus became the birthday of Israel, the anniversary of the day on which the Covenant had been concluded between God and His people and the Law first revealed. Such, ever since, has been its primary significance; it is known, in fact, as "the season of the giving of our Law."

The parallelism between the historical and agricultural aspects of the festival is far closer than might at first be suspected, and is carried through with rare ingenuity and resource. According to Jewish teaching, the important thing about the session at Sinai was not only the giving of the Law but also the receiving of it, the two acts of offer and acceptance constituting a Covenant (or contract) between God and Israel. Here too, therefore, the idea of collaboration is involved: if the Law issues from God, its fulfillment lies with Israel. Inspiration and aspiration, revelation and perception, are the two sides of a single coin: on the one side is the face of God; on the other, that of man. What Saint Theresa said of the relation of the Christian to Christ was expressed by Judaism, many centuries earlier, in its concept of the covenantal partnership of God and Israel: In the world of men, Israel is God's hands and feet and eyes.

Nor is it only in this major respect that the natural and historical aspects of the festival run parallel to each other. For if the former marks the end of seven weeks' collaboration between God and man in the reaping of the material harvest, what the latter celebrates is the end of a corresponding spiritual harvest, which began with the deliverance from Egypt and reached its climax with the conclusion of the Covenant. And just as the ingathering of the crops is the necessary condition of life and prosperity during the ensuing year, so the event at Sinai is the necessary condition of Israel's continuing existence and fortune. Moreover, if, in the primitive agricultural rite, man offers to God two loaves of the new bread as a symbol of cooperation, in the historical counterpart—by a fine and inspired inversion—God offer to man the two tablets of the Law.

Lastly, as the harvest is renewed from year to year, so too is the historic experience of Sinai. Jewish teaching (as we have pointed out repeatedly) is insistent on the point that the festivals are not mere commemorations. All the generations of Israel, say the sages, were released from Egypt, and all were present at the mountain. By this they did not mean, as is so often supposed, that all of time was telescoped into a single moment, but rather that a single moment was projected into all of time. Both the revelation of God and His covenant with Israel are essentially continuous and are no more confined to the single event at Sinai than is the process of nature to a single harvest.

29.

the sukkah and its meaning

isaac n. fabricant

The third festival of the trilogy is *Sukkot,* sometimes spelled *Succoth.* This festival celebrates the harvest in nature and the wandering of the people of Israel after the Exodus. The *Sukkah* is a frail booth or hut, decorated with flowers and branches, in which people are to eat their meals during the festival. The festival comes in October; in northern climates the weather is too chilly for spending an entire meal out of doors. The *Sukkah* provides the opportunity to link a great moment of history with the commemoration of nature's bounty. Like all Jewish holy days, the observance in the home is the center of the celebration. Families work together in making the *Sukkah.*

Rabbi Fabricant, a British scholar, here describes the observance of the festival.

From *A Guide to Succoth,* by Isaac N. Fabricant (London: Jewish Chronicle Publications, 1958), pp. 8–12. © 1958 by Isaac N. Fabricant. Reprinted by permission of Jewish Chronicle Publications.

It is a Mitzvah to begin building the Succah on the evening when Yom Kippur[1] ends. The great Fast has not exhausted but rather refreshed the individual and in a mood of dedication he applies himself to the task of building "the temporary residence." The impermanence of the Succah is stressed emphatically in the Talmud, where it is ruled that the Succah must not be built higher than twenty cubits so as not to give it a permanent character. It is further enjoined that the Succah should not be lower in height than ten handbreadths as such a structure would not be fit as a residence.

In the season of plenty the Jew rejoices in his prosperity and in the rewards which his labours have brought him. He is inclined to delude himself into thinking that life is secure and durable. The Psalmist describes those people who are misled by their phantasy "that trust in their wealth, and boast themselves in the multitude of their riches—their inward thought is that their houses shall continue for ever, and their dwelling places to all generations." (*Ps.* xlix.) The Bible, however, through the law of the Succah brings man face to face with the realisation of the frailty of human life and the transience of human existence.

A *Sukkah*

It is essential that the Succah is built in a manner which enables it to provide more shade than light. A Succah which does not allow this greater measure of shade is invalid—for the word Succah is derived from a verb which means "to cover" and the logical corollary of covering is that it should produce shade. There is an interesting and significant regulation . . . which declares that even if the tent or hut is not made with the intention of fulfilling the Mitzvah of Succah, so long as it is built with the purpose of providing "shade" the Succah is ritually proper for the Festival.

Those who were perplexed by the hazards and the sorrows of Jewish history could draw confidence from the thought that the nations which basked in the glaring brilliance of applause and which thought that their successes were to be eternal were to be outlived by a people who would survive because of their reliance on God and because they dwelt within "the shade of faith." Isaac Arama (15th c.) in his work *Akedath Yitschak* discussing this essential condition of "shade" regards the Succah as a vital symbol in Jewish ritual. It teaches that man must not have confidence in his own strength nor in his own fortunes but must place his faith in Divine Providence. For this reason the covering of the Succah of plants and leaves should not be laid on too thickly so that the heaven and the stars should be visible for "the heavens declare the glory of God." (*Ps.* xix.)

The medieval moralists found great scope for their religious teachings in the laws of the Succah. Rabbenu Bahya ben Asher (13–14th c.) speaks of the decision of Shammai to class as unfit an old Succah, i.e. a Succah that had been built earlier than thirty days before the Festival and without the intention that it would be used for the Festival that was to follow. This medieval moralist utilises the Succah to emphasise the profound lesson that symbols which have their roots in the ancient past must not be regarded as obsolete tradition but as observances which require renewal of interest and enthusiasm and even of language and terminology to engage the minds of each new generation.

Rabbi Joseph Caro, the celebrated author of the Shulchan Aruch of the sixteenth century, declared that the Succah provides a lesson on discipline. He argues that it would have been more appropriate that the Festival of Succoth should be observed in the month of Nisan since the Succah recalls the especial protection afforded by God to Israel when they left the land of bondage in Nisan. Nisan, however, is a month of intensely warm weather when people naturally leave their homes and retire to the booth in the field or garden where the shade can shelter them from the scorching heat of a relentless sun. Hence in Nisan the Succah would be ineffectual as a symbol. Tishri, the month of rains, was selected because whereas the rest of the world leaves the booth for the secure protection which the house offers, the Jew leaves the home and dwells in the Succah in order to show his readiness to fulfil the behest of his Creator.

It is worth noting that those customs which are interwoven with home and family ceremonial have survived through the ages. The Seder, the Succah and other similar "family" observances have captured the imagination of our people and have strengthened home and family ties. In the days of Nehemiah when the leaders of Jewry realised the necessity of revitalising Jewish life they pressed this "family" observance into service and soon the Succah made a dramatic appearance in garden, field, upon house roofs, in the house courts and in the broad places of the city gates.

To the mystic the Succah represented the ideal combination of physical and spiritual which is the mosaic of Jewish thought. It is a place where one eats and drinks in an atmosphere of the joy of the Festival. It is also the place where one meditates and prays. R. Moses Cordovero, the sixteenth-century mystic of Safed, instituted a series of talks on the Torah, which he held in his Succah not only for his family but also for members of the Community. The Succah gave ample opportunity for hospitality, and in the words of the Zohar: "It is necessary for man to rejoice within the Succah and to show a cheerful countenance to guests. It is forbidden to harbour thoughts of gloom and how much more so feelings of anger within the portals of the Succah, the symbol of joy."

The finest commentary on the Succah is the prayer which one recites on entering the Succah the first night of the Festival as an inauguration of the custom of dwelling in the Succah. "May it be Thy will, O my God and God of my fathers, that Thou mayest cause Thy Divine Presence to dwell amongst us and mayest

Thou spread the Tabernacle of Thy peace over us." The Succah rewards those who inhabit it with a sense of deep and abiding tranquillity.

Notes

1. See pp. 142ff.

30.

sukkot: the feast of booths, the festival of ingathering

theodor h. gaster

In this selection, Professor Gaster tells us about the development and meaning of *Sukkot,* The Feast of Booths.

From *Festivals of the Jewish Year. A Modern Interpretation and Guide,* by Theodor H. Gaster New York.: William Sloane Associates, 1952), pp. 80–81, 84–87. Copyright © 1952, by Theodor H. Gaster. Reprinted by permission of the author and William Morrow & Co., Inc.

Corresponding to the festival of Passover in spring is the Feast of Booths (*Sukkot*) in autumn. This, too, begins at full moon in the first month of the season; this, too, is a harvest festival; and this, too, is observed for eight days. Moreover, just as Passover marks the beginning of the summer dews, so Booths marks that of the winter rains.

The original name of the festival was Feast of Ingathering (*Asif*); it celebrated the ingathering of summer crops and fruits, and the close of the agricultural year. The date was at first variable and indefinite; the feast took place whenever the harvest happened to be in (Deut. 16:13). Later, however, when the year came to be determined on an astronomical basis, the Feast of Ingathering was made to begin either at the autumnal equinox (Exod. 34:22) or at full moon in the appropriate lunar month. The latter system is the one which has prevailed in Jewish practice.

The Feast of Ingathering was really but the concluding stage of a longer festive season, the three principal moments of which were: (*a*) the Day of Memorial: (*b*) the Day of Purgation; and (*c*) the harvest-home. The two former stages are now represented respectively by New Year, on the first day of the lunar month, and by the Day of Atonement, on the tenth. Prefaced by these two solemn occassions, on which all noxious and evil influences are ceremonially removed, the Feast of Ingathering marked both the successful issue of the preceding year and the "clean start" of the one which followed. It was therefore regarded as the most important of all the seasonal festivals, and came to be known as "*the festival*" *tout court.*

The principal features of the celebration were: (*a*) the actual reaping of crops and fruits and the bringing in of the vintage; (*b*) the performance of special ceremonies designed to induce rainfall; (*c*) the custom of dwelling in booths (*sukkot*) or trellis-roofed cabins throughout the period of the festival. Of these usages the most important was the last, and it was this that gave the feast its popular name.

The booths were originally functional in character; they were simply the wattled cabins in which the harvesters and vintners were wont to lodge during the time of the ingathering. Such booths, made of plaited twigs of carob and oleander and roofed with palm leaves, are still used in the Holy Land throughout the period (from June to September) when the reaping is in progress, and it is in this sense that the word *sukkah* is usually employed in the Hebrew Bible. . . .

Etrog (Citrus Fruit) and *Lulav* (Palm Branch) for *Sukkot*

For Israel, this purely agricultural aspect of the festival was not enough. Like Passover and Pentecost, so too the Feast of Booths had to possess a historical as well as a seasonal significance; it had to exemplify the presence of God not only in the world of nature but also in that of event; and it had in some way to symbolize and epitomize Israel's continuing covenant with Him.

The transformation was accomplished by an ingenious device: the traditional booths were interpreted as a reminder of those in which the ancestors of Israel had dwelt when they wandered through the wilderness on their journey from Egypt to the Promised Land! The festival thus became a logical sequel to Passover and Pentecost, which commemorated respectively the escape from bondage and the conclusion of the Covenant at Sinai. Moreover, by themselves dwelling in booths at this season, each successive generation of Jews could be said to be sharing in that experience and thereby endowing it with a perpetual character.

This interpretation was, of course, purely fanciful; the cold fact is that people who wander through deserts live in tents, not booths, wood and green leaves being unavailable except at rare and intermitten oases. To be sure, the point is not really important; the "myth" which is woven around a traditional institution is usually more indebted to fancy than to fact, and its validity lies not in its historical accuracy or authenticity but in the transcendental truths which it focuses and conveys. Nevertheless, throughout the ages Jewish scholars and teachers felt a little uneasy about the story of the booths in the wilderness, and alternative interpretations were therefore propounded.

It was observed, for instance, that in sundry passages of the Bible, the word *sukkah*—or, more precisely, its masculine equivalen, *sok*—serves, by poetic metaphor, to denote the temple of God in Jerusalem, and that both the First and Second Temples are said expressly to have been dedicated at the Feast of Booths. This at once suggested that the seasonal booths might be regarded as a symbol of that holy habitation. The idea finds repeated expression in the traditional liturgy of the festival. Typical is a medieval hymn chanted during the morning service of the first day, in which a sustained contrast is drawn between the heavenly and earthly tabernacles. The poem is full of recondite allusions and quaint conceits, but its general spirit and tenor may perhaps be conveyed by the following partial and paraphrastic rendering:

> Where flaming angels walk in pride,
> Where ministers of light abide,
> Where cavalries of heaven ride,
> Where souls have rest at eventide,
>   There, 'mid the sapphire and the gold,
>   God's tabernacle rose of old.
>
> Yet here, as in a mead aflower,
> Here, as in a bridal bower,
> Here, where songs of praise and power,
> Wreath Him, every day and hour,
>   Here, in an earthly booth as well
>   His glory did not spurn to dwell.

In the same way, in a poem recited on the eve of the second day, the ruined Temple is likened to a booth fallen to pieces:

> Thy tabernacle which is fallen down
> Rebuild, O Lord, and raise it once again!

Alternatively, the sukkah was given a continuing historical meaning by being identified with the protective providence of God, spread like a pavilion over His chosen people. Says the same poem, in reference to the Exodus from Egypt:

> Thy cloud enfolded them, as if that they
> Were shelter'd in a booth; redeem'd and free,

They saw Thy glory as a canopy
Spread o'er them as they marched upon their way.

And when dryshod they through the sea had gone,
They praised Thee and proclaimed Thy unity;
And all the angels sang the antiphon,
And lifted up their voices unto Thee.
   "Our Rock, our Savior He"—thus did they sing—
   "World without end the Lord shall reign as King!"

Whatever meaning be given to it, Jewish tradition insists that the seasonal sukkah must be in every sense a true booth; no mere token substitute will do. Specifications are laid down clearly in the Mishnah. The sukkah must not be lower than five feet, nor higher than thirty; and it must possess at least three sides. It may not be roofed with matting or burlap, but only with lightly strewn leaves or straw. It must be exposed to the elements and to a view of the stars. Moreover, since the task of erecting it is regarded as an essential part of the commandment, no permanent structure may serve.

The duty of eating and sleeping in the sukkah is incumbent upon all adult males; women and minors alone are exempt. Since, however, it is often impossible to observe this rule in modern cities, modifications of it have been introduced. According to some authorities, at least one meal must be taken in the booth each day and each night of the festival; according to others, it is sufficient if one eats in the sukkah on the first night only. In either case, nothing must be done to lessen the discomfort or even hardship which may attend the observance; rain water, for instance, may be baled out only if it "threatens to spoil the gruel"!

31.

the days of awe: sovereignty, remembrance, and redemption

The days of Awe, sometimes called "the high holy days," are the New Year, *Rosh Hashanah,* and the Day of Atonement, *Yom Kippur.* These come in the autumn, normally in September. They focus not upon the community so much as upon the life of the individual, his destiny in the coming year, and his atonement for deeds done in the year now ending. We shall attempt to evoke the spirit of the solemn and sacred days through contemplating synagogue prayers said on these occasions.

On the New Year, three great themes of the classical Judaic tradition, creation, revelation, and redemption, are expressed in a triplet of prayers on the themes of God's rule, as expressed through revelation; God's remembrance, beginning with the recollection of his creation of the world; and his coming redemption of mankind at the sound of the *shofar,* or ram's horn. Each of these prayers is concluded with the dramatic sounding of the *shofar.*

From *Mahzor for Rosh Hashanah and Yom Kippur,* edited by Jules Harlow (New York: The Rabbinical Assembly of America, 1972), pp. 241–2, 259–279. © 1972 by The Rabbinical Assembly of America. Reprinted by permission of The Rabbinical Assembly.

God reigns

We worship no earthly power. Only to the only King
do we bow and kneel, as a sign of ultimate loyalty to
Him alone, and awareness of our mortality.

We rise to our duty to praise the Lord of all, to acclaim the Creator. He made our lot unlike that of other people, assigning us a unique destiny.

We bend the knee and bow, proclaiming Him as King of kings, the Holy One praised be He. He unfurled the heavens and established the earth. His throne of glory is in the heavens above, His majestic Presence in the loftiest heights. He and no other is God, our faithful King. So we are told in His Torah: "Remember now and always that the Lord is God in heaven and on earth. There is no other."

And so we hope in You, Lord our God, soon to see Your splendor, sweeping idolatry away so that false gods will be utterly destroyed, perfecting earth by Your kingship so that all mankind will invoke Your name, bringing all the

earth's wicked back to You, repentant. Then all who live will know that to
You every knee must bend, every tongue pledge loyalty. To You, Lord, may
all men bow in worship, may they give honor to Your glory. May everyone
accept the rule of Your kingship. Reign over all, soon and for all time.
Sovereignty is Yours in glory, now and forever.

Our God and God of our fathers, cause Your sovereignty to be acknowledged
throughout the world. May Your splendor and dignity be reflected in the lives
of all who dwell on earth. Then all creatures will know that You created
them, all living things will comprehend that You gave them life, everything
that breathes will proclaim: The Lord God of Israel is King, and His dominion embraces all.

Our God and God of our fathers, . . . make our lives holy with Your commandments and let your Torah be our portion. Fill our lives with Your
goodness, and gladden us with Your triumph. . . .Cleanse our hearts to serve
You faithfully, for You are faithful and Your word endures forever. Praised
are You, Lord, King of all the earth who sanctifies . . . the people Israel and
the Day of Remembrance.

Today the world is born. Today all creatures everywhere stand in judgment,
some as children and some as slaves. If we merit consideration as children,
show us a father's mercy. If we stand in judgment as slaves, grant us freedom.
We look to You for compassion when You declare our fate, awesome, holy
God.

God remembers

Creation You remember, Lord, considering the deeds of all mankind from
ancient days. All thoughts are revealed to You, all secrets since the beginning
of time. For You there is no forgetting, from You nothing is hidden. You
remember every deed, You know every doer. You know all things, Lord our
God, and foresee events to the end of time. You have set a day for bringing
to judgment countless human beings and their infinite deeds. This You
ordained from the beginning, this You made known from of old.

This day is the birthday of Creation, a remainder of the first day. Its observance is a law for the House of Jacob, ordained by the God of our fathers.
And this is a day of decree for all nations: war or peace, famine or abundance.
Every single creature stands in judgment: life or death. Who is not called to
account on this day? The record of every human being is set before You, his
work and his ways, his designs and his desires.

Blessed is the man who forgets You not, who draws courage from You. Those
who seek You shall not stumble, those who trust You shall not be disgraced
when the record of all deeds is set before You and You probe every man's
deeds. Remember us as You remembered Noah in love, graciously saving him
when You released the flood to destroy all creatures because of their evil

deeds. You made his descendants numerous as the dust of the earth, as the sand of the sea.

Our God and God of our fathers, remember us favorably, grant us merciful deliverance for our sake, remember Your loving kindness and Your covenant with Abraham our father on Mount Moriah. Recall how Abraham subdued his compassion to do Your will whole-heartedly, binding his son Isaac on the altar; subdue Your wrath with Your compassion. In Your great goodness favor Your people, Your city and Your inheritance. Fulfill for us the promise contained in Your Torah transmitted by Moses:

"For their sake I will remember the covenant with their ancestors whom I brought out of the land of Egypt in the sight of the nations, to be their God. I am the Lord."

Leviticus 26:45

You remember all things forgotten; for You there is no forgetting. This day in mercy remember the binding of Isaac on behalf of his descendants. Praised are You, Lord who remembers the covenant.

God reveals. God redeems.

You were revealed to Your holy people at Mount Sinai. Your mysterious Presence revealed amid clouds of Your glory. All creation stood in awe, trembling, when You our King did manifest Yourself, teaching our forefathers Torah and *mitzvot.* Out of flaming fire, amid thunder and lightening, amid blasts of the *shofar* did You reveal Yourself to them.

Thus is it written in Your Torah:

On the third day, as morning dawned at Mount Sinai, there were peals of thunder and flashes of lightening, a dense cloud on the mountain, and loud blasts of the *shofar;* everyone in the camp trembled. The blare of the *shofar* grew louder and louder. As Moses spoke, God answered him in thunder.

Exodus 19:16, 19

So sang the Psalmist:

The God of judgment ascends His throne with shouts of acclamation; the Lord of compassion ascends with a fanfare of the *shofar.* With trumpets and *shofar,* acclaim the presence of the Lord our King. Sound the *shofar* on the New Moon, announcing our solemn festival. It is Israel's eternal ritual, the God of Jacob calls us to judgment.

Psalms 47:6, 98:6, 81:4–5

And thus proclaimed Your prophet:

All you who dwell in the world, inhabitants of the earth, shall see when the signal of redemption is hoisted on the mountains, and shall hear when the *shofar* is sounded.

Isiah 18:3

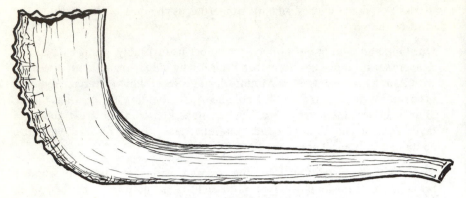

A *Shofar* (Ram's Horn)

Our God and God of our fathers, sound the great *shofar* for our freedom, raise high the banner to gather our exiles. Unite our scattered people, gather our dispersed from the ends of the earth. Lead us with song to Zion Your city, with everlasting joy to Jerusalem Your sanctuary, where our forefathers offered their sacrifices of well-being and their burnt offerings. And thus is it written in Your Torah:

"On your joyous occasions, your fixed festivals and new moon days, you shall sound the *trumpets* . . . They shall be a reminder of you before the Lord your God; I the Lord, am your God."

Numbers 10:10

There is none like You, hearing the *shofar* and attending to its sound. Praised are You, Lord who hears the sound of the *shofar* of His people Israel with compassion.

32.

the days of awe: god's compassion

Every day throughout the fall festival season, the Jew recites the 27th Psalm, which speaks of God's compassion and love of man. This is the season of judgment and deliverance. Man therefore prays for the forgiveness and acceptance of God.

From *Mahzor for Rosh Hashanah and Yom Kippur,* edited by Jules Harlow (New York: The Rabbinical Assembly of America, 1972), p. 297. © 1972 by the Rabbinical Assembly of America. Reprinted by permission of The Rabbinical Assembly.

A Psalm of David. The Lord is my light and my help. Whom shall I fear? The Lord is the strength of my life. Whom shall I dread? When evildoers draw near to devour me, when foes threaten, they stumble and fall. Though armies be arrayed against me, I have no fear. Though wars threaten, I remain steadfast in my faith.

One thing I ask of the Lord, for this I yearn: To dwell in the House of the Lord all the days of my life, to pray in His sanctuary, to behold the Lord's beauty. He will hide me in His shrine, safe from peril. He will shelter me, and put me beyond the reach of disaster. He will raise my head high above my enemies about me. I will bring Him offerings with shouts of joy. I will sing, I will chant praise to the Lord.

O Lord, hear my voice when I call; be gracious, and answer me. "It is You that I seek," says my heart. It is Your Presence that I crave, O Lord. Hide not Your Presence from me, reject not Your servant. You are my help, do not desert me. Forsake me not, God of my deliverance. Though my father and mother forsake me, the Lord will gather me in, and care for me. Teach me Your way, O Lord. Guide me on the right path, to confound those who mock me. Deceivers have risen against me, men who breathe out violence. Abandon me not to the will of my foes.

Mine is the faith that I surely will see the Lord's goodness in the land of the living. Hope in the Lord and be strong. Hope in the Lord and take courage.

33.

the days of awe: vows and forgiveness

The evening of the Day of Atonement is called *Kol Nidrei,* literally, "all vows," the first words in the opening prayer of the synagogue liturgy. Now the Jew, atoning for his sins and seeking God's forgiveness, divests himself of the grudges of the past year, regretting the vows and oaths which may preserve hatred for his fellow-man. Seeking God's forgiveness, he first forgives all who have wronged him and begs their pardon as well. At right with man, he then turns to God. The service begins with the removal of the Torah-scrolls from the ark. A formal court is convened, in the presence of the scrolls. The *Kol Nidrei* liturgy is sung by the cantor and congregation. Rabbi Harlow explains *Kol Nidrei* as follows.

From *Mahzor for Rosh Hashanah and Yom Kippur,* edited by Jules Harlow (New York: The Rabbinical Assembly of America, 1972), pp. 325–327. © 1972 by The Rabbinical Assembly of America. Reprinted by permission of The Rabbinical Assembly.

Our words, and especially our promises, must be taken seriously; our integrity must be unquestioned.

The Torah demands respect for vows: "When you make a vow to the Lord your God, you shall not delay in fulfilling it, for then you will have sinned, as the Lord requires fulfillment of all vows. But you do not sin if you refrain from vowing. You must be careful to fulfill any vow to the Lord which has passed your lips" (Deuteronomy 23:22–24). And Ecclesiastes further states: "Be not rash with your mouth, nor let your heart be hasty to utter a word before God."

In spite of such instruction and our own experience, we do make rash or foolish vows which can not or should not be fulfilled. Jewish tradition did not want to relieve an individual of the obligation to fulfill his vows; yet it did want to allow a person to annul a vow the fulfillment of which could cause harm. At the start of Yom Kippur in particular, tradition also wanted to relieve the individual of guilt he might feel for any unfulfilled vow, even a harmless one. It therefore devised a comprehensive legal formula of dispensation solemnly and publicly retracting all vows. The Rabbis teach, "Whoever wishes all the vows he may make throughout the year to be null and void shall say at the beginning of the year, 'May all vows which I shall vow be annulled' " *(Nedarim 23b). Kol Nidrei* is a development of that statement.

The *Kol Nidrei* formula is restricted to those vows which involve one's relationship with his conscience or with God, involving no other persons or their interests.

I hereby forgive all who have hurt me, all who have done me wrong, whether deliberately or by accident, whether by word or by deed. May no one be punished on my account.

As I forgive and pardon fully those who have done me wrong, may those whom I have harmed forgive and pardon me, whether I acted deliberately or by accident, whether by word or by deed.

Wipe away my sins, O Lord, with Your great mercy. May I not repeat the wrongs I have committed.

May the words of my mouth and the prayers in my heart be acceptable before You, O Lord, my Rock and my Redeemer.

While the Torah scrolls are taken from the Ark, the following verses are recited. (In some congregations they are recited while the Torah scrolls are carried in procession.)

Praised be He who gave the Torah to His people Israel.

Blessed the people who are so favored.
Blessed the people whose God is the Lord.

It is a tree of life for those who grasp it,
and those who uphold it are blessed.
Its ways are pleasantness, and all its paths are peace.

The Lord is gracious and compassionate,
surpassingly patient and merciful.

The Lord is good to all His creatures;
His tenderness extends to all His works.

Light is sown for the righteous,
joy for the upright in heart.

Kol Nidrei

The legal declaration of Kol Nidrei is recited in the setting of a formal court. Two men holding Torah scrolls stand at either side of the Hazzan, thus constituting a court (bet din) of three which is required for the legal procedure of granting dispensation from vows.

By authority of the court on high and by the authority of this court below, with divine consent and with the consent of this congregation, we hereby declare that it is permitted to pray with those who have transgressed.

All vows and oaths we take, all promises and obligations we make to God between this Yom Kippur and the next we hereby publicly retract in the event that we should forget them, and hereby declare our intention to be absolved of them.

Leader and congregation:

And all the congregation of the people Israel shall be forgiven, as well as the stranger who dwells among them, for all the people Israel acted in error.

Numbers 15:26

Leader:

In Your unbounded lovingkindness, please pardon the sin of this people. Forgive us as You have forgiven our people through all times.

Numbers 14:19

Congregation and Leader:

Then the Lord said to Moses: "I have pardoned them, as you have asked."

Numbers 14:20

Leader and congregation:

Praised are you, Lord Our God, King of the universe, for granting us life, for sustaining us, and for helping us reach this day.

The Torah scrolls are returned to the Ark.

34.

the days of awe: confession

Throughout the Day of Atonement, the community of Israel many times confesses its sins, collective and individual, before God. It is a time of contrition and remorse, humility and self-criticism. The confession goes as follows.

From *Mahzor for Rosh Hashanah and Yom Kippur,* edited by Jules Harlow (New York: The Rabbinical Assembly of America, 1972), pp. 351–353, 377–383. © 1972 by The Rabbinical Assembly of America. Reprinted by permission of The Rabbinical Assembly.

Our God and God of our fathers, hear our prayer; do not ignore our plea. We are neither so brazen nor so arrogant to claim that we are righteous, without sin, for indeed we have sinned.

We abuse, we betray, we are cruel.
We destroy, we embitter, we falsify.
We gossip, we hate, we insult.
We jeer, we kill, we lie.
We mock, we neglect, we oppress.
We pervert, we quarrel, we rebel.
We steal, we transgress, we are unkind.
We are violent, we are wicked, we are xenophobic.
We yield to evil, we are zealots for bad causes.

We have ignored Your commandments and statutes, but it has not profited us. You are just, we have stumbled. You have acted faithfully, we have been unrighteous. What can we say to You; what can we tell You? You know everything, secret and revealed.

You know the mysteries of the universe, the secrets of everyone alive. You probe our innermost depths, You examine our thoughts and desires. Nothing escapes You, nothing is hidden from You.

May it therefore be Your will, Lord our God and God of our fathers, to forgive us all our sins, to pardon all our iniquities, to grant us atonement for all our transgressions.

We have sinned against You unwillingly and willingly,
And we have sinned against You by misusing our minds.
We have sinned against You through sexual immorality,
And we have sinned against You knowingly and deceitfully.

151

We have sinned against You by wronging others,
And we have sinned against You through prostitution.
We have sinned against You by deriding parents and teachers.
And we have sinned against You by using violence.
We have sinned against You through foul speech,
And we have sinned against You by not resisting the impulse
to evil.
For all these sins, forgiving God, forgive us, pardon us, grant us
atonement.
We have sinned against You by fraud and by falsehood.
And we have sinned against You by scoffing.
We have sinned against You by dishonesty in business.
And we have sinned against You by usurious interest.
We have sinned against You by idle chatter,
And we have sinned against You by haughtiness.
We have sinned against You by rejecting repsonsibility,
And we have sinned against You by plotting against others.
We have sinned against You by irreverence,
And we have sinned against You by rushing to do evil.
We have sinned against You by false oaths,
And we have sinned against You by breach of trust.

For all these sins, forgiving God, forgive us, pardon us, grant us atonement.

Forgive us the breach of all commandments and prohibitions, whether involving deeds or not, whether known to us or not. The sins known to us we have acknowledged, and those unknown to us are surely known to You, as the Torah states, "The secret things belong to the Lord our God, but the things that are revealed belong to us and to our children forever, that we may fulfill all the words of this Torah." For You forgive and pardon the people Israel in every generation. But for You we have no King to pardon us and to forgive us for our sins.

At the conclusion of the Amidah, personal prayers may be added, before or instead of the following.

Before I was born, I had no significance. And now that I have been born, I am of equal worth. Dust am I though I live: surely after death will I be dust. In Your presence, aware of my frailty.

I am totally embarrassed and confused. May it be Your will, Lord my God and God of my fathers, to help me abstain from further sin. With Your great compassion wipe away the sins I have committed against You, though not by means of suffering.

Keep me far from petty self-regard and petty pride, from anger, impatience, despair, gossip and all bad traits.

Let me not be overwhelmed by jealousy of others; let others not be overwhelmed by jealousy of me. Grant me the gift of seeing other people's merits, not their faults.

May He who brings peace to His universe bring peace to us and to all the people Israel. And let us say: Amen.

part eight

torah in america: movements in american judaism

Judaism is represented in America by four major trends, or movements: Orthodox, Reform, Conservative, and Reconstructionist. They should not be regarded as fundamentally different sects; they have a great deal in common with one another. We shall review the main traits and beliefs of the four movements to observe the points on which they agree and how they formulate their differences. I do not mean to suggest that the varieties of Judaic religious expression are to be reduced to these four modes alone. Within each movement there are wide variations and differing emphases. Outside of the synagogue-movements are many Jews who regard themselves as religious, and beyond these are even more who regard themselves as Jewish but in no way religious. But within the four movements coalesce the larger number of Judaists—Jews who practice Judaism—and nearly all rabbis and most religious scholars find a place in one or another of the synagogue-movements.

In considering each of the movements, we shall ask two questions. First, what are the primary characteristics of this mode of Judaism? Second, what are the chief problems to be confronted within it? For the critique of the several movements, we shall turn to their participants. Theirs are criticisms from within and reflect a deep appreciation for the movement that is under examination.

35.

american orthodoxy

emanuel rackman

Orthodox Judaism remains closest to the letter and spirit of classical Judaism. Indeed, it makes every effort not to diverge from the historical formulation of the rabbis and sages of every age. Other movements in modern Judaism have to measure themselves and justify their programs against this dominant and entirely credible claim. The Orthodox sometimes call themselves "Torah-true," and it is difficult for the observer to reject that self-description. Yet Orthodoxy is very varied. It includes both people aware of and intimately involved in all phases of modern life and culture, on the one side, and men and women resolutely set against modernity on the other. The former are more easily accessible, for naturally they have the ability to express their ideals in terms easily accessible to the outsider, while the latter find it more difficult to explain to non-participants exactly what participation means to them. Their frame of reference is entirely separate from that of the contemporary secular person.

The so-called "modern" Orthodox are represented by Yeshiva University and the graduates of its rabbinical schools. They are formed into the Union of Orthodox Jewish Congregations and their rabbis constitute the Rabbinical Council of America. Their journal, *Tradition,* is widely read and contains essays which speak for those most attuned to the requirements of the classical *halakhah,* or law, and of the traditional "way of Torah" in general.

A second expression of Orthodoxy, not represented here, is shaped around the yeshivas, or traditional Talmudical academies, found in many major cities. The rabbis educated in these yeshivas do not plan to serve congregations; their studies are meant to make them into learned Jews, but they do not intend to make their living by what they have learned in the Talmud. The piety of the yeshiva movement is, as one might expect, less philosophical and abstract; it is expressed very much within the idiom and language of classical Jewish piety from the earliest times. The writings continue the issues of law and theology, including mysticism, just as they have been discussed for many centuries. The yeshiva movement within American Orthodoxy therefore constitutes the historically most perfect continuation of classical Judaism available in the Western world. But the modern Orthodox will not concede that their piety is less authentic or less attuned to the requirements of the tradition.

Rabbi Emanuel Rackman, a leading figure in modern Orthodoxy and in the Yeshiva University, provides two important statements. The first, which now follows, gives an account of the accomplishments of Orthodoxy, stressing the traits of piety and sacrifice characteristic of Orthodox Jewry. Rackman realistically faces the fact that not all American Jews today are Orthodox, but he stresses the hope that in time they will be and lays down the claim that they should be. Orthodoxy therefore cannot be represented as isolationist or separatist, indifferent to the Jews outside its framework. It faces the challenges of the present context but at the same time remains confident it can meet and master those challenges. Rackman's stress on halakhic problems will by now be entirely comprehensible, for it is within the law that the major issues of Jewish life are debated and resolved.

From "American Orthodoxy—Retrospect and Prospect," by Emanuel Rackman, *Judaism* III, 4, 1954, pp. 302–309. © 1954 by American Jewish Congress. Reprinted by permission of the author and American Jewish Congress.

The earliest Jewish settlers on American soil brought with them the only Judaism they knew—Orthodox Judaism. Two centuries later Reform Judaism took root and still fifty years thereafter Conservative Judaism was born. Under the circumstances, one would have expected that Orthodox Judaism would be the first to meet the challenge of the American scene, ideologically and institutionally. In fact, it was the last to do so. Paradoxically enough, it is only in the last few decades that Orthodoxy seriously came to grips with the problem of its own future.

For too long a time Orthodoxy relied upon the fact that the preponderant number of American Jews professed to be its adherents. Majorities supporting the status quo in many social situations often rely upon the force of their numbers and their inertia, while well organized and dedicated minorites make gains for change. The Orthodox Jewish community once was such a majority. It was slow to realize the extent to which it was losing its numerical advantage. Second, the ranks of American Orthodoxy were ever replenished with thousands of immigrants from abroad. The new arrivals more than compensated for the defections to other groups. Now the loss of the European reservoir of Jews has caused American Orthodoxy to become concerned. It must find the way to command the loyalty of American born Jews. Third, Orthodoxy by its very nature compromises less easily with new environments and new philosophies, so that it could not avail itself of that flexibility which aided the growth of the Reform and Conservative movements. The challenge of the American scene had to be met differently and the solution was later in its formulation and implementation. Nonetheless, significant and many were the contributions of Orthodoxy to our dual heritage as Americans and as Jews.

It fell to the lot of Orthodoxy to establish the legal status of Jews and Judaism in American democracy. To the everlasting credit of our pioneering forbears it must be said that they were not content with second-class citizenship in the United States. George Washington confirmed this attitude in his now famous letter to the Orthodox congregation in Newport, Rhode Island. However, the false dictum that America is a "Christian state" must be challenged again and again, even in the twentieth century, and while the battle is now waged by all Jews, and especially the defense agencies, it is usually one Orthodox Jew or another who creates the issue. The right of Sabbath observers to special consideration where "Blue Sunday" laws are in effect; their right to special treatment in the armed forces; their right to unemployment insurance benefits when they decline employment because of religious scruples—these are typical of many problems that Orthodox Jews raise in the hope that their resolution will insure maximum expansion of the American concept of equality before the law. In many instances, bearded Orthodox Jews who retain their eastern European dress are also a challenge to the sincerity of most Americans who boast that their way of life spells respect for differences. The resistance of many of our co-religionists to the leveling character of American mores, and its inevitable discouragement of diversity, is a healthy contribution to our understanding and practice of democracy. Altogether too often American Jews require the reminder even more than American Christians. . . .

It was, however, in the establishment and construction of thousands of synagogues throughout the country that Orthodox Jews made manifest not only their loyalty to their ancestral heritage but their appreciation of their grand opportunity in this blessed land of freedom. How truly pauperized immigrants managed, in cities large and small, to rear beautiful edifices for worship is a saga worthy of more attention than it has heretofore received. What is particularly noteworthy is that no central agency guided or financed the movement. In every case it was individual Jews who banded together and performed the feat, a remarkable tribute to the effectiveness of our tradition in inducing in individual Jews the capacity to act on their own initiative for the greater glory of God. Even today no central body guides or directs the establishment of Orthodox synagogues. Orthodoxy's synagogue organization—the Union of Orthodox Jewish Congregations of America—is still totally ineffective in this kind of work. The initiative must always come from Jews who desire an Orthodox synagogue, and not from any resourceful, missionary, national or international body. In part, this is also one of the weaknesses of Orthodox Judaism which its leaders want to correct on the threshold of its fourth century on the American scene. However, it remains to be seen whether it will be the Union of Orthodox Jewish Congregations or Yeshiva University that will blaze the new path.

The extent to which Orthodox Jews gave of their worldly goods for the establishment and construction of synagogues was exceeded only by their willingness to sacrifice for the cause of Jewish education. Their first venture in this direction, even before the era of the public school, was a Jewish all-day school under the auspices of Congregation Shearit Israel in New York. The more usual approach to the problem, however, was via the Talmud-Torah, the afternoon school in which children spent from five to ten hours weekly. In some instances the Talmud Torahs were successful, and many distinguished American Rabbis and scholars received their earliest instruction in Judaica in such schools. Yet altogether too often because of incompetent instructors, bizarre methods, and inadequate facilities, the Talmud Torahs failed to induce either a love or an understanding of Judaism. In the twentieth century, therefore, Orthodox Judaism countered with the Yeshiva movement. This movement has enjoyed a phenomenal growth. In the ranks of Conservative Judaism, too, it is receiving sympathetic attention and support, and even among Liberal Jews one occasionally hears it suggested that the all-day school is the most effective answer to Jewish illiteracy. Orthodox Judaism is endeavoring to recapture the loyalty of American Jews. However, it cannot "adjust" to the American scene. The term "adjust" too often implies man's right to trim religion to meet his personal desires. Such a right Orthodoxy denies any Jew, and notwithstanding even Dr. Kinsey, the sixth commandment of the Decalogue is binding no matter how high the percentage of spouses who flout it. Nonetheless, most American Orthodox Rabbis recognize that there has always been, and still are, different modes of Orthodox Jewish thought and practice, and that Orthodoxy has always admitted a great measure of innovation. The innovation, however, is always within the Halakhic process and pursuant to its revealed norms. The result, therefore, is organic development of God's will, not man's.

In order to communicate this point of view to American Jews Orthodoxy must have leaders who are not only articulate in English but also masters of western thought and its temper. That is why Yeshiva University and the Hebrew Theological College advocate the mastering of all western thought in order to create an ultimate synthesis with Jewish learning. This goal will be achieved as more of the graduates of these schools and other Yeshivoth become expert in the natural and social sciences.

There already exists a society of Orthodox Jewish scientists which is dedicating itself to the solution of problems created for Orthodoxy by modern technology. Many a Halakhic point of view is receiving support from the natural sciences, and what is more important, these scientists are demonstrating that there is no conflict between natural science—which has abandoned the notion that it can attain any absolute truths whatever—and religion which calls for faith in given absolutes. The greater challenges to Orthodoxy, however, come from the social sciences and an impressive group of Orthodox leaders, lay and Rabbinic, are coping with them.

Orthodoxy's position vis-a-vis the Higher Criticism of the Bible is one such area. While Orthodoxy is committed to no one conception of Revelation, all Orthodox Jews regard the Pentateuch as divinely revealed. Moses wrote it while in direct communion with God. Moreover, with Moses too, the Oral Law had its beginnings and its process was ordained by God. German Jewish Orthodoxy perhaps made more progress in its defense of this position than has American Jewish Orthodoxy to date. However, Orthodoxy relies heavily on the fact that modern archaeological research has bolstered the historicity of the Biblical narrative and Orthodoxy is confident that further progress in philology will precipitate the same kind of retreat from anti-Orthodox viewpoints that the Bible's erstwhile plastic surgeons have suffered. Rabbi Chayim Heller, at Yeshiva University, is stimulating both the confidence and the type of research necessary to sustain the

Orthodox position. Moreover, many Orthodox thinkers believe that with a retreat from humanism generally, humanism will no longer be the vantage point from which the revealed Word of God will be arrogantly evaluated. Man will not be the measure of God.

The greatest challenge of all, however, lies in the realm of Halakhah; first, the importance of its study, and second, the importance of living by its prescriptions. Is the Halakhah viable in the modern age? Can it and does it enrich our spiritual existence? Is it relevant to our yearnings and aspirations and can it edify and fulfill them? Only a small percentage of even Orthodox Jews are content with the mandate, "The Law is the Law and must, therefore, be obeyed." Philosophical approaches to Halakhah and philosophical analyses of the Halakhic process must be articulated. The undisputed leader of the Orthodox Jewish community in this domain is Dr. Joseph B. Soloveichik, of Yeshiva University, who is now also Chairman of the Halakhah Commission of the Rabbinical Council of America. In addition to his brilliant resolution of many involved Halakhic problems of the modern age, and his equally masterful analyses of Talmudic texts, he is demonstrating the viability of the Halakha, the relevance of its insights to abundant and adventurous spiritual living, and the intellectual harvests to be reaped from preoccupation with its study. Most of the great Halakhic scholars who adorn the faculties of America's Yeshivoth, and most of the distinguished Orthodox Rabbis who founded and still lead the Union of Orthodox Rabbis of the United States and Canada, deserve credit for their benign influence upon the loyalty of thousands of American Jews to our ancestral heritage. But they have done little more than transplant the Orthodoxy of Eastern Europe on American soil. It is to Dr. Soloveichik, his co-workers and students, the American Orthodoxy looks for the ideological content, the techniques and the conclusions required to stem the tide of defections to other groups by making it abundantly clear that Halakhic Judaism is eternal and has naught to fear from the challenges of western thought, present and future.

First, however, it wants to stimulate a renascence of Torah learning on American soil. Orthodoxy feels that until Jews are learned they cannot be pious. It insists that it sustained its greatest set-back in America because of Am ha-Arazuth, Torah illiteracy. For more than two and a half centuries America could not boast of a score of men learned in the Law. How could Orthodoxy then achieve here that synthesis that was once the glory of Spanish Judaism? The first task, therefore, is to spread the knowledge of Torah. As tens of thousands become masters of the Halakha, the Halakha will have a new birth in the new world.

Second, Orthodoxy does not believe that the modern contribution to progressive revelation can come until the modern age recaptures basic religious experience. The commitment of our age to material values has deadened our capacity for religious experience. Yet, there is evidence that as we face the atomic era in human history, there will be a resurgence of religious values and a reawakening of religious experience. In such atmosphere, Judaism will thrive. Particularly will Halakhic Judaism thrive as more and more Jews seek to apprehend God's will rather than merely indulging their own.

36.

a challenge to orthodoxy

emanuel rackman

Rabbi Rackman serves not only as an expositor and exponent of Orthodox Judaism, but also as a perceptive critic. Here he raises the central intellectual problem faced, and not entirely resolved, within Orthodoxy: the issue of changing philosophies and conceptions of the world within an unchanging discipline of religion and piety. His primary claim is that Orthodox Judaism does not stand against intellectual honesty and does not require that one turn his back to the ideas of his own time. This view, which is held within the yeshiva movement, is contrary to the historical realities of the classical tradition, Rackman says. In a sense he here takes up the perspective first encountered in Rabbi Fritz Rothschild's exposition of how the Bible has been interpreted over the centuries.

Rabbi Rackman's main point is that Orthodoxy is not monolithic or static, but varied and dynamic. There is ample room for different viewpoints and interpretations. Divergence of opinion in the past is sufficient warrant for freedom of interpretation and inquiry in the present. You cannot locate a great many fixed dogmas. You cannot find much agreement on many theological and metaphysical matters. You cannot impose a single conception of the nature and meaning of Revelation upon the entire theological corpus of Judaism. So why should people now suppose that there is only one, fixed viewpoint to be imposed on and adopted by everyone? Rackman's stress on the varieties and resilience of the classical tradition at the same time constitutes both a serious criticism of the obscurantism characteristic of some Orthodox circles and a responsible defense of, and apology for, modern Orthodoxy.

From "A Challenge to Orthodoxy," by Emanuel Rackman, *Judaism* XVIII, 2, 1969, pp. 143–158. © 1969 by American Jewish Congress. Reprinted by permission of the author and American Jewish Congress.

A group of Israeli intellectuals, Orthodox in practice and commitment, addressed an inquiry to one of the world's most pious and learned of rabbis. In their work and thought they had embraced scientific theories which appeared to contradict passages of the Bible when literally interpreted. The age of the earth was one example. From another rabbi they had heard that Orthodoxy requires that one believe the earth to be only 5728 years old. Were they to be regarded as heretics because of their disagreement with this view?

The twenty-five page reply prepared for them is not yet published. Its author (who prefers to be unnamed) sought the concurrence of three colleagues who had occasionally expressed progressive views. One declined to become involved because of advanced age and poor health; another declined concurrence because of fear of what he himself calls "McCarthyism" in Jewish Orthodoxy; the third felt that his status in the traditionalist community was not yet sufficiently secure to be of any value to the scholar soliciting approval, especially since the latter himself enjoyed so much more prestige than he.

The reply—with copious references to authorities—indicates that Orthodoxy is not monolithic: it requires acknowledgment of the divine origin of the Commandments and firm resolve to fulfill them; however, it also permits great latitude in the formulation of doctrines, the interpretation of Biblical passages, and the rationalization of *mitzvot.* It is not difficult to demonstrate that the giants of the Tradition held widely divergent views on the nature of God, the character of historic revelation, and the uniqueness of the Jewish faith. Not all of these views could possibly be true, and yet not one of them may be deemed heretical, since one respected authority or another has clung to it. The only heresy is the denial that God gave the Written and Oral Law to His people, who are to fulfill its mandates and develop their birthright in accordance with its own built-in methodology and authentic exegesis.

Often in the past, upon encountering new cultures or philosophical systems, Jewish scholars re-examined the Tradition and discovered new insights and interpretations. Their contemporary colleagues of a more conservative temperament resisted and attacked the creative spirits as heretics, though the impugned protested that they were deeply committed to the Tradition and had said nothing which was not supported by respected authorities who had preceded them. The resulting schisms were often no credit to the Jewish people and, in modern times, even yielded groupings among American Jews which are not based altogether on ideological differences.

Unfortunately, however, it is the reactionaries in Orthodoxy who bear much of the guilt for this tragic phenomenon. Their heresy is that they regard their own Biblical and Talmudic interpretation as canonized in the same measure as the texts themselves—which was never true. They are repeating this heresy again, in Israel and the Diaspora, so that already Jewish sociologists detect the possibility of further schisms in Orthodoxy. At least four groups are even now discernible, and the "rightists" are exercising pressure to brand the "leftists" as heretics and to force them either to create a new sect or to identify with Conservative Judaism. The founder of Reconstructionism did break with the Tradition, and his views, insofar as they deny the divine origin of Torah and *mitzvot,* are heresy. But this was unequivocally clear to his own colleagues on the faculty of the Jewish Theological Seminary fifty years ago, and Solomon Schechter must have had him in mind when he poked fun at those who observe the *mitzvot* and yet deny their God-given character. However, this does not mean that all who have new approaches are *ipso facto* non-Orthodox and must affiliate elsewhere. . . .

Even with regard to doctrine, divergence of opinion has prevailed among the giants of the Tradition that only one dogma enjoys universal acceptance: the

Pentateuch's text was given to the Jewish people by God. However, what its mandates are, their number, application, and interpretation—this is part of the Oral Law, also God-given, but its guardians were rarely unanimous on its legal norms and less so on matters theological. That a majority prevailed on any particular issue in the past does not necessarily mean that the minority view is heretical, for, while one must continue to fulfill the law as the majority decided, one may propagate the minority point of view in the hope that it will one day be accepted by a new Sanhedrin. Maimonides is less liberal on this point than his critical glossator, Rabbi Abraham Ben David, but even Maimonides accords this power to a Sanhedrin greater than its predecessors in quality and quantity. Therefore, how can one brand as a heretic anyone who in matters theological differs with his contemporaries and seeks to make normative a point of view once rejected or proscribed but for whose acceptance he continues to hope?

How many are the dogmas of Judaism? Maimonides said thirteen, but other scholars held that there were fewer. Even on so basic a point as to whether there can exist more than one divine law Albo differed with Maimonides. He denied that there is any evidence for Maimonides' contention that the immutability of the Mosaic Law is a pillar of the faith and opined that there may be a succession of divine laws, so that even Mosaic law is not beyond change or repeal. Jews generally have agreed with Maimonides—at least until the Messiah will come, and upon his coming they believe with Albo that new divine laws may be promulgated. The collective experience of the Jewish people may warrant the conclusion that the Maimonidean view is the more prudent—pragmatically to be regarded as true—but who can gainsay the right of a dissenter to agree with Albo or even a modification or extension of Albo's view and yet regard himself as a member of the family of the committed?

Agreement or even consensus is still more difficult to find in connection with such matters as the nature and mission of angels, the character of "the world-to-come" and how it differs from immortality of the soul, the precise role the Messiah will play when he comes and what events will be the most dependable credentials of his legitimacy, the form final judgment will take in a hereafter and the reward and punishments to be dispensed, the transmigration of souls, and a score of other issues with which ancient and medieval scholars were concerned. One discovers in their writings virtually every opinion known to man, ranging from the purest rationalism to the wildest fancy. Few Orthodox Jews try to be specific in formulating their own creeds. They are content with a few generalizations: that God endows every human being with a soul, which is His eternal spark within us and immortal; the human being—body and soul—is responsible and accountable for his performance on earth; one day nature will be made perfect, and as God fulfills His promise to make it perfect He will also have to do justice to the dead, who are the most helpless victims of nature's imperfections. Details are not only avoided, they are unthinkable. Except in most elusive form these sentiments can hardly be regarded as dogmas; they leave too much room for the play of the imagination of the individual believer. Therefore, it is incredible that moderns, who are committed to faith and the Law, should be excluded from the fold because of limited credulousness in this sphere. Indeed, it would be impossible for reactionaries to ignore the giants of the past who were equally skeptical. . . .

But the range of the diversity involves doctrines even more basic to the faith. To what extent, for example, is there any binding authority on the nature of God and His attributes? Here, too, Maimonides and Rabbi Abraham ben David differed so radically on God's corporeality that, were Jews prone to create sects because of doctrinal disputes, as Protestents do, each would have been responsible for a new sect in Judaism. Even with regard to so integral a part of Judaism as God's role as Creator, Maimonides retained an open mind. He believed that the correct interpretation of the Bible required a belief in *creatio ex nihilo,* but he admitted that if it could be proven conclusively—as Aristotle had failed to do—that this was impossible, one would then only be required to re-examine and correct one's interpretation of the Bible to make it consonant with the demands of absolute truth. Judaism is very much at peace with a host of antimonies regarding God's nature—His imminence and His transcendence, His prescience and His becoming, His absolutism and His vacillation. To deny that God is a personal God who communicates with all men, and especially with Israel, would be heresy according to Judaism, but any description of Him by rationalists, empiricists, intuitionists, or existentialists would hardly be without some warrant in the writings of the Sages.

Similarly, there is no substantial agreement with regard to the manner in which God communicated with Israel, its Patriarchs and Prophets. Somehow the Tradition preferred never to demand of Jews more than that they believe the text of the Pentateuch to be divine in origin. Otherwise, the widest latitude in interpretation was not only permitted but often encouraged. Even the authorship of the Five Books of Moses was not beyond the scope of the diversity. Several Sages held that Moses himself wrote the book of *Deuteronomy* but God dictated its inclusion with the earlier books. Moreover, much in the earlier books started also as the work of man. In their dialogues with God the Patriarchs spoke their own words. Jacob composed his own prophecy for his offspring. Moses sang his own song of triumph on the Red Sea. In the final analysis, then, the sanctity of the Pentateuch does not derive from God's authorship of all of it but rather from the fact that God's is the final version. The final writing by Moses has the stamp of divinity—the kiss of immortality. So stated, the dogma is a much more limited one than one would be led to believe it is when one listens to many an Orthodox teacher today.

If this is the situation with regard to the Pentateuch, is it wise to add dogmas that the books of the Prophets and the Writings were all authored by the men to whom the Tradition attributes them? The Talmud itself was not dogmatic, but contemporary Orthodoxy always feels impelled to embrace every tradition as dogma. The Talmud suggests that perhaps David did not write all the Psalms. Is one a heretic because one suggests that perhaps other books were authored by more than one person or that several books attributed by the Tradition to one author were in fact written by several at different times? A volume recently published makes an excellent argument for the position there was but one Isaiah, but must one be shocked when it is opined that there may have been two or three prophets bearing the same name? No Sage of the past ever included in the articles of faith a dogma about the authorship of the books of the Bible other than the Pentateuch. What is the religious, moral, or intellectual need for adding dogmas now when it is well known with regard to many such issues that there always prevailed *noblesse oblige* among scholars? It may be heresy to deny the possibility of prophetic prediction, but it is not heresy to argue about authorship on the basis of objective historical and literary evidence. How material is it that one really believes that Solomon wrote all three Scrolls attributed to him? Is the value of the writings themselves affected? And if the only purpose is to discourage critical Biblical scholarship, then, alas, Orthodoxy is declaring bankruptcy: it is saying that only the ignorant can be pious—a reversal of the Talmudic dictum.

True, a pious man has *emunat hakhamim,* faith in the dicta of the Sages. Yet Orthodox Jews do not rely on this principle in connection with their physical well-being. They are willing to be treated in illness by physicians who hold views that differ radically from those expressed in the Talmud for the treatment of disease. Certainly the Tradition condones this. Is it less forgiving of one who in his study of the Bible feels impelled to arrive at conclusions on the basis of evidence unavailable to his forebears?

No more than with regard to the authorship of the Biblical books did the Sages canonize interpretations of the Bible. For the purpose of the Halachah one interpretation may have to be followed until the Halachah, within its own processes, is altered; but the Sages recognized, offered, and delighted in many alternatives, frequently contradictory interpretations which had significance for their spiritual living. Especially was this true when they interpreted narrative portions of the Bible. Maimonides was the most revolutionary of all when he held that most Biblical history is allegorical. Whether Jacob only dreamed that he wrestled with an angel or actually did so was debated by sundry Sages. Nahmanides even held that it was God's intention that the *mitzvot* of the Torah were given for ultimate fulfillment in the Land of Israel, and our observance of them in the Diaspora is only preparation for our sojourn in the land of our fathers. Hardly any Orthodox rabbi agrees with him today—and perhaps none agreed with him in his day. Was he, therefore, deemed a heretic?

Even the historic fact of revelation was not specifically delineated. Whether God as much as spoke all the Decalogue so that everyone could hear it was controversial. One Rabbi dared to say that God did not descend to earth. Summing up the Talmudic and Midrashic texts available and the opinions of medieval philosophers, one modern scholar said that the best that could be said for the Jewish conception of revelation is that it is "elusive." Perhaps it is. But the net effect is a consensus on which the faith is founded. *Something* extraordinary happened—and the Jew begins with a text that is God's word. He may not always understand it. He may often question why God approved of much that He gave. Unlike Martin Buber, the Orthodox Jew does not reject any part of the text. If he finds it difficult to explain why the very God who ordered us never to take revenge also demanded the extermination of the Amalekites, he does not delete from the text the lines he does not fathom; he ponders them until divine illumination comes to him. He may discover that the Amalekites—unlike the Egyptians —merited destruction and continuing hate; he may regard Amalek as the symbol of militarism for the sake of militarism; or he may even conclude that what is meant is the id in every human being. Heresy begins not when interpretation is challenged but when the text is no longer considered divine. That is why Franz Rosenzweig did not consider himself un-Orthodox because of his theory of revelation but only because he could not bring himself to obey all the *mitzvot* until they spoke to him personally and became meaningful to his own existential situation. Unlike him, the Orthodox Jew obeys and does not wait. Obedience to God's will by itself is meaningful to his existential situation, and the more he obeys the more he discovers meaning and relevance.

If Jews differed with regard to their interpretation of the texts of Scripture, certainly they differed with regard to their interpretation of history. It has been demonstrated, for example, that Ashkenazim and Sephardim differed with regard to their positions on eschatology and the warrant that historical situations might provide for either activism or quiescence with regard to the coming of the Messiah.

Thus, even with respect to creed, the diversity is as legion as it is with respect to Law. To be counted among the devout and the committed never required unrelenting conformity in matters of the mind and heart. Judaism did not suffer as a result. On the contrary, it remained one of the most dynamic and spiritually satisfying of all religious traditions. In the last century and a half this magnificent Tradition was abandoned: in its encounter with the enormous diversity of the winds of doctrine prevailing in the modern world, Orthodoxy sought to guarantee its survival by freezing the Halachah and its theology. As a result, it now cannot realize its full potential in an age when more and more intellectuals are prepared for the leap of faith but hardly for a leap to obscurantism. . . .

37.

what is reform judaism?

abraham j. feldman

Rabbi Abraham J. Feldman, for many years a rabbi in Hartford, Connecticut, and a leader in many American Jewish organizations, here explains to his own congregation, Temple Beth Israel, what Reform Judaism is—and what it is not. He wishes to show his congregation that Reform Judaism is not meant as a mode of assimilation or a way out of either the Jewish tradition in general or Orthodoxy in particular. Rather, he holds, Reform Judaism here and now is the authentic continuation of classical Judaism. Reform is positive and affirmative; it stands for a serious commitment.

It would have been appropriate to consider Reform Judaism in advance of Orthodoxy, for historically the Reform movement in Germany raised the challenge that brought traditional Jews to self-consciousness and provoked the definition and organization of Orthodoxy. Reform Judaism met head-on the difficulties of modernization; it led the way for other groups, and while much criticized, it served as the pioneer in the effort to explore how people might be both Jews and modern men and women. What is interesting here, however, is the effort to link up Reform with its antecedents and to lay claim to the same legitimacy and authenticity that Orthodoxy regards as its justification.

From *Reform Judaism: A Guide for Reform Jews,* by Abraham J. Feldman (New York: Behrman House, 1956), pp. 5–10. © 1956 by Abraham J. Feldman. Reprinted by permission of the author.

Reform Judaism is a Jewish religious movement originating in Germany in the 18th century. It has sought and continues to seek so to interpret Judaism that it may meet the religious needs of the Jew in modern times. It clings to the basic concepts of historical Judaism. But it has made changes in some of the customs and ceremonies which have come to us from the past. In doing this, Reform Judaism remained true to the spirit and practice of traditional historic Judaism which, be it remembered, has always been both adaptable and progressive.

When we speak of Reform Judaism we are not speaking of a new kind of Judaism. It was only the name that was new as it came into being near the end of the 18th century in Germany. This name has become the label of that interpretation of Judaism which recognizes and emphasizes the dynamic character of the Jewish religion—*dynamic,* which is the opposite of arrested or static Judaism. Reform Judaism emphasizes what is inherent in all Judaism, the principle of progression in the concepts and forms of the Jewish religion. Reform has its roots in the past! It proudly acknowledges the glory, the dignity, the validity of Jewish tradition. It chooses to continue to identify itself with the tradition and it refuses to admit that Jewish tradition is something which is petrified, the crystallization of any one moment or era of Jewish religious thought and experience. This idea of a progressive Jewish tradition is not new. The Jewish tradition always was progressive but, especially in the 15th through the 18th centuries, an effort was made to freeze it. When the ghetto disappeared and the period of emancipation began, this frozen tradition failed to hold and to satisfy those generations because of its completely unbending and, in a very real sense, unorthodox position. It was then that a group of Jews, led by laymen at first, decided that it was time to unfreeze the tradition, and attempted the long overdue and the long dammed-up adjustments. This was the beginning of the modern Reform. The Reformers did not seek escape from Judaism. If they had, the road was open and a welcome awaited them elsewhere. They *wanted* to remain within the fold and orbit of Judaism but they wanted the tradition unfrozen and the processes of change speeded up.

This matter of adjustment of Judaism to contemporary needs was not anything new in our tradition. Why is it that Judaism *never* had any formal creed? Why were there controversies between the schools of Hillel and Shammai? What was the meaning of the great struggle between the Sadducees and the Pharisees? What was the meaning of the conflict between Maimonides, Ibn Daud, Nachmanides, etc.? Why the conflict in the 17th and 18th centuries between the Hasidim and their opponents, the Misnagdim? It was in all instances the insistence upon freedom of interpretation and emphasis. Movements, differences—these are nothing new in Judaism. To illustrate: the code of practice which largely governs authoritative Jewish Orthodoxy today is the *Shulhan Aruch,* a work compiled by Joseph Caro in 1555 and first printed in 1565. Caro was a Sephardic Jew, i.e., belonging to the Spanish-Portuguese Jewish tradition. Hence, his work recorded the practices of the Jewish tradition as they were known among Sephardim. But there were variant practices of Judaism, especially among Ashkenazic Jews, i.e., Jews in Germanic countries and in Russia and Poland. These were not included in Caro's code.

When his compilation (the *Shulhan Aruch)* appeared and came to the notice of Ashkenazim, a storm of protest broke out. The reason? Many of the practices which Caro represented as "authoritative" and obligatory were not current among Ashkenazim. They were unknown. And Caro did not even mention many which were "authoritative" in Central European and Eastern and Southern European Jewry.

So, in 1578, thirteen years after the first publication of Caro's code, a new edition of the *Shulhan Aruch* appeared which incorporated Ashkenazic practices. The additions were prepared by Rabbi Moses Isserles of Cracow, Poland. Both the Sephardic and Ashkenazic practices in their respective areas became, in time, authoritative, orthodox.

What is called "Traditional Judaism" is not all of one pattern or form.

Changes, variations, are continuous, although they are often long in becoming recognized or approved. In passing, it might be interesting to recall that Isserles' addenda were not immediately approved. It was not until the middle of the 17th century that the controversy about their authoritativeness died. In like manner, many other adjustments and adaptations were made in Jewish practices. Most of them were long in gaining general recognition. Nevertheless, these changes have helped keep Judaism alive.

Reform was thus not a new sect but a *movement* placing a strong emphasis upon a living, fluid tradition, and seeking to correct the damage done by centuries of ghetto isolationism and congealment.

Thus Reform is classical Judaism asserting anew the right and the duty of accelerating the process of progress and change where changes seem to be necessary. If some customs and practices are no longer meaningful, then they are no longer useful, and to cling to them mechanically or to acknowledge them as valid whilst they are largely neglected is to endanger the very survival of Jews and Judaism. In the absence of an authoritative legislative body continuing to function, and thus to be compelled to wait for the slow process of Halachic change through *responsa,* which often takes generations, is to expose the patient to danger. Therefore, Reform's principal contribution is the decision to keep Judaism forever contemporary, and to keep it responsive to the religious needs of successive generations. Its purpose is not to preserve, let us say, in Hartford, or in Brooklyn, or in Chicago, or even in the United States of America, all the forms of the Judaism of Poland, of Galicia, Hungary, Rumania or Lithuania, but to keep Judaism *Jewish* in content whilst adapting the traditional forms to contemporary life, and creating new forms as needs require. Some day, Judaism in the State of Israel might become adapted to the new life and challenge of its needs and ways.

Reform insists that changes be made *when* they are needed, *in* and *by* the generation that needs them, rather than wait generations or even centuries before any perceptible adjustments occur. Our generations today and the generations tomorrow have the right and, we think, the duty to keep Judaism alive by keeping it contemporary, and responsive to their spiritual needs. Our people can be Jewishly religious in America, for example, without being coerced into irreligion by attempting to mold American Jews into the religious pattern or forms of Warsaw or Kovno or the Chief Rabbis of Jerusalem. Reform in the United States has undoubtedly saved hundreds of thousands of Jews for Judaism and for Jewish life. Reform Judaism has saved Jews for Judaism in America by making it possible and proper to be religious Jews without strict and undeviating conformity to the minutiae of traditional practice. To the extent that these Jews were saved for Jewish life, Reform has made a vital contribution to all Jewish religious life. It stemmed the tide of assimilation away from Jewishness.

Moreover, Reform in America has taught both Orthodoxy and Conservatism the methodology for organizational survival in this country. Rabbi Isaac Mayer Wise, who came to this country in the middle of the 19th century and became the organizing genius of Reform, early realized that only through unified endeavor would there be survival of the Synagogue in America, for American

Jewish religious life in his day was in a state of chaos. He, therefore, organized the Union of American Hebrew Congregations, that is, the union of congregations which were inclined to the liberal and progressive interpretation of Judaism. It was the same Isaac Mayer Wise who realized that Rabbis for American Jews would have to be American-oriented to be effective, and that these men would have to be trained and experienced in both the general American culture and the disciplines of classical historic Judaism. Hence, two years after he founded the Union of American Hebrew Congregations, he proceeded to the founding of the Hebrew Union College for the training of Rabbis, men who were and are both college-bred and religiously-educated Jews.

Again. Jewish education for children in the United States in the middle of the 19th century was inconsequential. Hosts grew up without knowledge of Jewish history, without understanding of Judaism, with no appreciation of the content of Jewishness. There were no teachers and no textbooks. Reform Judaism, therefore, through the Union of American Hebrew Congregations and the Central Conference of American Rabbis (the association of Reform Rabbis of America), entered that field and have produced through the years a significant textbook literature and methodology.

As the Reform congregations grew, the women organized themselves into sisterhoods and then into a National Federation of Temple Sisterhoods. Men organized themselves into men's clubs or brotherhoods and then into the National Federation of Temple Brotherhoods. Youth groups were organized within the congregations and then these were united under the National Federation of Temple Youth.

Following the lead of this pattern of Reform, and observing its success, Orthodoxy and Conservatism adopted similar techniques. Orthodoxy and Conservatism proceeded to organize their congregations in accordance with the method and techniques and often even the names used by the Reform movement. Thus there are now the Union of Orthodox Jewish Congregations, and the United Synagogue of America. Each in turn developed similar departments of activity including sisterhoods, brotherhoods, youth education, etc. Modeling themselves on the Central Conference of American Rabbis, the Reform group, Orthodox and Conservative Rabbis also formed associations.

It is not only on the organizational level that Reform influenced the religious character of Jewry in America. Reform introduced the late Friday evening service and was attacked for introducing it. Today all Conservative synagogues have late Friday evening services and many Orthodox congregations do likewise. Preaching was re-introduced as part of the service of worship by Reform. Today this is the practice prevailing throughout Orthodox and Conservative congregations. Reading of prayers in English, the vernacular of America, was introduced into the services of Reform. Today English readings during the service are customary not only in the Conservative synagogues, but in many Orthodox synagogues as well. Confirmation for boys and girls on Shovuos was introduced by Reform Judaism. Today Conservative synagogues have introduced the same rite, and in many Orthodox synagogues girls are confirmed. Likewise we have, in the Conservative synagogues, men and women sitting together, a practice first introduced by Reform and for which it was vehemently attacked.

There have been modifications of the traditional prayer book in the Conservative synagogue. They have mixed choirs and organ music as part of the regular worship of the synagogue. They have modified their practices in the matter of dietary laws, Sabbath observance, and some of the theology of Judaism. In all these fundamental areas, the Reform attitude and practice have become the dominant pattern which is accepted and followed. It is a fact that even American Orthodoxy has been and is being influenced by Reform Judaism, and that Conservatism is a more moderate form of Liberal Judaism.

I am not saying that Orthodoxy and Conservatism will merge into Reform. That is neither possible nor desirable. But I am suggesting that Reform Judaism has pioneered in accelerating the process of change in traditional Jewish practice, and with it has stimulated the other branches of the Synagogue to do likewise and to do it more rapidly.

It was natural that there should be opposition. And it was equally natural for Reform to respond in kind. But the result of this conflict has been a remarkable revival of interest in the study of Judaism historically, and an intensification of zeal for religion.

. . . Some [changes,] like the introduction of the vernacular in prayer, are not discussed because they are so completely obvious. The abridgment of the prayer book and the continued revisions of it are part of this process of keeping Judaism always contemporary. Those who are familiar with the pattern of the traditional Jewish prayer book know that the essential traditional character of the prayer book has been preserved in the *Union Prayer Book.* The introduction of instrumental music was, again, an effort to enrich and beautify the always-musical service of the Synagogue.

It should be noted that most of the changes occurred largely in the area of ritual and ceremony. The Reform attitude towards these is different. In the fundamentals of Judaism, however, there is very little divergence. All religious Jews accept the traditional definitions and concepts of God, of the place of man in the divine scheme, of the place of the people of Israel in history, of the importance and significance and centrality of the synagogue in Jewish life. All religious Jews share the same ethics and all have the same Sabbath and Holy Days and Festivals.

Reform Judaism has been a positive, constructive influence on Jewish religious life in America, and much of the revitalization current in all branches of the Synagogue is directly traceable to the renewal of vigor which Reform gave to Judaism in this country. And in the new effectiveness thus acquired by all branches of the Synagogue, Jewish religious loyalty among American Jews has been greatly enriched.

Reform is not a different kind of Judaism. *It is Judaism,* historic, classical, traditional, but eager to remain always contemporary.

38.

guiding principles of reform judaism

In 1937 the Central Conference of American Rabbis, the reform rabbinical organization, formulated the following principles as a summary of reform Judaism. Since the meeting took place in Columbus, Ohio, the principles are called "the Columbus Platform."

From *Reform Judaism: A Guide for Reform Jews,* by Abraham J. Feldman (New York: Behrman House, 1956), pp. 11–14. © 1956 by Abraham J. Feldman. Reprinted by permission of the author.

I. Judaism and Its Foundations

1. *Nature of Judaism*. Judaism is the historical religious experience of the Jewish people. Though growing out of Jewish life, its message is universal, aiming at the union and perfection of mankind under the sovereignty of God. Reform Judaism recognizes the principle of progressive development in religion and consciously applies this principle to spiritual as well as to cultural and social life.

Judaism welcomes all truth, whether written in the pages of Scripture or deciphered from the records of nature. The new discoveries of science, while replacing the older scientific views underlying our sacred literature, do not conflict with the essential spirit of religion as manifested in the consecration of man's will, heart and mind to the service of God and of humanity.

2. *God*. The heart of Judaism and its chief contribution to religion is the doctrine of the One, living God, Who rules the world through law and love. In Him all existence has its creative source and mankind its ideal of conduct. Though transcending time and space, He is the indwelling Presence of the world. We worship Him as the Lord of the Universe and as our merciful Father.

3. *Man*. Judaism affirms that man is created in the Divine image. His spirit is immortal. He is an active co-worker with God. As a child of God, he is endowed with moral freedom and is charged with the responsibility of overcoming evil and striving after ideal ends.

4. *Torah*. God reveals Himself not only in the majesty, beauty and orderliness of nature, but also in the vision and moral striving of the human spirit. Revelation is a continuous process, confined to no one group and to no one age. Yet the people of Israel, through its prophets and sages, achieved unique insight in the realm of religious truth. The Torah, both written and oral, enshrines Israel's ever-growing consciousness of God and of the moral law. It preserves the historical precedents, sanctions and norms of Jewish life, and seeks to mold it in the patterns of goodness and of holiness. Being products of historical processes,

certain of its laws have lost their binding force with the passing of the conditions that called them forth. But as a depository of permanent spiritual ideals, the Torah remains the dynamic source of the life of Israel. Each age has the obligation to adapt the teaching of the Torah to its needs in consonance with the genius of Judaism.

5. *Israel*. Judaism is the soul of which Israel is the body. Living in all parts of the world, Israel has been held together by the ties of a common history, and above all, by the heritage of faith. Though we recognize in the group-loyalty of Jews who have become estranged from our religious tradition a bond which still unites them with us, we maintain that it is by its religion and for its religion that the Jewish people have lived. The non-Jew who accepts our faith is welcome as a full member of the Jewish community.

In all lands where our people live, they assume and seek to share loyally the full duties and responsibilities of citizenship and to create seats of Jewish knowledge and religion. In the rehabilitation of Palestine, the land hallowed by memories and hopes, we behold the promise of renewed life for many of our brethren. We affirm the obligation of all Jewry to aid in its upbuilding as a Jewish homeland by endeavoring to make it not only a haven of refuge for the oppressed but also a center of Jewish culture and spiritual life.

Throughout the ages it has been Israel's mission to witness to the Divine in the face of every form of paganism and materialism. We regard it as our historic task to cooperate with all men in the establishment of the kingdom of God, of universal brotherhood, justice, truth and peace on earth. This is our Messianic Goal.

II. Ethics

6. *Ethics and Religion*. In Judaism religion and morality blend into an indissoluble unity. Seeking God means to strive after holiness, righteousness and goodness. The love of God is incomplete without the love of one's fellowmen. Judaism emphasizes the kinship of the human race, the sanctity and worth of human life and personality and the right of the individual to freedom and to the pursuit of his chosen vocation. Justice to all, irrespective of race, sect or class is the inalienable right and the inescapable obligation of all. The state and organized government exist in order to further these ends.

7. *Social Justice*. Judaism seeks the attainment of a just society by the application of its teachings to the economic order, to industry and commerce, and to national and international affairs. It aims at the elimination of man-made misery and suffering, poverty and degradation, of tyranny and slavery, of social inequality and prejudice, of ill-will and strife. It advocates the promotion of harmonious relations between warring classes on the basis of equity and justice, and the creation of conditions under which human personality may flourish. It pleads for the safeguarding of childhood against exploitation. It champions the cause of all who work and of their right to an adequate standard of living, as prior

to the rights of property. Judaism emphasizes the duty of charity, and strives for a social order which will protect men against disabilities of old age, sickness and unemployment.

8. *Peace*. Judaism, from the days of the prophets, has proclaimed to mankind the ideal of universal peace. The spiritual and physical disarmament of all nations has been one of its essential teachings. It abhors all violence and relies upon moral education, love and sympathy to secure human progress. It regards justice as the foundation of the well-being of nations and the condition of enduring peace. It urges organized international action for disarmament, collective security and world peace.

III. Religious Practice

9. *The Religious Life*. Jewish life is marked by consecration to these ideals of Judaism. It calls for faithful participation in the life of the Jewish community as it finds expression in home, synagogue and school and in all other agencies that enrich Jewish life and promote its welfare.

The Home has been and must continue to be a stronghold of Jewish life, hallowed by the spirit of love and reverence, by moral discipline and religious observance and worship.

The Synagogue is the oldest and most democratic institution in Jewish life. It is the prime communal agency by which Judaism is fostered and preserved. It links the Jews of each community and unites them with all Israel.

The perpetuation of Judaism as a living force depends upon religious knowledge and upon the education of each new generation in our rich cultural and spiritual heritage.

Prayer is the voice of religion, the language of faith and aspiration. It directs man's heart and mind Godward, voices the needs and hopes of the community, and reaches out after goals which invest life with supreme value. To deepen the spiritual life of our people, we must cultivate the traditional habit of communion with God through prayer in both home and synagogue.

Judaism as a way of life requires, in addition to its moral and spiritual demands, the preservation of the Sabbath, festivals and Holy Days, the retention and development of such customs, symbols and ceremonies as possess inspirational value, the cultivation of distinctive forms of religious art and music and the use of Hebrew, together with the vernacular, in our worship and instruction.

These timeless aims and ideals of our faith we present to a confused and troubled world. We call upon our fellow Jews to rededicate themselves to them, and, in harmony with all men, hopefully and courageously to continue Israel's eternal quest after God and His kingdom.

39.

the limits of liberal judaism

jakob j. petuchowski

Rabbi Jakob J. Petuchowski, who teaches at Hebrew Union College-Jewish Institute of Religion, Cincinnati, here asks, How far? He stands as a critic from within the Reform movement and wonders whether there are limits to the willingness of Reform Jews and rabbis to experiment with, and to change, Jewish tradition. He asserts there should be limits, but in this excerpt does not specify what they are. The framework of discussion is the problem of theology. Petuchowski here criticizes those Reform rabbis who are not prepared to confess belief in God. He does not specify the particular traits or qualities of God, but rather the professed atheism of a small number of Reform rabbis, and the indifference of a somewhat larger number to the belief in God. In other words, to what degree is Reform Judaism prepared to accomodate itself to Jewish secularism—the belief that one may live a "good Jewish life" without reference to the divinity or the Torah as divinely revealed.

Petuchowski phrases matters in terms of those Reform Jews who hold that a liberal can never impose tests of belief or behavior, can never define the substance of his liberalism. To Petuchowski, "reform" is a verb. That is, one starts with the tradition and may, as need presents itself, revise or reshape it. He does not wish to see "reform" turned into a body of rigid, inflexible dogma, even the "dogma" of a dogma-less Judaism. He sees reforming as an approach to the classical tradition, not as a new and separate sect outside of the historical tradition. In phrasing matters in this way, he shows us one of the internal dilemmas faced within contemporary Reform Judaism.

From "The Limits of Liberal Judaism," by Jakob J. Petuchowski, *Judaism* XIV, 2, 1965, pp. 146–158. © 1965 by American Jewish Congress. Reprinted by permission of the author and American Jewish Congress.

A century and a half ago, some of the militant Orthodox opponents seemed to overstate their case when they denounced the slightest aesthetic reforms of synagogue architecture and of the worship service as the thin end of the wedge which would lead to the ultimate rejection of the God of Israel. Today we must credit them with more perspicacity than was possessed by their Reform contemporaries who tried so hard to justify all their innovations by appealing to the authoritative sources of Rabbinic Judaism itself. The latter-day heirs of the Reformers all but retroactively justify the exaggerated invectives of the benighted medievalists. But are they really the latter-day heirs of the early Reformers? That is the question on which the whole problem turns.

To answer it we would need criteria. But the establishment of criteria is itself tantamount to essaying definitions, and definitions, in turn, operate with limits. And we are back to the apparent *contradictio in adiecto* of speaking about " The *Limits* of Liberalism."

Liberalism can have no limits. It cannot be bound by any fealty to dogma or authority. It cannot move along the grooves of preconceived notions, nor can it be held back by the fetters of tradition. Such is the nature of Liberalism: try to fence it in, and you have deprived it of its essence. Part of today's confusion may be traced back to the fact that not a few rabbis, and a not insignificant number of laymen, owe their allegiance to Liberalism. Liberalism is their philosophy, and Liberalism is their religion. Let it lead where it may. Such Liberalism may even go hand in hand with a proud affirmation of Jewishness. But it is a Jewishness of the ethnic and cultural variety, a Jewishness of admitted background rather than of religious affirmation.

What the early Reformers had in mind would seem to have been something entirely different. For that matter, the very syntactical construction of the phrase, "Liberal Judaism" indicates that it was not Liberalism *per se* which they were after, but Judaism. Their Liberalism was a matter of the adjective, not of the noun. If anything, the liberal agnostic, or the liberal atheist, would have fitted far less into a Holdheim's or a Geiger's definition of the Jew than into the quasi-biological definition maintained by the Halachah. It was not an espousal of Liberalism *per se* which marked the contribution of the pioneers of Reform Judaism, but a liberal approach to *Judaism.* Judaism was both the starting-point and the goal. Liberalism was to be employed in the service of Judaism; and, to that extent, it was Judaism itself which set limits to the free and unbridled iconoclasm of conventional Liberalism. It was . . . Felix Goldmann's criticism that those limits were not always sufficiently defined and adequately maintained by the Reformers of the nineteenth century. But of this there can be no doubt, that the early Reformers at least had the good intention of preserving the "eternal verities" of classical Judaism for a new age.

By now, however, the very forces which they helped to set in motion have, on occasion, been turned against them. The relativization of both content and form, and loyalty to the very historicism which they regarded as the key to the truth, have brought it about that some of those who, today, preach from their pulpits and lecture in their academies insist that there never was such a thing as a "Judaism" which, in matters of cardinal belief and legal interpretation, was the same in all ages and climes. How easy it is to contrast the supposed Aristotelianism of Maimonides with the supposed anthropomorphism of Rabbi Akiba! How uncomplicated the process of demonstrating that economic factors, rather than an inherent dynamic, have been responsible for the forms in which Halachah clothed itself in different ages and environments! How perfectly obvious the discovery that one and the same classical text—say, the Bible—meant two entirely different things when read by Maimonides, on the one hand, and by the Baal Shem Tov, on the other! And from all this it follows, or is said to follow, that what has been common to all the various "Judaisms" is merely a certain vocabulary, a number of well-worn clichés. In reality, so it is being claimed, people— for some reason known as "Jews"—always created their own religions to meet their particular convenience, seeking to establish a link with the past only by clinging to a traditional vocabulary.

Of course, it is not being denied that, in ages past, a "God-concept" (though never the identical one) figured in all of the various manifestations of—what was called—"Judaism." It could not have been otherwise. After all, those Jews all lived in environments where belief in God was taken for granted. They merely shared a common universe of discourse with Islam and Christianity. But all of this happened before Darwin, and before Freud, and before Logical Positivism. *We* are living in an entirely different world today. *We* have to create our own "Judaism," one that will fit into our world, and that will bring us our this-worldly "salvation." And, with this goal in mind, we consciousy prefer the exclusion of the "God-concept" of our immediate or more remote predecessors. We pick those traditional insights which happen to suit our purposes. We can forget about all the others. After all, is it not enough that we identify ourselves as Jews, and that we even make use of the established "Jewish" institutions? We do call our assemblies "Jewish congregations," and our mentors, "rabbis." If Maimonides could pass off his Aristotelianism as Judaism, our humanism need fare no worse. Not to admit to our rejection of traditional superstitions would be intellectual dishonesty. We are committed to Truth and to Reason. What else do you want of us?! . . .

Does all this mean that we are accepting limits for Liberalism? The answer is an unequivocal "Yes!" We have nothing but profound respect for true, even radical, Liberalism: We recognize it as a viable philosophy of life. But we also recognize that an acceptance of Liberalism entails a definite commitment—a commitment which, by the way, has its source and origin outside of the sphere of mere Reason, even as a commitment to Reason as one's sole guide is itself a commitment undertaken beyond the bounds of Reason.

The rabbis we have in mind, and the Jews who would turn to them, are people who are likewise committed to the ideal of personal freedom. But they have an even prior commitment to Judaism. Here, factors of tradition, personal experience, and of reasoning interact in such a way that no dogmatic historicism or sophisticated semantics can shatter the conviction that "our God" is the very One Who was the "God of our fathers." It is not a question of whether that conviction çan be communicated to everybody and shared by everybody. Rather is it a *fact* that those who share that particular conviction do manage to understand one another and to relate their lives to that shared conviction. Our suggestion, therefore, that those who, for similar reasons, have made the same commitment now unite in a recognizable body is a suggestion which has been made for the purpose of greater effectiveness. It is liable to be fiercely opposed by all those who would feel threatened by any departure from the accustomed policy of "religious neutrality," by all those, that is to say, who now "feel at ease in Zion" on the strength of expanding membership rolls. The religious leaders of Judaism have weathered such storms before. They can do so again.

40.

the conservative approach to judaism

theodore friedman

For many years Rabbi Theodore Friedman served a Conservative congregation in South Orange, New Jersey, and now lives in Jerusalem. He was a president of the conservative rabbinical group, the Rabbinical Assembly. He is an authoritative exponent of the Conservative approach to contemporary Judaism.

Conservative Judaism is in some ways the least well defined of the three major movements, and that is as it should be, for Conservatism seeks for itself a moderate and middle position between Orthodoxy, which it sees as rigid and unbending, and Reform, understood to be without limits and indifferent to the classical tradition. But Conservative Judaism takes within itself the problems faced by both extremes. It is deeply committed to traditional law traditionally expounded. But it also wishes to take seriously the difficulties and challenges facing contemporary Jews.

The claim of Conservative Jews, we will by now expect, is going to be that they are the natural outgrowth of the classical tradition. If the great rabbis of old were alive today, they would be in our group. That claim stresses the same fact important to Rackman, the suppleness and flexibility of the tradition. It ignores the difficulty of preserving flexibility in the face—not of a new problem—but of an entirely hostile environment. It is easy to be "liberal" in a stable and enduring setting. It is difficult to agree to changing the law in some detail, when the entire context seems to require giving up the law entirely. Orthodoxy will not admit to rigidity, but it must say in its defense that this is not the time for radical change at all. Conservative Judaism indeed made various modifications of the law, but it has discovered that the people for whom it proposed to liberalize the law did not plan to keep the law to begin with. So the context of its moderate modernism is awry. Stressing common consensus, Conservatism ignores the absence of any agreement at all. Changing details of the law, it prefers to bypass the issue of whether there can be *halakhah* at all. Clearly, matters are not uncomplicated for the several movements in modern Judaism.

From "Jewish Tradition in Twentieth-Century America: The Conservative Approach," by Theodore Friedman, *Judaism* III, 4, 1954, pp. 310–320. © 1954 by American Jewish Congress. Reprinted by permission of the author and American Jewish Congress.

One searches in vain through the vastness and variety of Jewish history for a convincing precedent for the Jewish experience in America. Here, a totally new constellation of forces, social, economic and intellectual swirled around the Jewish immigrant. The full potential of their impact on the forms, concepts and organizational expressions of Judaism cannot as yet be fully judged if only for the fact that the preponderant majority of American Jews stands but one generation removed from their immigrant forebears. Another generation, at least, must elapse before the process of integration will have worked itself out with any degree of finality. That is not to reduce the rise and growth of Conservative Judaism in American to a resultant of sociological forces. The American environment, for all its massive, determinative character, embodies but one factor in the equation to be solved. The other, and no less potent factor, is the body of ideas, loyalties and practices with which the leaders and ideologues of Conservatism confront the environment in their efforts to perpetuate and advance an historic faith. It would be fatuous, however, to deny that the impress of the American milieu, inclusive of Reform Judaism, lies deep on both the thinking and practice currently obtaining in Conservative Judaism, and for that matter, on other schools of thought. It would, however, be equally blind not to see the roots of the Conservative interpretation of Judaism in ideas and tendencies whose rise are not to be attributed to the American experience, and indeed, long antedate it. In sum, the law of multiple causes operates here as elsewhere.

It has long been customary to locate the genesis of the Conservative interpretation of Judaism within the context of the Historical School of Jewish Scholarship of the nineteenth century. The influence on the rise of Conservative Judaism of that galaxy of Jewish scholars who for the first time turned the full revealing light of modern historical methodology on the Jewish past is clearly decisive; decisive enough to warrant the somewhat extended analysis to which we shall presently subject it. For all its pervasiveness, still at work, one would miss the essential timbre of Conservatism if one did not recognize that, in almost every instance, it was an influence that played on personalities originally steeped in and stamped by the traditional Jewish life and learning then prevailing in Eastern Europe. . . .

The stage is most quickly and adequately set for our discussion of the ideological problems that have constituted the agenda of Conservative Judaism by two quotations; the first from the writings of [Solomon] Schechter and the second from an essay on Zachariah Frankel by Louis Ginzberg.

Its (the Historical School) theological practices may perhaps be thus defined: it is not the mere revealed Bible that is of first importance to the Jew, but the Bible as it repeats itself in history, in other words as it is interpreted by Tradition . . . Since, then, the interpretation of Scriptures or the Secondary Meaning is mainly a product of changing historical influences, it follows that the center of authority is actually removed from the Bible and placed in some living body, which, by reason of its being in touch with the ideal aspirations and the religious needs of the age is best able to determine the nature of the Secondary Meaning. This living body, however, is not represented by any section of the nation or any corporate priesthood or Rabbinhood, but by the collective conscience of Catholic Israel, as embodied in the Universal Synagogue. This Synagogue, the only true witness to the past, and forming in all ages the sublimest expression of Israel's religious life, must also retain its authority as the sole true guide for the present and the future . . . Another consequence of this conception of Tradition is that it is neither scripture nor primitive Judaism, but general custom which forms the real rule of practice. Holy Writ as well as history, Zunz tells us, teaches that the Law of Moses was never fully and absolutely put in practice. Liberty was always given to the great teachers of every generation to make modifications and innovations in harmony with the spirit of existing institutions . . . The norm as well as the sanction of Judaism is the practice actually in vogue. Its consecration is the consecration of general use or, in other words, of Catholic Israel . . .

Speaking of the positive—historical school, a position he clearly shares, the late Professor Ginzberg writes:

For an adherent of this school, the sanctity of the Sabbath reposes not upon the fact that it was proclaimed on Sinai, but on the fact that the Sabbath idea found for thousands of years its expression in Jewish souls. It is the task of the historian to examine into the beginnings and developments of the numerous customs and observances of the Jews; practical Judaism on the other hand is not concerned with origins, but regards the institutions as they have come to be. If we are convinced that Judaism is a religion of deed, expressing itself in observances which are designed to achieve the moral elevation of man and give reality to his religious spirit, we have principle, in observance of which, reforms in Judaism are possible. From this point of view the evaluation of a law is independent of its origin, and thus the line of demarcation between biblical and rabbinical law almost disappears.

What Schechter expresses in the foregoing in terms of broad generalization and proposes as the norm for contemporary Judaism, had been spelled out in learned and illuminating detail in the researches of the historical school. I. H. Weiss, Graetz and Zachariah Frankel, followed by others, in their studies of the Oral Law, had established beyond argument that what Schechter terms the Secondary Meaning could only be understood in developmental terms. Moreover, that development was ever subject to a variety of historical forces, inner and external. But whatever the past viability of the Oral Law and the degree of sensitivity of its masters and fashioners to the needs, social and spiritual of their time, one thing was crystal clear. Halakhah was the method par excellence of Judaism. In the millennial sweep of Jewish history, those groups that broke with the Halakhah eventually found that they had thereby severed themselves from the body of *Klal Yisrael*. To assert as much is to merely set the stage for the problem of Halakhah in modern times, not to solve it.

Once the affirmation of Halakhah as indispensable to a continuing, historically grounded Judaism has been granted, what has been and continues to be the Conservative approach to the problems involved in the effort to render the Halakhah normative in the life of the Jew in the twentieth century? Actually, there have been two concurrent methods at work, methods that have characterized the history of the Halakhah.

The first has been that of a common consensus arrived at not by formal deliberation and decision based on the Halakhah, but rather by a natural unconscious process into which there have entered in varying proportions the force of tradition and the influence of the environment. Thus, virtually all Conservative congregations maintain family pews though the history of the Conservative movement reveals no official decison permitting such practice, a decision which could hardly be warranted by even the most liberal interpretation of the Halakhah. By a similar consensus, no Conservative congregation has ever even discussed the question of worshipping bareheaded unless it was preparing to leave the ranks of Conservatism. Yet, even from the strictest Halakhic viewpoint, a convincing case could be made out for the legitimacy of worshipping bareheaded. Other examples might be adduced of this process of common concensus which has given a fairly uniform character to the Conservative Synagogue and its practices.

The other method of meeting the problems of Halakhah in a technological society, has been the two-fold process of deliberate interpretation and enactment *(Takkanah)*, the "classic" methods of the Halakhah. This has been the province of the Committee on Jewish Law and Standards of the Rabbinical Assembly of America.

As an indication of the spirit animating the approach of the Committee to the contemporary problems of Jewish religious observance, one aspect of its decisons should be noted. Where the Committee, counting twenty-three members, is unanimous in a decision, such a decision is considered binding on all members of the Rabbinical Assembly. Where a minority and majority decision are reported a member may follow either opinion.

Several factors, all worthy of consideration, coincided to bring about this unique practice of permitting members an option between two conflicting opinions. Historically, it is a conscious return to the method and practice of the ancient Halakhic literature. Again, it is a recognition that certainly today, if indeed ever in the past, Jewish religious practice in its detail cannot possess a universally uniform character.

Equally determinative in the adoption of the above described practice was the implicit recognition that if its decisions were to genuinely represent the thinking of present-day Conservatism, then in certain areas, mostly peripheral in nature, the Committee could not speak authoritatively with a single voice. For truth to tell, within Conservatism three tendencies in regard to the application of the Halakhah to modern life are discernible. That their respective advocates have shown no inclination to turn these tendencies into schismatic lines is proof of the power and centrality of the ideological commitments held in common, despite diversity of viewpoint on certain specifics.

One group may be said to oppose any approach to the Halakhah that would yield decisions that would depart from what is commonly regarded as the Orthodox norm. Any change in religious practice, it is argued, must be initiated by bodies or individuals whose authority is recognized by all Jews professing loyalty to the tradition. Otherwise, Conservatism is certain to become a sect and ultimately go the way of all sects in the history of Judaism. In practice, this group has refused to make few, if any, of the adjustment commonly found in the preponderant majority of Conservative congregations. At the other end of the ideological arc, are those who while favoring most of the traditional practices would regard them not as Halakhah and hence subject to modification and adaptation by the accepted canons of Jewish law, but rather as sanctified religious folk-ways. The forms of these observances, it is maintained, must ultimately be determined by the people themselves in consultation with their spiritual leaders; presuming, of course, that the former are committed to Judaism and are anxious to employ its resources to the maximum in spiritually enhancing their lives and expressing themselves Jewishly.

Midway between these two schools of thought, though by no means a compromise between the two—a quite inconceivable ideological construction—there stands a third group which may be said to constitute a palpable majority. It regards the traditional Halakhah as an instrument viable enough to meet the changed situation of the modern world in which the American Jew lives. The fact that it has not, on the whole, been so adapted to date argues not for its inherent intractability but reveals rather the spiritual outlook of those who have been its prime authorities and exponents. That outlook and mood were marked by a natural suspicion of the modern world as inherently subversive of Judaism. Every added constriction of the area of the permissible, it considered a manifestation of piety. Primarily, however, it was its refusal to employ the broad powers implied in the method of *Takkanah* that led to the inertness of the Halakhah in the face of radically altered conditions. In its truly creative periods, the Halakhah, in the hands of a Rabbi Yochanan ben Zakkai, for example, had proven itself capable of meeting the challenge of the cataclysmic changes in the life of the Jewish people that followed the destruction of the Second Temple and the loss of national autonomy. Similarly, it is held that the power of Takkanah, wisely used, could re-align traditional Jewish law with the social realities of our times and, at the same time, set realistic standards of observances that would render the tradition capable of becoming a living force in the daily life of the American Jew. . . .

41.

conservative judaism in search of identity

jacob neusner

From *Judaism in the Secular Age,* by Jacob Neusner (New York: Ktav Publishing House, 1970) pp. 139–163.

Conservative Judaism began with the claim that it would constitute not a denomination but "Catholic Israel." Solomon Schechter declared:

> This living body . . . is not represented by any section of the nation, or any corporate priesthood or rabbihood, but by the collective conscience of Catholic Israel as embodied in the Universal Synagogue. The Synagogue, with its continuous cry after God for more than twenty-three centuries, with its unremittent activity in teaching and developing the word of God, the only true witness to the past, and forming in all ages the sublimest expression of Israel's religious life, must also retain its authority as the sole true guide for the present and the future. . . . Another consequence of this conception of Tradition is that it is neither Scripture nor Primitive Judaism, but general custom, which forms the real rule of practice. . . . The norm as well as the sanction of Judaism is the practice actually in vogue. Its consecration is the consecration of general use—or in other words, of Catholic Israel.

This concept is now wanting for several reasons. First of all, whether or not "Catholic Israel" existed in Schechter's day, it certainly does not exist today. There is no consensus, no collective conscience, and hence no authority to be located within the "Universal Synagogue." Further, the collapse of Jewish observance among masses of Jews renders unacceptable the criterion of "the practice actually in vogue." As Arthur A. Cohen points out:

> As he [Schechter] defined Catholic Israel, history could educate consciousness and form conscience, but it could command neither. Catholic Israel has no apodictic force. It is that fitful, unpredictable, indeed on occasion capricious, response of the Jewish people to its collective history and obligation. "Catholic Israel" represents, therefore, the ratification of the given. In no generation can the condition of Israel, the Jewish people, have so severely called into question such a possibility as the present one.

Conservative Judaism has given little serious thought to its relation, as a movement, with Reform or Orthodox Judaism in the United States and Canada, with the Establishment of Israeli Orthodoxy, with the religious organizations of Jewries in other parts of the world, and with the community as a whole. Conservative Jews rather have continued to act as if these groups do not exist. If we Conservative Jews can no longer behave so indifferently towards other groups, however, we need to think our way towards a less inchoate and more consistent attitude towards them. We need to formulate the principles by which many of our movement in fact now act. We need to specify policies which will guide day-to-day relations, both in local communities and in comprehensive, national agencies, between the Conservative movement and other groups, both religious and secular, within Jewry.

It should be quite clear at the outset that we are seeking to define not only the attitudes of our own movement towards other Jews, but also the limits within which, to our way of thinking, any Jewish group, including our own, may find its legitimate place. It is quite obvious, for example, that we seek no peculiarly Conservative-Jewish attitude to apostates; we share with all Jews an instinctive attitude that, however we may respect the sincerity of their convictions, they no longer concern Jewry as Jews. With similarly instinctual agreement we include within the Jewish consensus—and within broad limits there is such a consensus —a secular Messianist such as David Ben-Gurion; and within our movement we find an honorable place, quite obviously, for much divergent thought.

If these are facts, however, how do we as Conservative Jews explain them? Upon what basis, according to the theological presuppositions of our movement, do we include divergent thinkers, indeed place them at the forefront of our movement, *and at the same time* exclude others? Part of the answer to these questions requires a definition of what makes a Jew into a Conservative Jew; of what excludes the Orthodox, on one hand, and the Reform Jew, on the other, from our movement's consensus; of what, by our own theology, we approve in the theology of other groups of religious Jews, and in the ideology of secularists. We must therefore propose a statement of what constitutes Conservative Judaism, the criterion by which we are going to be able to find answers to the questions of relationship to other Jews. The answer cannot be found, however, by contrast to others, but rather within our own resources and historical affirmations. . . .

Self-respect, dignity, and self-acceptance are qualities basic to mental health, and the mental health of our movement depends upon them. When one does not accept himself, his commonplace response is pomposity, pretentiousness and delusions of self-importance. Our unrealism about the rest of Jewry, our spurious claim to constitute "Judaism" when we are only a part of it at best, our willingness to abjure our own principles for the sake of "unity" with those who hold us in utter contempt—these are facts which reflect lack of self-respect, dignity, and self-acceptance. It is futile to proceed further in any inquiry into our policies towards Jewry at large unless we recognize these facts.

The chief issue is, by what criteria shall we form judgments of the rest of the Jewish world? The obvious answer is, by the criteria of the *truth* as we perceive it. We need to formulate, and affirm, the principles of our movement, and having done so, we need to judge by them the rightness or wrongness of other phenomena within Jewry and Judaism. I have no doubt that within the Conservative movement, both rabbinical and lay, there are, in fact, great areas of common agreement.

1.   We affirm the continued vitality of Jewish tradition and the abiding relevance of its major apprehensions concerning God, Torah, and Israel.

2.   We affirm with equal vigor the need rigorously and unsentimentally to investigate what these words and ideas mean in the light of reality as we perceive it in this time and place.

3.   We deny that the tradition can continue intact without requiring an unacceptable division in our minds between the tradition and all our other sources of knowledge about the world, our other patterns of thinking about the truth.

4.   We deny that the tradition, unmodulated by the right and proper contribution of this generation, can or ought to lay a claim upon the life of the next.

Rabbi Robert Gordis stated at the Rabbinical Assembly convention of 1965:

> In spite of the claims made in other quarters, it is we who are the authentic heirs of rabbinic Judaism. Professor Salo W. Baron, in his first edition of his great History, written when he was completely unassociated with our movement and in fact had affiliations elsewhere, stated: "Neo-Orthodoxy, equally with Reform, is a deviation from historical Judaism. No less than Reform, it abandoned Judaism's self-rejuvenating historical dynamism. For this reason we may say that . . . the positive-historical Judaism of Frankel and Michael Sachs and the "Conservative" Judaism of America have been much truer to the spirit of traditional Judaism. By maintaining the general validity of Jewish law and combining with it freedom of personal interpretation of the Jewish past and creed, Frankel and his successors hoped to preserve historical continuity. . . . It is Conservative Judaism which seems to show the greatest similarities with the method and substance of teaching of the popular leaders during the declining Second Commonwealth, inasmuch as, clinging to the traditional mode of life, it nevertheless allows for the adaptation of basic theological concepts to the changing social and environmental needs." Many of those who attack our movement as "deviationist"—a term totally repugnant to the authentic Jewish tradition—and who demand unswerving adherence to the written letter of the Law are actually the Sadducees of the twentieth century. Had they lived in the days of Hillel, Rabbi Yohanan ben Zakkai, Rabbi Akiba, Rabbi Meir or Rabbi Judah Hanasi, they would have condemned every creative contribution that the Sages made to the living Judaism of their age and ages.
>
> Nor are we in a position to accept the standpoint of those who abrogate the authority of the Law. Ours is therefore the very creative task of preserving tradition creatively, and utilising its resources for growth, so that it may function in the modern world as significantly as it did in ancient and medieval times. It is perfectly true that Conservative Judaism has a more difficult role than that of our two sister movements. It is easy to affirm and accept a tradition in toto if only pro forma, and, of course, it is even easier to reject a tradition completely. Our path calls upon all our resources of creative learning, practical wisdom and genuine piety. The road is long, arduous and fraught with hazard.

We do not, as Rabbi Gordis' statement makes clear, see ourselves as heretics, or as in any degree deviating from the historical Jewish tradition. We see ourselves as the true heirs of those who, in times past, affirmed both the Revelation at Sinai and the imperatives of the world since then. So far as other groups ignore the tradition in the formation of their values and ideas about Judaism, we deny their authenticity. So far as other groups refuse to reflect upon all truth relevant to the issues inherent in the tradition, persist in regarding as authoritative judgments and attitudes which we now know to be false, we hold them to be in error. ....

If we regard Orthodoxy and Reform as in some ways in error, we find it possible to respect the achievements of each. We are not half so angry at Orthodoxy, or contemptuous of Reform as they are of us. Measuring Orthodoxy by our own criterion, we find that it wins high praise indeed for its devotion to Jewish learning at all levels and for all ages, though not to scholarship; for its loyalty to the tradition, though in a form we regard as historically inauthentic and in some ways contemporarily unviable; and for its willingness to sacrifice where necessary to keep the ritual commandments. We admire the capacity of Reform Judaism to stress the needs of the current generation and to keep to the fore the issues of contemporary meaning and relevance, though we find these issues too often resolved in terms of anomic individualism, or, in politics, of doctrinaire liberalism alone. We admire its courage in recognizing the need for the tradition to continue its growth, though we regret its having evolved its own Reform tradition in forms almost as rigid as the inherited ones. We respect the emphasis of Reform Judaism upon mutual understanding and tolerance within the Jewish community, though we find it hard to distinguish between its forms of tolerance and a latitudinarian accommodation of everyone and anything. We regret, however, that the Reform movement has not yet taken a firm stand in favor of Jewish tradition. In no respect do Reform Jews start with a presumption in its favor.

Our view of the other two movements in modern Judaism cannot so easily be exhausted, but it should be clear that we do make judgments about them, and that these judgments are based upon criteria we hold to be valid for all of Judaism, and to be most nearly approximated within our movement. We should not regret the day on which Orthodoxy and Reform would recognize their errors and resolve to pursue the path we have followed, and we do not think that day is so very distant. We see with pleasure the growing tendency among elements of Orthodoxy to affirm our affirmation and to deny what we deny, to accept without regret the data of America and of the twentieth century, and to deny the continuing possibility of ignoring contemporary realities and sustaining anti-intellectualism. We note with satisfaction each painful step taken by Reform Judaism towards a renewed dialogue with Jewish tradition, towards a recovered tension between the necessities of the tradition and the requirements of the current age, and towards the revived appreciation, which we have never lost, of the infinitely interesting potentialities of inherited theology and inherited practices.

We see no difficulty in co-operation with other movements within Judaism towards achieving goals which Conservative Judaism affirms. We regard our co-operation as contingent, however, upon the values of our own movement, just as we expect that of others to be similarly judged by their own criteria. We shall expect to be treated with unfailing courtesy and not contempt. We shall not expect anyone to relinquish, for the purposes of co-operation, his own self-respect or sincere convictions, nor shall we give up ours. We regard Reform and Orthodox Jews as wholly legitimate Jews by the criteria we have suggested: they are loyal to the tradition and faithful to God, by their own word, just as we hope to be. We regard their rabbis as rabbis, because they are men of learning and faith.

We regard their laymen as motivated by the same high resolves as are Conservatives. We understand that they have much to teach us. We regard their views of Judaism with reverence and their success in deepening Jewish knowledge and commitment with rejoicing. We stress that we relate to Orthodox, Reform, and other religious Jews as brothers. They are not our "separated brethren." Our disagreements are real, but they are disagreements among people who see one another as parts of the same tradition, and who do not question the integrity or sanctity of one another's religious understanding. We are not discrete denominations, talking to one another from our separate reservations. We are Jews together, pledges for one another, responsible for one another, aspiring to live with one another in concerned compassion. It is this very brotherliness which lends vigor and sharpness to our conversations. No one should misunderstand or misinterpret matters: we speak in love, and criticize, when we do, in a loving spirit. . . .

These statements presuppose that Conservative Judaism constitutes a movement within Judaism. They assume that we do have within our midst a broad but precise, objective consensus upon major Jewish and existential issues, and that we come together not merely because we find one another's prejudices congenial, but because we want through our collective life to embody and to advocate important principles. The Rabbinical Assembly is more than an *alumni* association; the United Synagogue more than an institutional convenience to support the Seminary. The facts that the Rabbinical Assembly has a Membership Committee and that the United Synagogue expels congregations guilty of reprehensible practices support these presuppositions. At the same time, we have yet to articulate the major elements of our consensus. Bingo and violations of Sabbath and dietary laws do not exhaust our conception of Conservative sins; but we have never said what else matters. The reason is that, though not alone, we have laid greater stress upon the "need for unity" than the need for clarity and specificity. We have too readily avoided divisive issues, and glossed over major perplexities. We have preferred to hide ourselves from the realities of our movement, to ignore not only *what* we are, but what many *think* we are, an easy compromise between "something" and "nothing," a sloppy and slipshod convenience for those who find Orthodoxy too taxing, and Reform insufficient. . . .

42.

the temper of reconstructionism

harold m. schulweis

The fourth movement in American Judaism, Reconstructionism, is the newest and least widely known. It was founded by Rabbi Mordecai M. Kaplan, for many years professor at the (Conservative) Jewish Theological Seminary of America. In the recent past, Reconstructionist rabbis and their congregations have broken away from the Conservative movement; those who are graduates of Reform seminaries have likewise drawn closer to the Reconstructionist movement. The Jewish Reconstructionist Foundation, which publishes a theological journal as well as important books and prayerbooks, now has created a rabbinical seminary, located in Philadelphia, The Reconstructionist Rabbinical College. A federation of congregations and fellowships has been in existence for many years. But, despite its growth, the movement remains devoted not only to the theological method, but also to the specific theological convictions of its founder. It has not interpreted the theological method in such a way as to generate new ideas and approaches. Thus, in the minds of its critics, it is the most dogmatic movement in American Judaism.

Rabbi Kaplan's theological system centers upon a naturalist and wholly this-worldly interpretation of theology and upon a religious understanding of the nature of Jewish peoplehood. Here Rabbi Schulweis explains these two central conceptions of Jewish Reconstruction its "God-idea" and its doctrine of Jewish peoplehood.

Rabbi Schulweis, who serves a synagogue in California, gives us the most difficult account we have faced. That is because Reconstructionism has deliberately confronted the philosophical and theological issues of the day and proposed to deal with them in accord with the modes of thought of the age.

Later we shall consider how Kaplan himself explains his God-idea, but it first seems best to follow a balanced and thorough account of the entire system, for Schulweis makes explicit not merely the content, but the way of thinking, of Kaplan's theology. He then shows why Jewish peoplehood is central to Kaplan's thought and explains the importance of the folk within the theology of Reconstructionism. Later we shall listen to an Orthodox critique of this viewpoint.

From "The Temper of Reconstructionism," by Harold M. Schulweis, *Judaism* III, 4, 1954, pp. 321–332. © 1954 by American Jewish Congress. Reprinted by permission of the author and American Jewish Congress.

... Based upon a temperate naturalism, Reconstructionism has from the start, reacted with discomforture to the theologically orthodox approach which appears to rupture the universe into unbridgeable realms of natural and supernatural phenomena. Reconstructionist holism seeks a more comprehensive interpretation of reality in which events achieve relatedness; and it welcomes a continuity of inquiry which is not paralyzed by the supernaturalist's indignation whenever religious sancta are made subject to examination. The perspective of a single, unbifurcated universe of natural events, Reconstructionism insists, needs not blur the empirical distinctions of "higher" and "lower" values of existence. But "higher" values have natural histories and do not require the mystification of *ad hoc* supernatural explanation which makes of religion "a refuge of ignorance."

God and the world, God and man, live in one world. God is not the estranged, "totally other" of rekindled neo-orthodoxy, dwelling with "cosmic snobbishness" beyond man's reach. The approach to an understanding of God is through God's highest creature, endowed with His image. The beginning of the knowledge of God is the knowledge of man, his aspirations and dreams and needs. In this regard, Reconstructionist theology accepts man's ego-involved predicament as a blessing, not as an obstacle in man's urge to reach out and touch the face of God. Unless the anthropocentrism of our theology is made conscious, our fallibility will be disguised for indisputable revelation. To speak the word of God without knowing it is man who speaks, is to attempt jumping out of one's very own skin.

One of the discomforts with Kaplan's theology may be attributed to his disconcern with the traditional methods of talking God into existence through professional arguments. Assuming an unfathomable and ineffable Deity, supernaturalists yet seek "the proof" in a worn logic which either begs the question (e.g., cosmological, ontological, ex gradibus) or demands an anxious leap from partial analogy (e.g., teleological). Kaplan's initial theological question is not, "How can I prove that God exists" but "what do I want my God-idea to be like." "What will I worship, and for what values will I be willing to lay my life down" is prior, in Kaplan's approach to theology, to the search for proof of an assumed revelation. In Weiman's language, our task is "so to formulate the idea of God that the question of God's existence becomes a dead issue." While God cannot be pointed to and thereby exhausted, He is still in this world and knowable. We must seek Divinity not however as one seeks material substance but through the predicates attributed to God. We learn of God through discovery of Goodness and Holiness which are then properly ascribed to Divinity.

The critics protest: if God be conceived as a "power which endorses what *we* believe ought to be and that guarantees that it will be," is not God a mere intra-psychic projection, an hypostatized image of the human self? Milton Steinberg states it bluntly. "Does God really exist or is He only man's notion? Is there anything objective which corresponds to the subjective conception?" And Jacob Agus regards Kaplan's theological position as anomalous since "the 'force of life' which causes plants to grow and flowers to bloom is not divine in itself, but when human beings are around that 'force' of a sudden, becomes a part of God." The criticism is not entirely unanticipated. To appreciate Kaplan's position we must look at the God-idea afresh. God is not an isolable object which may be given ostensive definition. God is witnessed in Process, in the context of the constant *transactions* which take place between man and the *compulsive* forces in the environment; divinity is discovered in the *interaction* between man's needs, wants, ideals, and the possibilities for their this-worldly fulfillment. God, then, is not a humanistic "work of human imagination and will" (Dewey), but remains as real as "a stone-wall or a toothache." Men's ideals may be made of whimsy and caprice, but they will soon crumble when placed before the teeth of obstinate reality. Man, if he is to live creatively, *must* adjust himself to the compulsive factors of life which often disregard his will. The universe is not as flexible nor human aspirations as quickly assured for man to live unconscious of Powers "operating in ways over and above the plans and purposes of men, bringing forth values men cannot foresee and often developing connections of mutual support and mutual meaning in spite of or contrary to the efforts of men."

Neither must the universe be accepted quietistically as in aesthetic naturalism. Much of what was once considered hostile, unalterable fact has been turned into an instrument for man's advancement. God is *discovered* neither through a passive reception of Revelation plunging down through the heavens nor through shallow humanism granted theological poetic license. Constant changes in man's ideals and the modification of the energies of the environment is the lot of man's struggle to utter God's name more clearly. In his creative responses to the obdurate demands of his self and his environment, man experiences "the force of a controlling datum . . . (an) awareness of an ordered cosmos, in which we, and all whom we recognize as human are presented with conditions which must be met and laws which must be obeyed as a prerequisite to our salvation of human self-fulfillment." The proper study of man and his quest for this worldly salvation (soterics) turns out to be the ground of Kaplan's empirical theology. In this sense the "nearer we get to knowing the actual conditions essential to genuine salvation, the truer is bound to be our concept of God."

There is much faith in Kaplan's concept of a universe which is an organic totality, conditioning man's choice, yet responsive to his efforts. In Kaplan's soterics there is a faith-presupposition that each event somehow carries within it its own natural and ideal realization. The world is congenial to the human quest for stable and secure elements which illumine man's life. Belief in such Power "predisposing man to his ultimate good" is frankly not "a reasoned faith but a willed faith." It plays the role of a pragmatic working hypothesis, as indispensable to human progress as the principles of induction or the uniformity of nature are for the scientist, and as undogmatic as both.

But, Kaplan's critics demand: "Can a belief so provisional and tentative support a faith to die for?" If this alone be the criterion of true faith, the critics' argument stands unopposed. Kaplan's religious temper will certainly not test truth "with the sacrifice of man's life ... or by staking the lives of all the generations."

But the value of a religion which inhibits man from such fanatic zeal is not negligible. And it is questionable whether the ability to call upon men to sacrifice their lives and their society is to be valued greater than the restraint which undogmatic faith places upon man.

The faith in Powers which are said to "endorse what we believe ought to be and that guarantee that it will" and which make cosmos out of chaos raises query as to the metaphysical status of these forces. Granted our interactional view of Divinity in Process, are the non-human forces purposive, conscious agents for human salvation? Or, as the question is put more often, is Kaplan's God personal?

In regard to the problem of the Powers consciousness, the answer must be predicated upon Kaplan's concept of God viewed not isolated but within the context of the natural order; with man taken seriously as a "partner with God," created with an aspect of divinity. "Insofar as consciousness and purpose are indispensable to man's salvation, they are veritable manifestations of God as the Power that makes for salvation." Here again is illustrated Kaplan's theological method of inverting the place of the subject with that of its predicate.

But may not the criticism be turned about? Is not the ascription of consciousness or personality a most blatant form of anthropomorphism? And does not the supernaturalist when put to test to explain his concept of God as "Mind," "Spirit," or "Person," invariably take cover behind the Maimonidean apologia of negative attributes? Wieman pursues the counter attack. He insists that eliminating "personality" from God makes religion more truly theocentric since the attribution of personality to God is argued either on the anthropocentric grounds that within it "man can find no satisfaction of his needs" or that "personality is the highest form of existence that we know."

Many critics have questioned: is Kaplan's God-idea Jewish; is his concept of salvation Jewish? Few arguments are felt to be as devasting as those doubting the "Jewishness" of an ideology or characterizing it as *"Chukas Ha-Goi"* (the way of the non-Jew). "How fantastic," writes Agus, "to compare the living God of Israel with the name given to those processes and relationships that make for human welfare."

Despite the emotive charge behind the outcry, the history of Jewish thought itself testifies to the fact that the Aristotelianism of Maimonides, the neo-Platonism of Gabirol, the Hegelian spirit of Krochmal, the Kantianism of Cohen, or the existentialism of Rosenzweig and Buber, were all challenged as to their Jewishness. Yet, whom do we call upon to exhibit Jewish theology or philosophy if not these?

Judaism is what Jews believe and practice, and the test of the Jewishness of an idea remains ultimately its acceptance by Jews. Kaplan, like many Jewish theologians in their own day, attempts to reconcile and integrate the inherited tradition with the worthwhile spirit of the contemporary environment and this method of "non-imitative assimilation" has traditionally enriched Judaism.

43.

judaism without supernaturalism

mordecai m. kaplan

Here Rabbi Mordecai M. Kaplan, founder of the Jewish Reconstructionist movement and for many years a professor at the Jewish Theological Seminary of America, answers some of the basic questions about his theological viewpoint and therefore clarifies for us the account and analysis just now given by Rabbi Schulweis. His primary problem is to deal with the idea, or concept, of God, and from here he answers the question of miracles and other matters raised within the context of a supernatural idea of God.

From *Judaism Without Supernaturalism: The Only Alternative to Orthodoxy and Secularism,* by Mordecai M. Kaplan (New York: The Reconstructionist Press, 1958), pp. 109–115. © 1958 by Jewish Reconstructionist Foundation, Sponsor of Reconstructionist Press. Reprinted by permission of the Reconstructionist Press, 15 West 86 Street, New York, N.Y. 10024.

You speak of God as the Power that makes for salvation, and yet you adopt the traditional concept and locution of "God reveals Himself." Is that consistent?

We do not "adopt" traditional concepts and ways of speaking, any more than we "adopt" our native language. We are born into a tradition as we are born into a particular culture with its language. We make use of both, though not necessarily in the way they were used by our forebears. We speak the same language as they did to express our own thinking. In almost like manner we have to make use of their religious tradition to express our own ideas about religion. Even "the fool (who) says in his heart there is no God," has to use the word "God" to express his negative attitude toward religion.

We take this remarkable phenomenon of cultural continuity altogether too much for granted. We seldom appreciate its profound significance for the civilization and humanization of man. We find, to be sure, that we can no longer understand the great words that have come down from the past in the same sense as they were understood then. Is that, however, a good enough reason for throwing them out of our vocabulary, and for repeating the old trick of throwing the baby out with the bath? Shall we no longer use the term "spirit," because to the ancients it denoted breath, or "soul" because it meant to them some ghost-double of a human being, or "holy" because they associated it with anything they believed to be untouchable, or "revelation," because they thought of it in terms of thunder and lightning, or "God," because it suggested to them a venerable "ancient of days" seated on a throne in the heavens?

The purpose of speaking of God as "the Power that makes for salvation" is to identify the particular human experiences which enable us to feel the impact of that process in the environment and in ourselves which impels us to grow and improve physically, mentally, morally, and spiritually. That process is *Godhood.* It reveals itself in those particular experiences. That is the meaning which the traditional statement that God reveals Himself should convey to us. For the sake of that cultural continuity which is itself a manifestation of Godhood, we should continue to speak of God as "revealing Himself."

What does it mean to believe in God, if we do away with the belief in a God who performs miracles?

The mere fact that we cannot accept as historical the record of miraculous events in the Bible and elsewhere does not imply that we regard the miracle stories as of no significance in our thinking about God and human life. The question raised, however, does pose a general difficulty which has to be met. Disbelief in the traditional account of the miracles has, undoubtedly, created a religious void. How is that void to be filled?

To fill that void we must put ourselves, first of all, in the position of those who lived at a time when belief in miracles was not questioned. In those days people lacked all understanding of natural law. They had no way of realizing that inner necessity which compels things to be what they are, at the same time that they are subject to immutable laws of cause and effect. Whatever occurred in nature or in human life was to them the manifestation of some personal will. That personal will was a projection of their inner purposive drives, magnified to a cosmic scale. They accepted literally the notion that God was a king whose kingdom was the world. In that kingdom He was conceived as enacting the laws whereby all things in heaven and on earth were governed. Everything that took place was regarded as fulfillment of those laws. On rare occasions, however, for the sake of His chosen People, or of any individual whom He loved, He would suspend the laws by which the entire universe was governed. Such personal decrees were conceived not figuratively but literally; they were thought to emanate from God as they would from a king.

All of this is completely out of gear with the thinking of the average intelligent person at the present time. We can hardly expect him to accept as literally true the traditional accounts of miraculous events. This is what has caused the religious vacuum.

The modern-minded person must be made to realize that the purely naturalistic approach to reality is true as far as it goes, but does not go far enough. From the standpoint of salvation, or making the most of human life, the strictly scientific account of reality can help us only *in providing the conditions* necessary to our achieving that goal. But the very notion of salvation, in any sense whatever, is entirely beyond its scope. It cannot even justify our striving for that goal, much less assure that it is attainable. All values or ideals, though they do not deny natural law as understood by scientists, do point to a phase of reality, of which natural law does not take account.

To believe in God means to accept life on the assumption that it harbors conditions in the outer world and drives in the human spirit which together impel man to transcend himself. To believe in God means to take for granted that it is man's destiny to rise above the brute and to eliminate all forms of violence and exploitation from human society. In brief, God is the Power in the cosmos that gives human life the direction that enables the human being to reflect the image of God.

That conception of God does not require our believing in miracles, which imply the suspension of natural law. Does that mean, then, that we can afford to ignore the tradition which affirms such miracles? Not at all. On the contrary, we need that tradition to realize that we have come upon our present idea of God after considerable groping and searching for the truth. That tradition records the gropings and searchings which went on in the consciousness of our ancestors. Would we want to forget our own childish notions? Are they not essential to our experiencing our personal identity? Likewise, our tradition is indispensable as a means to our experiencing our continuity with our ancestry and our Jewish People. If we study that tradition carefully, we are bound to discover nuances and anticipations of attitudes toward life that are not only tenable but well worth cultivating. Those are the permanent values in our tradition, which we cannot afford to ignore.

44.

reconstructionism as the ideology of american jews

charles s. liebman

A major analysis of the Reconstructionist movement comes from Professor Charles S. Liebman, presently at Bar Ilan University, Ramat Gan, Israel, and formerly at Yeshiva University. Liebman brings to bear upon Reconstructionism some of the analytical categories of sociology of religions, in particular trying to understand the folk-centeredness of the movement and its stress upon Jewish peoplehood. He first shows the striking correspondence between the ideas held by the generality of American Jews—religious or otherwise—and the particular assertions of Reconstructionism. Then he argues that Reconstructionism articulates the folk-religion of American Jews, while Orthodoxy, Reform and Conservatism constitute the elite-religion. These terms are carefully explained and are not meant to denigrate Reconstructionist theology, but to understand its place and context within American Judaism.

From "Reconstructionism in American Jewish Life," by Charles S. Liebman, *American Jewish Year Book, 1970,* Vol. 71 edited by Morris Fine and Milton Himmelfarb (New York: American Jewish Committee; Philadelphia: Jewish Publication Society of American, 1971), pp. 68–71, 90–97. © 1970 by American Jewish Committee and Jewish Publication Society of America. Reprinted by permission of the author and American Jewish Committee.

A comparison of the major values or principles of most American Jews, as gleaned from their behavior, with the major values or principles of Reconstructionism suggests that many of them are potential Reconstructionists. Here, in brief, and not necessarily in order of importance, are what this author believes to be the major ideas, symbols, and institutions arousing the deepest loyalties and passions of American Jews. At a later point we will seek to demonstrate that most American Jews share these values. Here we merely assert them:

1. There is nothing incompatible between being a good Jew and a good American, or between Jewish and American standards of behavior. In fact, for a Jew, the better an American one is, the better Jew one is. If, however, one must choose between the two, one's first loyalty is to American standards of behavior, and to American rather than to Jewish culture.

2. Separation of church and state is an absolute essential. It protects America from being controlled by religious groups; it protects Judaism from having alien

standards forced upon it, and, most importantly, it protects the Jew from being continually reminded of his minority status. Only the separation of church and state assures the existence of religiously neutral areas of life, where the status of the Jew as a Jew is irrelevant to his function.

3. The Jews constitute one indivisible people. It is their common history and experience, not a common religious belief, that define them as a people. What makes one a Jew is identification with the Jewish people, and this is not quite the same as identification with the Jewish religion. Denominational differences within Judaism must not be allowed to threaten the basic unity of the people.

4. One consequence of defining Judaism as a shared history and experience is that problems of theology are not only likely to be divisive, they are also somewhat irrelevant. On the one hand, God is not some supernatural being, some grandfather image; but, on the other hand, there is a force in the universe besides man. But whatever one's definition of God, the entire matter is not terribly crucial. There are many more important things of a Jewish nature for the Jew to do, i.e., insuring the physical and spiritual survival of the Jewish people, than to expend his energy or attention on theological matters.

5. Jewish rituals are nice, up to a point. Going to a synagogue a few times a year, or lighting candles on Friday evening, having the family together for a Seder, or celebrating a son's *bar mitzvah* are proper ways of expressing one's Jewishness and keeping the family united. But Jews cannot be expected to observe all the rituals and practices of traditional Judaism. These were suitable, perhaps, to different countries or cultures, but not to the American Jew of the 20th century. Many rituals ought to be changed; it is up to each person to decide for himsef what he should or should not observe.

6. Among the major tasks facing Judaism is insuring the survival of the State of Israel. This is every Jew's obligation. But support for Israel does not necessarily mean that one must settle there, or that living outside Israel is wrong, or that living in Israel makes one a better Jew.

Reconstructionism shares these basic values, standards, and attitudes of American Jews. In fact, they constitute the bulk of the Reconstructionist program, shorn of its philosophical underpinning. As we have seen, Reconstructionism maintains that:

1. Jews must live in two civilizations or cultures, Jewish and American, but their first loyalty must be to American civilization.

2. Separation of church and state is more than merely desirable as a practical matter; it is a religious principle.

3. Judaism is defined by peoplehood, not religion. Religion must serve Jews, and not the other way around. Since religious differences tend to be divisive, the community must be organized and unified on a nonreligious basis; particular denominational identifications must be secondary to the unifying principles of one community.

4. God is the Power that makes for salvation, not a supernatural being. But a person's theology is generally unimportant, as long as he is active in some way in the Jewish community.

5. Ritual represents the folkways of the people, and should be retained for communal and personal needs. Rituals that are not functional, or that conflict with prevailing ethical standards, or that are hard to observe should be modified or abolished.

6. Jews have a religious obligation to support Israel, but they have no obligation of *'aliyah* [emigration to Israel]. The notion of *shelilat ha-golah* (negation of the diaspora) is wrong.

What, one asks, could be more Jewish-American that Reconstructionism? With some minor exceptions, it virtually embodies the major values and attitudes of American Jews. By this we do not intend to vulgarize Reconstructionism. Certainly Mordecai Kaplan, who has been so critical of American Judaism, would be the last to welcome the idea that the majority of American Jews actually accept his principles. We do not mean to imply that Kaplan, or Reconstructionism, is understood by the American Jews. Most of them surely have never heard of Kaplan, or of Reconstructionism. But we do maintain that by extracting and oversimplifying the principles of Reconstructionism one arrives at the grass-roots or folk religion of American Jews. Folk religion is often an oversimplification of a more complex religious system.

But if this is so, why is it that most Jews do not identify with Reconstructionism?

It may be argued that the other groups in American Judaism—Orthodoxy, Reform, and especially Conservatism—also embody most, if not all, these values. However, none has articulated them so explicitly as Reconstructionism, so elevated them to the status of basic principles, or so incorporated them into ideology and prayer. Only Reconstructionism really has made them into a religion. Also, the agreement with these principles among non-Reconstructionist leaders is much lower than among Reconstructionist leaders. For example, in the questionnaire mentioned above,[1] Reconstructionist rabbis were in greater agreement than non-Reconstructionist rabbis with the statements embodying these basic values. Not all differences between Reconstructionist and non-Reconstrictionist rabbis were statistically significant, but they were always in the expected direction. That is, Reconstructionist rabbis always expressed greater agreement with statements reflecting Reconstructionist ideology than did Orthodox, Conservative, and Reform rabbis. The only issue on which Reconstructionist rabbis did not stand at an extreme of the attitudinal continuum was Israel. They were more sympathetic to the role of Israel in Jewish life than were Conservative and Reform rabbis, but less than the Orthodox. This is consistent with Reconstructionist ideology, which transformed Zionism into a religious ideology earlier and more radically than Conservatism and Reform, but which, unlike Orthodoxy, adopted a position against negation of the diaspora and did not stress the religious importance of *'aliyah* . . .

Reconstructionist ideology is an articulation of the folk religion of American Jews. Orthodoxy, Conservatism, and Reform represent the three *elitist* ideologies of the American Jewish religion. Folk religion can be thought of as the *popular* religious culture. The elite relgion is the ritual, belief, and doctrine which the acknowledged religious leaders teach to be the religion. Thus the elite religion includes rituals and ceremonials (the cult), doctrines and beliefs (ideology), and a religious organization headed by the religious leaders. Their authority, the source of their authority, and the rights and obligations of the members of the organization are part of the beliefs and ideologies of the elite religion.

When we refer to Christianity, Islam, or Judaism, or when within Judaism we distinguish Orthodoxy, Conservatism, and Reform, we are really referring to the elitist formulations of these religions or groups. But not all who identify or affiliate with a religion accept its elitist formulation in its entirety. A subculture may exist within a religion, which the acknowledged leaders ignore or even condemn, but in which many, and perhaps a majority, of the members participate. The subculture may fall into the category of folk religion.

What, we may ask, is the difference between folk religion and denominationalism? Why call folk and elite religion two aspects of the same religion, rather than two separate religions? The answer is that both share the same organization, and both recognize, at least nominally, the authoritative nature of the cult and ideology, which the elite leadership affirms. Folk religion is not self-conscious; it does not articulate its own rituals and beliefs, or demand recognition for its informal leaders. Therefore, in the eyes of the elite religion, folk religion is not a movement but an error, or a set of errors, shared by many people. . . .

Most East European Jews who came to the United States between 1880 and 1920 identified in some way with Orthodox Judaism, though they did not necessarily accept its elitist formulation. They acquiesced to its authority structure (recognizing the religious authority of those who were ordained in accordance with elitist standards). They even accepted, though passively, its belief structure. What they demurred at, in practice, was its elaborate ritual structure. They developed their own hierarchy of the rituals—accepting some, modifying others, and rejecting still others, on the basis of values that had little to do with the elite religion itself. Those values were, preeminently, integration and acceptance into American society, but also ingrained customs and life styles, and superstitions of East European origin. Thus, at the turn of the century, there existed in the United States both an elite and a folk religion of Orthodox Judaism.

As the century advanced, the Orthodox folk found themselves increasingly uncomfortable. The elitist leaders were too rigid, uncompromising, and foreign in outlook. The synagogue those rabbis controlled was aesthetically unattractive. Even the belief and ideological system became increasingly intolerable, particularly as it seemed to foreclose the possibility for any modernization. As most Jews moved from older areas of Jewish settlement and established new synagogues in middle-class neighborhoods, they were physically freed from the constraint of the Orthodox elite, who tended to remain in the older neighborhoods. The Orthodox folk began withdrawing from Orthodoxy. But they neither desired nor could they articulate their own brand of Judaism. Rather, they sought a new elitist formulation with which they might be more comfortable. Others, socially more mobile, found it in Reform. Many, probably most, found it in Conservative Judaism.

However, the folk religion cut across Conservative, Reform, and many non-religious organizational lines. Its adherents reshaping all the institutions with which they affiliated, a greater uniformity now emerged in Jewish life. To some extent, the immigrants' children were differentially socialized by their different institutions, and a certain divisiveness resulted. But in general the homogenizing process was the more pronounced. By the end of World War II virtually all major non-Orthodox organizations expressed the six major attitudes and values of the Jewish folk. The Orthodox alone were excluded, because only an elite or the most passive remained Orthodox.

Our special concern here is with Conservatism, which rapidly became the dominant religious institution and expression of American Jews. However, the fact that the folk identified with Conservative Judaism did not mean that they were Conservative Jews as the Conservative elite, [Jewish Theological Seminary] leaders and alumni, understood Conservatism. An elaboration of the differences and tensions between the rabbinate and the congregants of the early Conservative synagogues would take us too far afield, and besides much of the basic research remains to be done. Suffice it to point out here that while the folk were more traditional in some respects and less so in others, in most respects they tended to be indifferent to Conservatism's elitist formulations.

Coincident with this development, and not entirely unaffected by it, was the effort to formulate the folk religion in elitist terms. This, we suggest, is Reconstructionism. We do not suggest that Kaplan deliberately fashioned an ideology to suit the basic attitudes of most American Jews. We do suggest that this is what Reconstructionism is. But the very nature of folk religion makes it unsuitable for elitist formulation. In an elitist formulation folk religion is often unrecognizable to the folk.

Elite religion is expressed in ideology, folk religion in ritual and symbol. Indeed, the beliefs and ideas underlying the different folk rituals may be incompatible. This becomes a problem only if one actually bothers to formulate them philosophically. Then, with their contradictions apparent, the ideologist of the folk religion seeks to adjust them. He does this by establishing the primacy of ideology over ritual and ceremony. But that negates the essence of folk religion.

The constituents of early Reconstructionism were the religious left wing among the JTS alumni. It was these men who pressed their congregations for change and innovation. It was they who insisted on seating men and women together, shortening services, abolishing the second day of festivals, introducing organ music, abolishing the priestly blessing, and, in a later period, inviting women to recite the blessings before the reading of the Torah. To the left wing these changes were consistent with their ideology and with their understanding of Judaism. They never perceived why many of their congregants, who had ceased to observe such basic Jewish practices as Sabbath and *kashrut* in their private lives, were reluctant to accept changes in the public sphere. The failure to perceive derives from the elitist assumption that authority systems, belief systems, and ritual or cultic systems within a religion must be consistent. Also, what an elitist system may consider to be superficial or secondary—food styles, recreational and leisure styles, a spouse's family background, status of Jews, the celebration of *bar mitzvah,* or funeral services—a folk system may consider to be essential.

Influenced by prevailing Western thought, the left-wing rabbis sought to modify their congregants' beliefs. Kaplan holds that God, as Judaism understands Him, does not exist, but that there are forces in the universe that help man to be good, creative, free. These Kaplan calls God. He was not the only Jew who had gone to college and stopped believing in the traditional God of Western religion. When he redefined God to his own satisfaction, that was also apparently to the satisfaction of most American Jews who had never heard of him.

Kaplan drew certain consequences from his definition: If there was no traditional God, one could not pray to Him for help or direct intervention. But what follows for Kaplan does not necessarily follow in folk religion. One may admit in one's living-room that there is no supernatural God, no miracle, no divine intervention in the affairs of men. But this, after all, is living-room talk. When a folk Jew's child is sick, or when he is concerned about the safety of Israel, or even when he is grateful and elated to be alive, he can still open his *siddur* and pray to God—not a living-room God but the traditional God. Who can say that conclusions reached in one's living-room are more compelling than what one *knows to be true* when one prays? If one has doubts as to which is the more compelling, one must reject Reconstructionism—precisely because it demands the supremacy of rational formulations of ideology. On the other hand, complete reliance on intellectual consistency, the rejection of what one's heart knows to be true, also leads to a rejection of Reconstructionism—because its very foundation lies in undemonstrable sentiments about man, progress, Judaism, Zionism. Reconstructionism is midway between religious belief and intellectual rigor, based on a minimum of axiomatic postulates. It is most likely to appeal precisely to those who waver. In fact, it has served as a two-way bridge between Jewish commitment and marginalism.

If people took seriously the intellectual formulation of their religion as a basic *Weltanschauung,* Reconstructionism might be a more significant alternative for some Jews. Certainly, its critique of Orthodoxy, Conservatism, and Reform would be more compelling. But most people today, recognize, at least implicitly, that different institutions provide them with sources of understanding or cues to proper behavior, each in a different segment of life. Neither Orthodoxy nor Conservatism nor Reform has much to say about aspects of life that most American Jews take very seriously, such as social relationships, politics, economics, and war. But most Jews do not really expect their synagogue to have anything to say about these beyond elementary moralizing. The intellectual thinness of American Judaism is a tragedy only to the elite.

There are other reasons for Reconstructionism's failure. It may be a religion by a sociologist's standards, but it is not quite a religion by American standards of what religion ought to be. After all, it denies belief in a supernatural God. The fact that most American Jews do so, too, is immaterial. For most Jews their denial is a personal attitude; but affiliation with a synagogue which accepts their own theology will cause them embarrassment. Synagogue affiliation is more than a private act. It is public identification with a major American religion, and the *American* thing to do. But how American is it if, by American standards, the synagogue is not really *religious?*

American Jews no doubt are more ethnic, or peoplehood-oriented, than religion-oriented. But only Reconstructionism makes a virtue of this, and most American Jews are not quite willing to admit to this virtue publicly. The entire basis of Jewish accommodation to America, of the legitimacy of Jewish separateness, has been that Judaism is a religion, like Catholicism and Protestantism, and that the Jews are not merely an ethnic group, like the Irish or the Italians. America tolerates Jewish afternoon or Sunday schools, interdictions on intermarriage, and a fair degree of social isolation and exclusiveness. Would these be tolerated if Jews were considered to be an ethnic group like the Irish, Italians, or even Negroes? Though there are many more Negroes than Jews in the United States, the desire of some Negro Spokesmen for separatism still has not attained the legitimacy of Jewish separatism precisely because Negroes are not defined as a religious group. Although Jews may know in their hearts that their identity stems from peoplehood and ethnicity, they are reluctant to display this truth in public. This is not a matter of deluding the American public. Above all, Jews delude themselves.

Reconstructionism's response has been to redefine religion. Kaplan has argued the need to redefine the symbolic nature of American public life and to express it in a civic non-supernatural religion that all Americans could share. Thus, since every American lives in two civilizations, he would also have two religions. Jews could then acknowledge that they are civilization rather than a religion. At the same time, it would be understandable that the Jews' civilization must also have religious expression. At this point, one suspects, the folk find themselves "turned off."

Reconstructionism's problems are compounded by the fact that its ideology has greatest appeal to the Jews least interested in synagogue activity or organized religious life. The outstanding difference between potential Reconstructionists and all other respondents, as revealed by the answers to our questionnaire, is that proportionately fewer of the former said religion plays a very important role in their lives. *De facto,* Reconstructionism is widespread among leaders of Jewish Community centers and secular Jewish organizations—all of them people who have found, for expressing their Jewish and Reconstructionist values, quite acceptable alternatives to the synagogue.

Finally, once Reconstructionism institutionalized itself, once it became a denomination, it violated a cardinal principle of Jewish folk religion: the unity of the Jewish people and the consequent irrelevance of denominational distinctions. Reconstructionism can demand that its ideology be taken seriously, but it cannot make the same demand for its distinctive institutional claims without asserting that differences between itself and other demonimations are significant. And this is precisely what folk religion abjures. . . .

Notes

    1. [Deleted from this excerpt].

part nine

torah in the state of israel

Although modern Zionism was regarded as primarily a political movement, intended to establish a national homeland for the Jewish people, and although the State of Israel is a secular, modern democratic state, nevertheless the State is still Jewish, still *of Israel*. The question naturally arises, In what ways is the Judaic tradition important in the formation of the national life of the Jewish state? While some Israelis call themselves religious, by which they mean entirely traditional and orthodox, and still more call themselves traditional, which would correspond in terms of observance to the patterns of Conservative Judaism in America, still others do not see themselves as religious at all, and do not regard being Jewish as a matter of a religious orientation toward life. All together, the Jews of the State of Israel constitute an important datum in the study of modern Judaism. A consideration of the way of Torah in the modern world is far from complete without asking about the character and meaning of that datum.

45.

how jewish is the jewish state?

louis i. rabinowitz

Louis I. Rabinowitz was a rabbi in South Africa and today pursues Jewish scholarship in Jerusalem.

From "How Jewish Is the Jewish State?" by Louis I. Rabinowitz, from *Conservative Judaism,* Vol. XXVI, No. 2, Winter 1972, pp. 1–13. © 1972 by the Rabbinical Assembly of America. Reprinted by permission of The Rabbinical Assembly.

For some thirty years, from Hitler's rise to power until the 1960s, the entire energies of the State of Israel "on the way" and of the State itself after its establishment, were directed toward the sheer human necessity of saving Jewish bodies from destruction and extermination. This tremendous effort inevitably led to a distortion of the essential purpose of Zionism and of the ultimate justification of Israel's existence—which is not so much the survival of the Jewish body, as of the Jewish soul.

There is no objective need for such a justification of the State. The twentieth century will stand out in history as that era which established the principle of the inalienable right of every people to self-determination, to live in accordance with its own chosen way of life. The determination of the Jewish people to develop a way of life and a civilization in Israel which will reflect the highest ethical and social ideals of Judaism is the fruit of an internal, subjective urge.

That urge has become even more acute as a result of the increasing spiritual erosion within the ranks of the Jewish people. This is a subject in itself; for the present it suffices to state that throughout its history the Jewish people has ever been faced with the possibility of annihilation from one of two sources—outside persecution and pogroms on the one hand, and inner spiritual lethargy and assimilation on the other. Paradoxical though it may seem, when the danger of physical extermination recedes, its place is taken by the danger of spiritual death. One destroys the Jewish body; the other the Jewish soul. We lost six million of our people by the one; who will be optimistic enough to reject the possibility that if the present process of intermarriage, alienation, and rejection of Judaism continues, the loss to the Jewish people may be even larger?

The State of Israel, offering the possibilities of a full Jewish life, free from external pressures, may be the answer. In that context the moving words in the last chapter of Maimonides' *Mishneh Torah* take on added meaning. Daringly identifying the messianic age with the this-worldly attainment of political independence and unfettered sovereignty of the Jews in their own land, he declares that "the Sages and Prophets did not long for the days of the Messiah that Israel might exercise dominion over the world, or rule over the heathen or be exalted by the nations, or that it might eat and drink and be merry. Their aspiration was that Israel be free to devote itself to the Torah and its wisdom, with none to oppress or nullify it" (*Laws of Kings* 12.4). That is surely the most sublime expression of the justification of the Jewish State.

Let it be said at once that this theory of the role of the Jewish State, as preserving Jewish values among Jews, and contributing to the progress of civilization as a whole, runs counter to a doctrine which, since the era of Emancipation, has been sedulously propagated as a bolster to Jewish self-esteem in the diaspora. Throughout the centuries, Jewish thought, theology and prayers viewed the *galut* as an unmitigated misfortune and tragedy, the punishment meted out to the Jewish people for their lack of loyalty to God—"because of our sins we were exiled from our land and kept far away from our soil"—and held that the time would yet come when the Jewish people would expiate those sins, and God in His mercy would return them to their land. The post-Emancipation philosophers seized hold of what may be called "an orphan statement" to the effect that "Israel was exiled among the nations only that converts might be added to them." On this they built the concept that the exile, far from being a tragedy, was a blessing in disguise for mankind. This was the birth of the theory of the "Jewish mission." The role of the Jew in the diaspora was to permeate the world with the ethical ideas of Judaism and the principles of social justice preached by the prophets of Israel, and so gradually bring the world "under the wings of the *Shekhinah.*"

Reviewing this theory in the light of facts, one must come to the rueful conclusion that if that has been the appointed role of the Jewish people, either we have been very bad teachers, or the world has shown itself to be a very bad pupil! Stripped of all apologetics and ingenious "proofs" of Jewish influence, it would be difficult to point to any substantial contribution whereby Jews *as Jews,* as a body upholding certain tenets, have decisively influenced the course of world civilization in the ethical sphere.

The "Jewish State" theory flatly denies this "Jewish mission" idea. It views the dispersion of the Jews and their existence as a vulnerable minority within a non-Jewish majority as providing those circumstances which bring about the diminution of the Jewish spirit. This is the "oppressor and nullifier" to which Maimonides refers. Only with the concentration of the Jews in their own land, where they will constitute a sovereign, independent entity able to direct its life in accordance with its own ideals, can Jewish ideals become a viable reality; only then can their influence ultimately make itself felt in the world. That, in brief, is the theory of the Jewishness of the Jewish State; it is that theory which this article will attempt to evaluate in the light of fact.

Before moving from the theoretical to the practical, I must make one point. In the *Midrash Sifre Zutta* published by Professor Saul Lieberman, there is a statement, more or less to the effect that "the Holy One blessed be He acted mercifully with Moses in not allowing him to enter the Land of Israel." For it is sometimes better that a person should die with all his glorious visions un-affected by harsh facts, than be brought face to face with reality. There is always a gap between promise and fulfillment, between expectation and reality. Better that Moses die with the promised vision of Israel entering into a land flowing with milk and honey, living "each man under his fig tree and each under his vine, with none to make him afraid," in peace, tranquility, and in accordance with God's revealed will, than go through all that Joshua was to experience, and emerge disillusioned.

No one, I hope, expects that in this imperfect world the newly established State of Israel, born out of chaos, faced with multiple internal and external problems, desperately if confidently fighting for its survival, would emerge full-grown as a model of all the virtues, giving expression in its daily life to the highest and most sublime ideals of Judaism, a noble example to the world. One can only expect that it direct its actions toward that ultimate goal. Twenty-four years of the State's existence can provide a basis for the examination of that direction.

With that important reservation, it is possible to turn from blueprint to clinical diagnosis. By what yardstick does one measure the "Jewishness," actual or potential, of Israel? For reasons of convenience, it is proposed to discuss the question under five heads. They are: certain national formalities, legislation, ethics, education, and the overall atmosphere of the country.

It can confidently be claimed that the State of Israel is Jewish in its calendar, and in the official observance of the dietary laws. The official days of rest and holidays are those laid down in the twenty-third chapter of Leviticus: Sabbath, and the five festivals—Pesah, Shavuot, Rosh Hashanah, Yom Kippur, and Suk-kot. It is remarkable that there have been only two additions to this list—one religious, and the other secular. Rosh Hashanah is observed for two days, as in the diaspora, and *Yom Ha-Atzmaut* (Independence Day) has been declared the only civil holiday of the whole year. (A proposal that *Rosh Hodesh,* the New Moon, be reinstituted as a holiday, as it was during the days of the First Temple, will almost certainly not be adopted.)

There is no difficulty in observing Jewish holidays in Israel. Indeed, an immigrant from England even complained to me about the ease of observing these days! In the diaspora, he argued, the determination to observe the Sabbath and festivals in a non-Jewish environment constituted a challenge which, to his regret, was entirely missing in Israel! Freedom from the necessity to work is, of course, quite independent of the manner in which these days are observed, which will be referred to later.

Similarly, *kashrut* is officially observed in Israel—in the armed services, the airlines, ships and railways, absorption centers, and other government institu-tions. The fact that the Ministry of Tourism does not give an "A" certificate to a hotel unless the food is kosher, has had the effect of making all first-class hotels kosher. However, the *formal* nature of this Jewishness is reflected in the fact that, apart from *kashrut,* the atmosphere of these hotels is wholly non-Jewish.

These formal structures do not guarantee the quality of their inner content.

Thus, it is by no means beyond the bounds of possibility that the Sabbath in Israel could become indistinguishable from Sunday in Paris, Los Angeles or Berlin, with the sole difference of being observed on a different day; that the sanctity of the Sabbath, which is the most characteristic feature of the Jewish day of rest, may perhaps disappear in Israel. Nor is it improbable that, with a further decline in culinary standards, the hotels will merely become luxurious lodging houses for tourists, with the latter joining the growing number of Israelis who frequent non-kosher restaurants for tasty food.

It is obvious that legislation in a democratic state cannot be effected unless it is based upon the general will of the electorate. (I ignore the actuality of a minority exercising influence out of all proportion to its numbers or representation, because it holds the balance of power between two opposing parties.) Thus, the legal system and norms of a country reflect the cultural, ethical and civilizational attitudes of the nation, especially in a country like Israel where the system of proportional representation ensures that all points of view are represented in the Knesset.

The legal system of Israel, however, started off at a disadvantage. When the State was established, the legal system consisted of an amazing hodgepodge of ancient Ottoman law and certain principles of English law introduced by the British Mandatory Government, on which a mass of Emergency Regulations was superimposed. In order for Israel to function, in 1948, that muddled system was declared the operative law of the State until such time as it would be superseded by laws passed by the Knesset. The most striking and symbolic of these laws was the Law of Return, which at one fell swoop abolished all the restrictions on Jewish immigration enacted by the Mandatory Government, going to the other extreme of giving every Jew the right to immigrate and conferring automatic Israeli citizenship on him the moment he set foot on the soil of Israel. In view of this, the Jewishness of the State in the legal sphere must be gauged not by the corpus of law as it exists, but by the extent to which new legislation passed by the Knesset (a) is in accordance with the spirit of Jewish law, and (b) has penetrated into and affected existing law in the direction of "Jewishness."

This fascinating subject deserves a much more detailed and scientific examination than can possibly be given in this review. Broad outlines, however, may be indicated. For example, the Knesset legislated that in all matters of personal status, particularly marriage and divorce, Orthodox Jewish law was to be the law of the country and was to be applied by the rabbinic courts. Jewish law, however, is not confined either to ritual law or to laws of personal status. The *Hoshen Mishpat,* the civil law, the law of *meum* and *teum,* of contracts, of conveyancy, of partnership, of evidence, are as much part of the corpus of Jewish religious law as are *kashrut* and the laws of forbidden sexual relationships. And it is here that we come up against the anomaly of the legal system of Israel. An almost tacit agreement has developed between the civil and religious authorities of the State, whereby as a *quid pro quo* for the former keeping "hands off" in the sphere of personal status, the rabbinic authorities have agreed to keep "hands off" in civil law! In the civil sphere, the Knesset apparently has a free hand in enacting legislation which may run completely counter to the established principles of Jewish civil law. . . .

Probably more than any other statesman in Israel, Mr. David Ben-Gurion has been consistently conscious of the spiritual purpose of the State of Israel as "a light unto the nations." In accordance with this principle, when the State was established, he issued instructions to the nascent diplomatic service that it was their duty, as official representatives of the Jewish State, to uphold the ideals of social justice, peace, and democracy, especially in the forum of international world opinion, the United Nations.

For some time, in fact, an attempt was made to keep this "light" burning. The most noble example of it was the instruction given to Israel's representative at the UN to vote for the independence of Libya (1950), on the grounds that Israel upholds in all circumstances the right of every national entity to independence, and despite the fact that the security of the 40,000 Jews of Libya would be endangered. Ironically, Israel's vote in favor of Libya was the decisive one cast; and on the morrow, Libya set up an anti-Israel boycott office!

Similarly, Israel has consistently voted against South Africa on the issue of *apartheid,* despite the fact that this would considerably embarrass the 120,000 Jews of that country. The grounds were that a Jewish state would be untrue to its justification for existence unless it vigorously opposed discrimination on grounds of religion or color. Alas, in the political jungle of international relationships, Israel could not continue to maintain this altruistic attitude and, with few exceptions, it has adopted the yardstick of the other nations of the world—self interest. Apart from the now formal vote against South Africa, one would be hard put to find a clear example of Israel's vote at the UN exemplifying the role of "a light unto the nations." With unconcealed regret, principle has had to give way to expediency.

Perhaps the most pleasing aspect of the ethical stance in Israel is the treatment accorded the non-Jewish minorities. The wholly praiseworthy attitude of the Government toward minorities goes far beyond the mere formal granting of electoral representation (for those who are Israeli citizens), providing education which takes full cognizance of their national traditions, and guaranteeing complete religious freedom. There is a conscious, determined effort to improve the minorities' economic and social conditions, and to prevent anything which smacks of discrimination. The Histadrut has successfully insisted that Arabs living outside the 1967 borders and working in Israel shall receive the same rates of pay as Israeli workers. Teams of advisors are engaged in improving Arab agricultural methods, providing cultural and social amenities, and seeking to raise their standard of living.

It can be stated confidently that the record of Israel's treatment of its minorities is in accordance with the finest principles of Jewish ethics. There is a conscious desire to fulfill "and ye know the soul of the stranger, for ye were strangers in the land of Egypt," and it is in every way to be deplored that outside the borders of Israel, the opposite opinion prevails.

A far more important question is how to improve the present level of "Jewishness" in Israel. To a great extent, this will depend on the kind of education that is provided. The unfortunate division of the school system into two trends, "non-religious" and "religious," has completely deprived the seventy percent of the school population who attend "non-religious" schools of any vestige of Jewish education. The advocates of this arrangement maintain that "Jewishness" is independent of religious virtues, and that they are producing citizens imbued with a way of life which, though wholly secular, reflects the essence of Jewish ethical values. Their confidence, however, was rudely disturbed by the realization that the products of this education were completely devoid of any knowledge—as distinct from practice—of Jewish tradition, even in its most rudimentary form. An attempt was made some years ago to undo the evil by introducing a course called "Jewish consciousness," the aim of which was to acquaint pupils with Judaism, without any suggestion of commitment to it. It has been universally conceded that the experiment has failed miserably.

More germane to the subject of this article is the contribution of the institutions of higher learning, both secular and religious, to the "Jewishness" of Israel. Let us set aside the purely scientific schools like the Weizmann Institute and the Haifa Technion, and consider the Hebrew University, Tel Aviv University, and Bar-Ilan which, in addition to their departments of science, have faculties of arts and humanities. Do these "arts" affect the art of living and, more specifically, the art of *Jewish* living? Do the "humanities" lead to a specific Jewish humanitarianism?

Let it be said at once that the universities in Israel reflect the tendency toward vocationalism as against the acquisition of knowledge for its own sake which characterizes universities the world over. Thus, other than in their chosen field, Israeli students are shielded from general, as well as specifically Jewish, culture.

These universities do have Faculties of Jewish Studies, but it is still too early to determine whether these studies are purely intellectual or whether they are also affective; whether the Jewish student of Judaica becomes more of a Jew than the Jewish student of Russian becomes a Russian. The potential for influence, however, undoubtedly exists, for some of the finest minds of the Jewish intelligentsia occupy the chairs of these faculties.

The position of the *yeshivot* in Israel is different. With the almost unique exception of Yeshivah Mercaz Ha-Rav in Jerusalem, it can be said of all the traditional *yeshivot* that they are "in Israel, but not of Israel." They provide the most intensive of Jewish studies—in a strictly restricted sphere—but they deliberately dissociate themselves from the current of normal daily Jewish life in Israel, and their influence in the emergence of a general sense of Jewishness in the State is consequently negligible. They constitute a closed society.

Some years ago, during a visit to South Africa, I was asked to approach the Government to allow the transfer to Israel of funds collected for the *yeshivot* there. (The Government, as a protest against Israel's consistent vote at the UN against *apartheid,* had forbidden the transfer of funds which "would assist the Government of Israel.") I succeeded. With a clear conscience I was able to make the point that although these *yeshivot* were situated in Israel, they were not part of the general life. They could just as well be in England or Williamsburg, a fact which is symbolically underlined by their names—the Mir, the Slobodka, the Ponevez, the Karlin Yeshivah—and the fact that their language of instruction is still Yiddish.

A striking exception is provided by the "new" *yeshivot,* particularly in the B'nei Akiva movement which are, incidentally, looked at askance by the older *yeshivot.* The students usually enter them from *yeshivah* secondary schools where they receive a secular education in addition to a broad Jewish education. They are entirely integrated into the national life of Israel, and their students enter military service—which the students of the traditional *yeshivot* avoid. In addition, there is a close link between these *yeshivot* and the religious kibbutzim of the Poel Mizrahi movement with their admirable ethical standards. These factors combine toward the emergence of what are undoubltedly the most Jewish of Israeli Jews—with equal emphasis on the words Jewish and Israeli.

That a specific way of life, and with it a specific character, is emerging in the State of Israel, is beyond question. It is in some ways sharply different from the character which the Jew has developed in the diaspora. This can be specially appreciated by a person like myself, who has spent most of his life in the diaspora, and the last eleven years in Israel. For instance, I am not quite sure that the traditional value traits which have characterized the Jew throughout the ages—*rahmanim b'nei rahmanim, gomlei hasadim b'nei gomlei hasadim* (The merciful children of merciful ancestors, full of kindness as their ancestors were") or "a good eye, a humble mind, and a lowly spirit" (*Ethics of the Fathers* 5.22)—particularly characterize the Jew of Israel today.

On the other hand, one can point to distinctive characteristics which constitute almost a complete psychological metamorphosis from the diaspora personality. One is the sturdy and almost exaggerated independence of the individual Jew. He stands four square on his rights; he refuses to submit. "No one is going to tell me what to do" has become his password. This admirable trait has its unlovely side: a certain lack of discipline in civil life and a throwing about of one's weight.

To give another example: Uzi Narkiss, conqueror of Jerusalem and now head of the Aliyah Department, addressed a meeting of the Actions Committee of the Zionist Organization during a spate of terrorist activities in Israel. Narkiss spoke with withering scorn of the fact that many potential tourists had cancelled their trips because of these troubles. His voice trembling with indignation, he exclaimed, "Jews afraid? When, in the whole course of Jewish history, has one ever heard of a Jew being afraid?" For him, as for others, particularly *sabras,* Jewish history begins with modern Israel.

There is no doubt that the superb fearlessness and courage of the Jew in Israel is a positive trait. We who were brought up in the diaspora refer to it as the revival of the long dormant Maccabean tradition; the Israeli see it as part of his nature. Again, it has its obverse side; its degeneration into foolhardiness is, I am sure, one of the main contributory factors to the mounting toll of road accidents!

Lastly, one notes the all pervading sense of equality in Israel, and the almost complete absence of social barriers between employers and employees, housewife and *ozeret* ("helper"—heaven forfend that one use the word servant!), officer and private, manager and office boy. There is a universal tendency to address everyone by his or her first name. All this is evidence of an egalitarian society to which there are few, if any, parallels in the world.

I confine myself to these three examples, and ask a pertinent question: To what extent are these phenomena the distilled essence of the fruit of Jewish ethical and social doctrine, and to what extent are they the result of the special circumstances in which the Jew in Israel finds himself? I would like to think, and I believe I am right, that the spirit of independence to which I have referred is the result of two thousand years of Jewish teaching of the worth of every individual soul; it is also possible that it is the reaction to the dreadful events of the holocaust and the helot-like conditions of the Jews in Arab countries. The indomitable courage and spirit of self-sacrifice may be the fruit of the teachings of the doctrine of martyrdom for the name of the Lord, which Jews gave to the world; it may possibly be the sober realization that the survival of Israel depends upon this spirit. The egalitarianism may be a florescence of the essential spirit of democracy which is part of Judaism; perhaps a sociologist could propound a less admirable cause for it.

Reference should be made to what may be termed a "new mitzvah" which has evolved in Israel. Some thirty years ago, my late father-in-law, Rabbi M. A. Amiel, Chief Rabbi of Tel Aviv, noted that the traditional division of the biblical precepts into "commandments between man and God," and "commandments between man and his fellow" is not comprehensive. He maintained that there is a third category, for which he coined the phrase "commandments of the Jew towards his country." Whether that category can be theologically maintained or not, it is a fact that this has become perhaps the most outstanding expression of "Jewishness" in Israel. It pervades every aspect of life and embraces every section of the population, with the exception of the extreme religious elements referred to above. It is not confined to military service, but to service in every sphere of life; it has become almost the supreme commandment of the Jews of Israel.

In conclusion, therefore, it may be stated that out of the ingathering of the exiles from over a hundred countries, a distinct civilization is emerging with its own way of life, traditions and distinctive features, which differentiate it from other countries and other Jewish communities. The formal framework is that of a Jewish state, with a distinctive language and an outer adherence to the norms of Judaism. It is too early to state with confidence whether its inner spirit will reflect a specific Jewish ethic or whether other factors—the desire to be "like all the nations," or the demands of defense and the sheer need of physical survival —will bring about a deviation from or even a denial of these ideals.

In the last analysis, as related above, it is a question of education in the broadest sense of that word. An educational system extending from the elementary school to the universities, geared to the conscious aim of inculcating specifically Jewish values in every sector of the population, outside the bounds of the purely religious framework, alone can ensure that the Jewish State will indeed be Jewish. And for that, a complete rethinking, amounting to a veritable spiritual revolution, will be necessary.

part ten

zionism and judaism

Thus far we have considered modern Judaism within the narrow framework of religious belief and behavior. We have laid out the issues of contemporary Jewish theology as they are formulated by participants in the major expressions of the classical tradition in America. We therefore have ignored two important aspects of contemporary Jewish piety.

First, we have not given attention to the nonreligious Jews and the points at which their perception of "being Jewish" intersects with that of the professing Jews. Yet many millions of Jews do not understand "being Jewish" as a matter of piety and faith at all. And at the same time their view of themselves as Jews has much in common with the self-understanding of religious Jews.

Second, we have ignored the place of Zionism and the State of Israel in contemporary Jewish piety, although that place is very large indeed. The profound concern of religious Jews for the welfare of the Jewish people in the land of Israel, the belief that the State of Israel is not an entirely secular phenomenon but is of deep religious significance, the centrality of the land and of Jerusalem in both the classical symbolism of Jewish liturgy and the contemporary piety of ordinary Jews—these explain why Zionism must enter into any account of Judaism.

And it is with Zionism that the religious and the secular circles intersect and become one. Therefore, in our discussion of the place of Zionism in Jewish piety, we shall have to refer not only to the pious Jew and to the classical tradition, but also to the Jew whose piety consists in seeing himself as a member of the Jewish people and in preserving and participating in its culture and its history.

The following essays take up two sides of the same problem. The first considers the ways in which Zionism poses a problem for Judaism and attempts to resolve the dilemmas attendant upon the interrelationship between a worldly and an other-worldly heritage. The second then tries to explain in what ways Zionism has solved the "Jewish problem" for modern Jews and how Zionism has therefore come to occupy so central a place both in the imagination of pious life of religious Jews and in the program and policy for the Jewish people of secular Jews.

It is appropriate that we should conclude our account of contemporary Jewish piety with that movement in modern Jewish life which is most ambiguous with respect to the classical tradition: religious in its corpus of symbols and aspirations, secular in its mode of operation and plan of action. If, as we have observed, the classic tradition held that one may use profane means in the service of the sacred and in doing so one makes the profane holy, then there will be nothing surprising in the mixed religious and secular character of Zionism or in the combination of pious fervor and secular practicality with which the vast majority of world Jewry respond to the call of Zion and Jerusalem.

46.

judaism and the zionist problem

jacob neusner

From "Judaism and the Zionist Problem," by Jacob Neusner, *Judaism* XIX, 3, 1970, pp. 311–323. © 1970 by American Jewish Congress, and reprinted with their permission.

The success of Zionism in solving the central Jewish problems of the modern age also creates new dilemmas for the Judaic religious tradition. Since Zionism functions for Jewry in much the same way as religions do for other peoples, the role and function of *Judaism*—the complex of myths, rituals, social and cultural forms by which classical Jews experienced and interpreted reality—now prove exceptionally ambiguous. Because Zionism appropriates the eschatological language and symbolism of classical Judaism, Judaists face an unwanted alternative: either to repudiate Zionism or to acquiesce in the historicization, the politicization, of what had formerly stood above politics and beyond history. The choice to be sure was recognized and faced by small reform and orthodox circles, as everyone knows. The classical reformers repudiated Zionism in the name of the mission of Israel, which, they held, required Jewry to take a decisive role in the universal achievement by all men of the Messianic age. Their last, and unworthy, heirs accurately repeat the rhetoric, but do not possess the moral authority, of the nineteenth-century reformers. Likewise, orthodox leadership in Eastern Europe and the U.S.A. quite early discerned what they understood to be the heretical tendency of Zionism: the advocacy that Jews save themselves, rather than depend on the Messiah, and return to Zion before the foreordained end of time. Their repulsive continuators present no interesting differences from the anti-Zionist reformers.

For the great mass of American Jews, who take literally the Zionist interpretation of Jewish history and innocently identify Zionism with Judaism, but regard themselves also both as Americans by nationality and Jews by religion, naive belief substitutes for and precludes close analysis. They have yet to come to grips with the inner contradictions recognized by the extremists of reform and orthodox Judaism. Indeed, they exasperate Israeli Zionists as much as Diaspora anti-Zionists. If Zionist, then why American? If the end has come, why not accept the discipline of the eschaton? If the end has not come, how to justify the revision of the Judaic consciousness and its reformation along Zionist lines? Nor has U.S. Jewry taken seriously the demands of logic and intellect for the formation of a credible ideology to explain the status quo and justify it. . . .

A Hostile View

Zionism solves "the Jewish problem." Its success lies only partially in politics. The more profound problems for which it serves as a satisfactory solution are inward, spiritual, and, ultimately, religious. Just as the Judaic tradition had formerly told Jews what it meant to be Jewish—had supplied them with a considerable definition of their identity—so does Zionism in the modern age. Jews who had lost hold of the mythic structure of the past were given a grasp on a new myth, one composed of the restructured remnants of the old one.

The Jew had formerly been a member of a religious nation, believing in Torah revealed at Sinai, in one God who had chosen Israel, hoping for the Messiah and return to the land in the end of days. Jews who gave up that story of where they came from and who they are tell a new story based on the old, but in superficially secular form. To be Jewish means to live in the land and share in the life of the Jewish nation, which became the State of Israel.

To a hostile observer, things look like this: the elements of "Jewishness" and the components of "Israelism" are to be one and the same—sacrifice, regeneration, resurrection. The sacrifice is no longer in the Temple; no prophets need decry the multitudes of fatted beasts. What now must be sacrificed is the blood of Israelis and the treasure of the Diaspora. The regeneration is no longer to be the turning of sinners to repentence—*teshuvah*—but rather the reformation of the economic and cultural realities of the Jewish people. No longer 'parasites,' but farmers, no longer dependent upon the cultural achievements of the nations but creators of a Hebrew, and 'enlandised' culture, the Jews would be reborn into a new being and a new age. The resurrection is no longer of the dead at the end of time, but of the people at the end of the Holocaust.

The unfriendly witness sees matters this way: The new Zionist identity, like the old Judaic one, supplied a law for the rituals and attitudes of the faith. The old *halakhah* was made irrelevant, the object of party-politics. The new was not partisan at all. All believed in, all fulfilled the law, except for sinners and heretics beyond the pale. The new law requires of Jewish man one great commandment: support Israel. Those who do it best, live there. Those who do not, pay a costly atonement in guilt and ransom for the absent body. The ransom is paid through the perpetual mobilization of the community in an unending campaign for funds. The guilt is exorcised through political rituals: letters to Congressmen and—for bourgeois Jews, what would normally be unheard of—mass rallies and street demonstrations. The guilt of Auschwitz and the sin of living in the Diaspora become interwined: "On account of our sin do we live today, and in the wrong place at that!" Above all, the guilty and the sinner forever atone by turning to . . . the land: There is no land but Israel, and the Jewish people are its product. The development of an American Jewish, or Judaic, culture is seen as irrelevant to the faith. The philanthropists will not support it, for no funds are left after allocations for Israel and for domestic humanitarian institutions. The rabbis will not speak of it, for the people will not listen. The people will hear of nothing but victories, and victories are won in this world, upon a fleshly battlefield, with weapons of war.

The old self-hatred—the vile anti-Semitism of an Alexander Portnoy—is left behind. No longer weak, one hardly needs to compensate for weakness by pretensions to moral superiority, and then to pay the price of that compensation by hatred of one's own weakness. Jews no longer look down on *goyim,* for they feel like them. The universal humanism, the cosmopolitanism of the old Jew are abandoned in the new particularism. The old grandmother who looked for Jewish names in reports of plane crashes has given way to the new grandson who turns off the news after the Middle Eastern reports are done with.

The Jew no longer makes contradictory demands on society. He no longer wants to be accepted into the tradition of society. In the new ethnicism of the hour, he seeks only his share. The liberal dilemma has been resolved. Jews now quite honestly interpret the universe in terms of their particular concerns. Self-hatred, liberalism, the crisis of identity—the three characteristics of the mid-twentieth century American Jew—all fade into the background. The end of the old myths no longer matters much, for new ones have arisen in their place. The American Jews who did not want to be so Jewish that they could not also be part of the undifferentiated majority have had their wish fulfilled. Some have indeed ceased to be Jewish at all, and no one cares. Many others have found a place in the new, well-differentiated majority—so goes the hostile view.

Against Religious Reaction

In my view, it is reactionary to cavil at these developments. Only an antiquarian cares about the end of old myths and the solution of the dilemmas that followed. Zionists need make no apologies to those who point out the profound changes Zionism effects in Jewish existence. They need only ask, Is self-hatred better than what we have done? Is a crisis of identity to be preferred over its resolution? Are people better off living among the remnants of disappointed other-worldly hopes, or shaping new aspirations? Surely it is healthier for men to recover a normal life than to lament the end of an abnormal one. Granted that the Jewish situation has radically changed, I contend it is no worse, and a good deal better, than what has been left behind. All the invidious contrasts in the world change nothing.

Zionism has had a uniformly beneficial effect upon Jewry. It achieves the reconstruction of Jewish identity by its reaffirmation of the nationhood of Israel in the face of the disintegration of the religious foundations of Jewish peoplehood. Zionism indeed supplies a satisfactory explanation for the continued life of the Jewish group. It reintegrates the realities of Jewish group life with an emotional, intellectual, and mythic explanation for those realities. If Zionism really is a new religion for the Jews, then I think, on that account, it is not obligated to apologize for its success. On the contrary, Zionism works a miracle by making it possible for the Jewish group to renew its life. It redeems the broken lives of the remnants of the Holocaust. But it also breathes new life into the survivors of a different sort of holocaust, the erosion of Jewish self-respect, dignity, and loyalty throughout the Western Diaspora. Jews who want more than anything else to become Americans are enabled to reaffirm their Jewishness. Throughout the world, Jews who had lost a religious, Judaic way of viewing reality regain a Jewish understanding of themselves.

Zionism indeed serves as a religion because it does what a religion must do: it supplies the meaning of felt-history; it explains reality, makes sense of chaos, and supplies a worthwhile dream for people who find in Jewishness nothing more than neurotic nightmares. Neither metaphysics nor theology proves necessary, for Zionism explains what the people already know and take for granted as fact. Zionism legitimates what Alexander Portnoy observed but could not accept: that Jews are men of flesh and blood, that (in Portnoy's phrase), *there is an id in Yid.* What is remarkable is that the early Zionists sought to do just that: to normalize the existence of the Jewish people.

The Zionist Problem

In what way, then, does Zionism constitute a problem for Judaism? In my view, it is not its secularity and worldliness, but the mythic insufficiency of Zionism that renders its success a dilemma for contemporary American Jews, and for Israeli ones as well.

Let us begin with the obvious. How can American Jews focus their spiritual lives *solely* on a land in which they do not live? It is one thing for that land to be in heaven, at the end of time, or across the Sambatyon for that matter. It is quite another to dream of a far-away place where everything is good—*but* where one may go if he wants. The realized eschaton is insufficient for a rich and interesting fantasy life, and, moreover, in this-worldly terms it is hypocritical. It means American Jews live off the capital of Israeli culture. Reliance on the state of Israel furthermore suggests that to satisfy their need for fantasy, American Jews must look forward to ever more romantic adventures reported in the press, rather than to the colorless times of peace. American Jews want to take their vacations among heroes, and then come home to the ordinary workaday world they enjoy and to which Israelis rightly aspire but do not own. The 'enlandisement' of American Judaism—the focusing of its imaginative, inner life upon the land and State of Israel—therefore imposes an *ersatz* spiritual dimension. We live here *as if* we lived there—but do not choose to migrate.

It furthermore diverts American Judaism from the concrete mythic issues it has yet to solve: Why should anyone be a *Jew* anywhere, in the U.S.A. or in Israel? That question is not answered by the recommendation to participate in the spiritual adventures of people in a quite different situation. Since the primary *mitzvot* of U.S. Judaism concern supplying funds, encouragement, and support for Israel, one wonders whether one must be a Jew at all in order to believe in and practice that form of Judaism. What is 'being Jewish' now supposed to mean?

The underlying problem, which faces both Israeli and American Jews, is understanding what the ambiguous adjective *Jewish* is supposed to mean when the noun *Judaism* has been abandoned. To be sure, for some Israelis and American Jews to be a Jew is to be a citizen of the State of Israel—but that definition hardly serves when Israeli Moslems and Christians are taken into account. If one ignores the exceptions, the rule is still wanting. If to be a Jew is to be—or to dream of being—an Israeli, then the Israeli who chooses to settle in a foreign country ceases to be a Jew when he gives up Israeli citizenship for some other. If all Jews are on the road to Zion, then those who either do not get there or, once there, choose another way are to be abandoned. That makes Jewishness depend upon quite worldly issues: This one cannot make his living in Tel Aviv, that one does not like the climate of Affula, the other is frustrated by the bureaucracy of Jerusalem. Are they then supposed to give up their share in the "God of Israel?"

More seriously still, the complete 'enlandisement' of Judaism for the first time since 586 B.C.E. forces the Judaic tradition to depend upon the historical fortunes of a single population in a small country. The chances for the survival of the Jewish people have surely been enhanced by the dispersion of the Jews among differing political systems. Until World War II Jews had stood on both sides of every international contest from most remote antiquity. Now, we enter an age in which the fate of Jewry and destiny of Judaism are supposed to depend on the fortunes of one state and one community alone.

That, to be sure, is not a fact, for even now the great Jewish communities in the U.S.S.R., Western Europe, Latin America, and North America, as well as smaller ones elsewhere, continue to conform to the historical pattern. But, ideologically, things have vastly changed. With all the Jewish eggs in one basket, the consequence of military actions is supposed to determine the future of the whole of Jewry and Judaism. So the excellence of some eight hundred pilots and the availability of a few dozen fighter-bombers are what it all comes down to. Instead of the thirty-six righteous men of classical myth are seventy-two phantoms—mirages—a curious revision of the old symbolism.

A Judaic Answer

Just what is *important* about being Jewish and in Judaism? In my view, the answer must pertain both to the State of Israel and to the *Golah exilic* communities in equal measure. It cannot be right only for American Jewry, for we are not seeking a *Galut*-ideology and no one would accept it. Such an ideology—right for here but irrelevant to Israelis—would obviously serve the selfish interests and the peculiar situation of American Jews alone. But the answer cannot pertain only to the situation of the Israeli Jews, for precisely the same reasons.

What is important about being Jewish is the capacity of the Jewish people and its mythic creations to preserve the tension between the intense particularities of their life and the humanity they have in common with the rest of mankind. That tension, practically unique to Jewry, derives from its exceptional historical experience. Until now, it has been the basis for the Jews' remarkable role in human history.

Others have not felt such a tension. To be human and to be English—or Navaho—were hardly differentiated. And why should they have been, when pretty much everyone one cared for and knew was English, or Navaho? To be a Jew in any civilation was, and is, to share the values held by everyone *but* to stand in some ways apart (not above) from the others. It was, and is, to love one's native land with open arms, to preserve the awareness of other ways of living life and shaping culture.

To be sure, before the destruction of the First Temple, Jewish people may well have been much like others. But from that time forward the land was loved with an uncommon intensity, for it had been lost, then regained, therefore could never again be taken for granted. And alongside land, the people found, as few have *had* to, that Jews live by truths that could endure outside a single land and culture. Jewry discovered in itself an international culture, to be created and recreated in every land and in every language. It found in its central moral and ethical convictions something of value for all civilizations. Its apprehension of God and its peculiar method of receiving and spelling out revelation in the commonplaces of everyday life were divorced from a single place, even the holiest place in the world where they had begun. . . .

. . . Zionism . . . posits in new and more incisive form the old question of universality, *but it also answers that question.* In the Jewish state Jews lose their sense of peculiarity. They re-enter the human situation common to everyone but Jews. In the State of Israel everyone is Jewish, therefore no one is the Jew. And this, in my view, opens the way to an interesting development: the reconsideration of Jewish humanity in relationship with the other sorts of humanity in the world. It is now possible for the normal to communicate with the normal.

What the Israelis have to communicate is clear to one and all. They have not divorced themselves from important elements of the Jewish past, but have retained and enhanced them. The possession of the land, after all, represents such an important element. What does it mean to believe that one's moral life is somehow related to the destiny of the land in which one lives? In times past the question would have seemed nonsensical. But today no people is able to take its land, its environment, for granted. Everyone is required to pay attention to what one does with one's blessings. Today each land is endangered by immoral men who live upon and make use of it. The moral pollution of which the prophets spoke may infect not only a society but the way a society makes use of its resources. So the intimate relationship between Israel and the land is no longer so alien to the existence of other nations. And the ecological-moral answers found in the land and State of Israel are bound to have universal meaning.

I choose this example because it is the least obvious. The record of the State of Israel is, in my view, not ambiguous about "the final questions of the universal meaning and obligation of the chosen people." One need not be an Israeli apologist to recognize the numerous ways in which the State of Israel has sought to make war without fanaticism, to wage peace with selflessness. Only indifference to the actual day to day record of the State of Israel, with its technical assistance, its thirst for peace, its fundamentally decent society at home, and above all its hatred of what it must do to survive, justifies questions concerning Israel's "universal duty." On the contrary, it seems to me that Israeli society has, within the limits of its wisdom and power, committed itself to the benediction of all peoples, and with its loyalty to that very blessing its very particularity is verified and justified.

I therefore do not agree that the new 'enlandisement' has betrayed the old. It has fulfilled it.

The other half of the question pertains to the Diaspora. The Diaspora was neither the true symbol nor the tragic negation of Israel's vocation. "Chosen-ness and law, obligation to God and duty to man," are still proper and feasible clues to Jewish existence *both* at home and abroad. The land never was, and is not now, merely the territorial locus of a secular nationality. The existence of the Diaspora guarantees otherwise. The Diaspora supplies the certainty that men of many languages and civilizations will look to Zion for more than a parochial message, just as the Israelis make certain the Diaspora Jews will hear that message. But, as I said, things are the reverse of what al-Tafāhum supposes. The Diaspora brings its acute consciousness of being different from other men, therefore turns to the State to discover the ways in which it is like the others. The Diaspora contributes its variety and range of human experience to the consciousness of the State of Israel. But the State offers the Diaspora the datum of normality.

One cannot divide the Jewish people into two parts, the 'enlandised' and the 'disenlandised.' Those in the land look outward. Those outside look toward the land. Those in the land identify with the normal peoples. Those abroad see in the land what it means to be extraordinary. But it is what happens to the whole, all together, that is decisive for the Judaic tradition. And together, the Diaspora Jew and the Israeli represent a single tradition, a single memory. That memory is of having had a land and lost it—*and* never having repudiated either the memory of the land *or* the experience of living elsewhere. No one in the State of Israel can imagine that to be in the land is for the Jew what being in England is to the Englishman. The Englishman has never lost England and come back. So one cannot distinguish between the Israeli and the Diaspora Jew. Neither one remembers or looks upon a world in which his particular values and ideals are verified by society. Neither ceases to be cosmopolitan. Both preserve a universal concern for *all* Israel. Both know diversities of culture and recognize therefore the relativity of values, even as they affirm their own.

This forms what is unique in the Jewish experience: the denial of men's need to judge all values by their particular, self-authenticating system of thought. In this regard the Diaspora re-enforces the Israeli's view of the world, and the Israeli reciprocates. Both see as transitory and merely useful what others understand to be absolute and perfected. Behind the superficial eschatological self-confidence of Zionism lies an awareness everywhere present that that is just what Zionism adds up to: a *merely* secular eschatology. No one imagines that Zionism has completed its task or that the world has been perfected. The world is seen by both parts of the Jewish people to be insufficient and incomplete.

The Israelis' very sense of necessity preserves the Jews' neatest insight: without choice, necessity imposes duty, responsibility, unimagined possibilities. The Jews are not so foolish as to have forgotten the ancient eternal cities—theirs and others—which are no more. They know therefore that it is not the place, but the quality of life within it, that truly matters. No city is holy, not even Jerusalem, but men must live in some one place and assume the responsibilities of the mundane city. But if no city is holy, at least Jerusalem may be made into a paradigm of sanctity. Though all they have for mortar may be slime, Jewish men will indeed build what they must, endure as they have to. The opposite is not to wander, but to die.

But have Diaspora Jews strayed so far from those same truths? In sharing the lives of many civilizations, do they do other than to assume responsibility for place? Do they see the particular city as holy, because they want to sanctify life in it? Or do they, too, know that the quality of life *anywhere* is what must truly matter? Men must live in some one place, and so far as Jewish men have something to teach of all they have learned in thirty centuries, they should live and learn and teach in whatever place they love. And one may err if he underestimates the capacity of the outsider, of the Diaspora Jew, to love.

I therefore see no need either to repudiate Zionism or to give up the other elements that have made *being Jewish* a maginificent mode of humanity. Zionism, on the contrary, supplies Jewry with still another set of experiences, another set of insights into what it means to be human. Only those who repudiate the unity of Israel, the Jewish people, in favor of either of its segments can see things otherwise. But viscerally American Jews know better, and I think they are right in refusing to resolve the tensions of their several commitments. Zionism creates problems for Judaism only when Zionists think that all that being Jewish means is 'enlandisement' and, thereby, redemption. But Zionists *cannot* think so when they contemplate the range of human needs and experiences they as men must face. Zionism is a part of Judaism. It cannot be made the whole, because Jews are more than people who need either a place to live or a place on which to focus fantasies. The profound existential necessities of Jews—both those they share with every man and those they have to themselves—are not met by Zionism or 'enlandisement' alone. Zionism provides much of the vigor and excitement of contemporary Jewish affairs, but so far as Jews live and suffer, are born and die, reflect and doubt, raise children and worry over them, love and work—so far as Jews are human, they require Judaism.

47.

zionism and "the jewish problem"

jacob neusner

From "Zionism and 'The Jewish Problem,' " by Jacob Neusner, *Midstream* XV, 9, November 1969, pp. 34–53. © 1969 by Theodor Herzl Foundation, Inc., and reprinted with their permission.

When Herzl proposed Zionism as the solution to the Jewish problem, the "Zionism" of which he spoke and the "Jewish problem" which he proposed to solve constituted chiefly political realities. But, as Arthur Hertzberg trenchantly argues in *The Zionist Idea,* Zionism actually represented not a merely secular and political ideology, but the transvaluation of Jewish values. If so, the same must be said of the "Jewish problem" to which it addresses itself. Zionism as an external force faced the world, but what shall we say of its inner spirit? The inwardness of Zionism—its "piety" and spirituality—is not to be comprehended by the world, only by the Jew, for, like the Judaism it transformed and transcended, to the world it was worldly and political, stiff-necked and stubborn (in Christian theological terms), but to the Jew it was something other, not to be comprehended by the gentile. . . .

The Zionism of which I speak is the effort to realize through political means the hope supposed to have been lost in the time of Ezekiel, proclaimed imperishable in the time of Imber, the continuous hope of restoration and renaissance first of the land of Israel, then of the people of Israel through the land, finally, since 1948, of the people and the land together, wherever the people should be found. This Zionism did not come about at Basel, for its roots go back to the point in the ages at which Jewry first recognized, then rejected, its separation from the land. Zionism is the old-new Judaism, a Judaism transformed through old-new values. It is a set of paradoxes through which the secular and the religious, separated in the nineteenth century, were again fused—re-fused—in the twentieth. Zionism to be sure is a complex phenomenon; within it are tendencies which are apt to cancel each other. But all forms of Zionism are subsumed under the definition offered here, which represents, I think, the lowest common denominator for all Zionist phenomena.

The Jewish problems which Zionism successfully solved were the consequence of the disintegration of what had been whole, the identity, consciousness, and the culture of the Jew. It was, as I said, Zionism which reconstructed the whole and reshaped the tradition in a wholly new heuristic framework.

In former times it was conventional to speak of the "Jewish problem." Most people understood that problem in political and economic terms. What shall we do about the vast Jewish populations of Eastern and Central Europe, which live a marginal economic life and have no place in the political structures of the several nations? Herzl proposed the Zionist solution to the "Jewish problem." Dubnow wished to solve the "Jewish problem" by the creation of Jewish autonomous units in Europe. The Socialists and Communists proposed to solve the "Jewish problem" by the integration of Jewry into the movement of the international proletariat and to complete the solution of the problems of the smaller group within those of the working classes.

Today we hear less talk about the "Jewish problem" because Hitler brought it to a final solution: by exterminating the masses of European Jews, he left unsolved no social, economic, or political problems. The Western Jewries are more or less well-integrated into the democratic societies. The State of Israel has no "Jewish problem" in the classic sense. The oppressed communities remaining in the Arab countries are relatively small, and the solution of their problems is to be found in migration to the West and to the State of Israel. The "Jewish problem" to be sure continues to confront Soviet Russia, and there the classic Marxist formulation of the problem still persuades people. But, for the rest, the "Jewish problem" does not describe reality or evoke a recognized, real-life perplexity. (That does not mean Jews do not have problems, or that gentiles do not have problems in relating to and understanding both Jews and Judaism.) . . .

For Jews the secular revolution is not new. From the Haskalah, the Jewish Enlightenment in the eighteenth century onward, Jews have come forward to propose a non-religious interpretation of "being Jewish," an interpretation divorced from the classic mythic structure of Judaism. The God-Is-Dead movement evoked little response among Jewish theologians and ideologists because they found nothing new in it. If the issue was naturalistic, instead of supernatural, theology, Jewish theologians had heard Mordecai Kaplan for half-a-century or more. If the issue was atheism, it had been formulated by Jewish secularists, socialists, and assimilationists in various ways from the mid-nineteenth-century forward. If the secular revolution means that large numbers of people cease to look to religion, or to religious institutions, for the meaning of their lives and cease to practice religious traditions and to affirm religious beliefs, then this is neither news nor a revolution. Jews have participated in that sort of "revolution" for two centuries. They have done so without ceasing to regard themselves, and to be regarded by others, as Jews. That does not mean the Jews have found antidotes to the secular fever, but it does mean that they by now have a considerable heritage of experience, a substantial corpus of cases and precedents, for what Christians find to be new and revolutionary: the loosing of the world from all religious and supernatural interpretations.

The secular revolution has imposed upon Jews a profound crisis of identity. In former times everyone knew who who was a Jew and what being a Jew meant. A Jew was a member of a religious nation, living among other nations by its own laws, believing in *Torah* revealed at Sinai and in one God who had chosen Israel, and hoping for the coming of the Messiah. The gentile world shared the philosophical presuppositions of Jewish beliefs. Everyone believed in God. Everyone believed in prophecy, in revelation, in the Jews' holy book. Everyone believed in the coming of the Messiah. Above all, everyone interpreted reality by supernaturalist principles. To be sure groups differed on the nature of God, the particular prophets to be regarded as true, the book God had revealed. But these differences took place within a vast range of agreement.

When religious understandings of the world lost their hold on masses of Western men, "being Jewish" became as problematical as any other aspect of archaic reality. If to be Jewish meant to be part of a Jewish religious community, then when men ceased to believe in religious propositions, they ought to have ceased being Jewish. Yet that is not what happened. For several generations Jewish atheists and agnostics have continued to take an active role in the Jewish community—indeed, functionally to constitute the majority in it—and to have seen nothing unusual either in their participation in Jewish life or in their lack of religious commitment. Indeed today the American Jewish community is nearly unique in interpreting "being Jewish" primarily in religious, or at least rhetorically-religious, terms. Other Jewish communities see themselves as a community, a nation, a people, whether or not religion plays a role in defining what is particular about that community. The secular revolution immensely complicated the definition of Jewish identity, not only by breaking down the uniform classical definition, but also by supplying a variety of new, complex definitions in its place.

Today, therefore, if we ask ourselves, "What are the components of 'Jewishness'?" we are hard put to find an answer. What are the attitudes, associations, rituals both secular and religious, psychology and culture, which both Jews and others conceive to be Jewish? The truth is, today there is no such thing as a single Jewish identity, as there assuredly was in times past an identity one could define in meaningful terms. Jewishness now is a function of various social and cultural settings, and is meaningful in those settings only.

The Jews obviously are not a nation in the accepted sense; but they also are hardly a people in the sense that an outsider can investigate or understand the components of that peoplehood. There is no "Jewish way" of organizing experience and interpreting reality, although there was and is a Judaic way. There is no single Jewish ideology, indeed no single, unitary Jewish history, although there once was a cogent Judaic theology and a Judaic view of a unitary and meaningful progression of events to be called "Jewish history." Only if we impose upon discrete events of scarcely related groups in widely separated places and ages the concept of a single unitary history can we speak of "Jewish history." Jewish peoplehood in a concrete, secular, this-worldly historical sense is largely a matter of faith, that is, the construction of historians acting as do theologians in other settings. There once was a single Jewish ideological system, a coherent body of shared images, ideas and ideals, which provided for participants a coherent over-all orientation in space and time, in means and ends. There once was such a system, but in the secular revolution it has collapsed.

It is indeed, the secular revolution that has imposed on Jewry a lingering crisis of identity. Jews today may find in common a set of emotions and responses. These do not constitute an "identity," but rather, a set of common characteristics based upon differing verbal explanations and experiences. That does not mean no one knows what a Jew is. In particular settings Jews *can* be defined and understood in terms applicable to those settings. But as an abstraction the "Jewish people" is a theological or ideological construct not to be imposed upon the disparate, discrete data known as Jews or even as Jewish communities in various times and places. Lacking a common language and culture, even a common religion, the Jews do not have what they once had. Today Jewish identity so greatly varies that we need to reconsider the viability of the very concept of "Jewishness" as a universal attribute, for today Jewishness cannot be defined in neutral, cultural terms.

If there are no inherent and essential Jewish qualities in the world, then nothing about "being Jewish" is natural, to be taken for granted. Being Jewish becomes something one must achieve, define, strive for. It is today liberated from the forms and content of the recent past, from the "culture-Judaism" of the American and Canadian Jewish communities. If the artifacts of that "culture-Judaism"—matters of cuisine, or philanthropy, or cliquishness—are not part of some immutable and universal Jewish identity, then they may well be criticized from within, not merely abandoned and left behind in disgust. One can freely repudiate them in favor of other ways.

Omissions in contemporary Jewish "identity" are as striking as the inclusions. Among the things taken for granted are a sense of group-loyalty, a desire to transmit "pride in Judaism" to the next generation, in all a desire to survive. But the identity of large numbers of Jews, whether they regard themselves as secular or not, does not include a concept of God, of the meaning of life, of the direction and purpose of history. The uncriticized, but widely accepted Jewish identity syndrome is formed of the remnants of the piety of the recent past, a piety one may best call residual, cultural, and habitual, rather than self-conscious, critical, and theological (or ideological). That identity is not even ethnic, but rather a conglomeration of traits picked up in particular historical and social experiences. It is certainly flat and one-dimensional, leaving Jews to wander in strange paths in search of the answers to the most fundamental human perplexities.

. . . The "Jewish problem" is most commonly phrased by young Jews as "Why should I be Jewish? I believe in universal ideals—who needs particular ones as well?"

Minorities feel themselves "particular," see their traditions as "ritual," and distinguish between the private, unique, and personal and the public, universal, and commonplace. Majorities do not. Standing at the center, not on the fringe, they accept the given. Marginal men such as the Jews regard the given as something to be criticized, elevated, in any event as distinguished from their own essential being.

Jews who ask, "Why be Jewish," testify that "being Jewish" somehow repels, separates a person from the things he wants. American society, though it is opening, still is not so open that men who are different from the majority can serenely and happily accept that difference. True, they frequently affirm it—but the affirmation contains such excessive protest that it is not much different from denial. The quintessential datum of American Jewish existence is anti-Semitism, along with uncertainty of status, denial of normality, and self-doubt. The results are many, but two stand out. Some over-emphasize their Jewishness, respond to it not naturally but excessively, to the exclusion of other parts of their being. Others question and implicitly deny it. The one compensates too much; the other finds no reward at all.

As Kurt Lewin pointed out (in *Resolving Social Conflicts. Selected Papers on Group Dynamics* [N.Y., 1948: Harper & Bros.], p. 164), ". . . every under-privileged minority group is kept together not only by cohesive forces among its members but also by the boundary which the majority erects against the crossing of an individual from the minority to the majority group." An underprivileged group-member will try to gain in social status by joining the majority—to pass, to assimilate. The basic fact of life is this wish to cross the boundary, and hence, as Lewin says, "he [the minority-group member] lives almost perpetually in a state of conflict and tension. He dislikes . . . his own group because it is nothing but a burden to him. . . . A Jew of this type will dislike everything specifically Jewish, for he will see in it that which keeps him away from the majority for which he is longing." Such a Jew is the one who will constantly ask, "Why be Jewish?" who will see, or at least fantasize about, a common religion of humanity, univer-salism or universal values that transcend, and incidentally obliterate, denomina-tional and sectarian boundaries. It is no accident that the universal language, Esperanto, the universal psychology, Freudianism, all were in large measure attractive to marginal Jews.

True, Jews may find a place in social groups indifferent to their particularity as Jews. But a closer look shows that these groups are formed chiefly by deraci-nated, deJudaised Jews, along with a few exceptionally liberal non-Jews standing in a similar relationship to their own origins. Jews do assimilate. They do try to blot out the marks of their particularity, in ways more sophisticated, to be sure, than the ancient Hellenist-Jews who submitted to painful operations to wipe away the marks of circumcision. But in doing so, they become not something else entirely, but another type of Jew. The real issue is never, to be or not to be a Jew, any more than it is, to be or not to be my father's son.

Lewin makes this wholly clear: "It is not similarity or dissimilarity of individ-uals that constitutes a group, but interdependence of fate." Jews brought up to suppose being Jewish is chiefly, or only, a matter of religion think that through atheism they cease to be Jews, only to discover that disbelieving in God helps not at all. They still are Jews. They still are obsessed by that fact and compelled to confront it, whether under the name of Warren or of Weinstein, whether the society of Jews or elsewhere.

Indeed, outside of that society Jewish consciousness becomes most intense. Among Jews one is a human being, with peculiarities and virtues of one's own. Among gentiles he is a Jew, with traits common to the group he rejects. That is probably why Jews still live in mostly Jewish neighborhoods and associate, out-side of economic life, mostly with other Jews, whether or not these associations exhibit traits supposed to be Jewish. And when crisis comes, as it frequently does, then no one doubts that he shares a common cause, a common fate, with other Jews. Then it is hardest to isolate oneself from Jews, because only among Jewry are these intense concerns shared.

The Jewish community has yet to face up to the self-hatred endemic in its life. Jews are subtle enough to explain they are too busy with non-Jewish activities to associate with Jews. Students coming to college do not say to themselves or others, "I do not want to be a Jew, and now that I have the chance not to be, I shall take it." They say, "I do not like the Hillel rabbi; I am not religious so won't go to services; I am too busy with studies, dates, or political and social programs to participate in Jewish life." From here it is a short step to the affirmation of transcendent, universal, values, and the denial of particular "religious" identity. That those who take that step do so mostly with other Jews is, as I said, proof of the real intent.

The organized Jewish community differs not at all from the assimilationist sector of this student generation. Indeed, it shows the way. Leadership in Jewry is sought by talented and able people, particularly those whose talents and abilities do not produce commensurate results in the non-Jewish world. Status denied elsewhere is readily available, for the right reasons, in Jewry, but in Jewry status is measured by the values of the gentile establishment.

Lewin says, "In any group, those sections are apt to gain leadership which are more generally successful. In a minority group, individual members who are economically successful . . . usually gain a higher degree of acceptance by the majority group. This places them culturally on the periphery of the underprivileged group and makes them more likely to be 'marginal' persons. . . . Nevertheless, they are frequently called for leadership by the underprivileged group because of their status and power. They themselves are usually eager to accept the leading role in the minority, partly as a substitute for gaining status in the majority. As a result, we find the rather paradoxical phenomenon of what one might call 'the leader from the periphery.' Instead of having a group led by people who are proud of the group, who wish to stay in it and to promote it, we see minority leaders who are lukewarm toward the group . . ." This, I think, is very much true of U.S. Jewry.

American Jews want to be Jewish, but not too much so, not so much that they cannot be just "people," part of the imaginary undifferentiated majority. And herein lies their pathology: they suppose one can distinguish between one's Jewishness, humanity, personality, individuality, and religion. A human being, however, does not begin as part of an undifferentiated mass. Once he leaves the maternity ward, he goes to a home of real people with a history, a home that comes from somewhere and that was made by some specific people. He inherits the psychic, not to mention social and cultural, legacy of many generations.

What has Zionism to do with these Jewish problems? It is, after all, suposedly a secular movement, called "secular messianism," and the problems I have described are the consequences of secularity. How then has an allegedly secular movement posited solutions to the challenges of secularity faced by the formerly religious community?

Zionism provides a reconstruction of Jewish identity, for it reaffirms the nationhood of Israel in the face of the disintegration of the religious bases of Jewish peoplehood. If in times past the Jews saw themselves as a people because they were the children of the promise, the children of Abraham, Isaac, and Jacob, called together at Sinai, instructed by God through prophets, led by rabbis guided by the "whole Torah"—written and oral—of Sinai, then with the end of a singularly religious self-consciousness, the people lost its understanding of itself. The fact is that the people remained a community of fate, but, until the flourishing of Zionism, the facts of its continued existence were deprived of a heuristic foundation. Jews continued as a group, but could not persuasively say why or what this meant. Zionism provided the explanation: The Jews indeed remain a people, but the foundation of their peoplehood lies in the unity of their concern for Zion, devotion to rebuilding the land and establishing Jewish sovereignty in it. The realities of continuing emotional and social commitment to Jewish "group-hood" or separateness thus made sense. Mere secular difference, once seen to be destiny—"who has not made us like the nations"—once again stood forth as destiny.

Herein lies the ambiguity of Zionism. It was supposedly a secular movement, yet in reinterpreting the classic mythic structures of Judaism, it compromised its secularity and exposed its fundamental unity with the classic mythic being of Judaism. If, as I suggested, groups with like attributes do not necessarily represent "peoples" or "nations," and if the common attributes, in the Jewish case, are neither intrinsically Jewish (whatever that might mean) nor widely present to begin with, then the primary conviction of Zionism constitutes an extraordinary reaffirmation of the primary element in the classical mythic structure: salvation. What has happened in Zionism is that the old has been in one instant destroyed and resurrected. The holy people are no more, the nation-people take their place. How much has changed in the religious tradition, when the allegedly secular successor-continuator has preserved not only the essential perspective of the tradition, but done so pretty much in the tradition's own symbols and language?

Nor should it be supposed that the Zionist solution to the Jews' crisis of identity is a merely theological or ideological one. We cannot ignore the practical result of Zionist success in conquering the Jewish community. For the middle and older generations, as everyone knows, the Zionist enterprise provided the primary vehicle for Jewish identity. The Reform solution to the identity-problem—we are Americans by nationality, Jews by religion—was hardly congruent to the profound Jewish passion of the immigrant generations and their children. The former generations were *not* merely Jewish by religion. Religion was the least important aspect of their Jewishness. They deeply felt themselves Jewish in their bone and marrow and did not feel sufficiently marginal as Jews to *need* to affirm their Americanness/Judaism at all. Rather they participated in a reality; they were in a situation so real and intimate as to make unnecessary such an uncomfortable, defensive affirmation. They did not doubt they were Americans. They did not need to explain what being Jewish had to do with it. Zionism was congruent to these realities, and because of that fact, being Jewish and being Zionist were inextricably joined together. . . .

. . . The Zionist stood between the religious party, which utterly rejected Emancipation and its works, and the secular-reform-liberal party, which wholly affirmed them. He faced the reality of Emancipation without claiming in its behalf a messianic valence. Emancipation is here, he thought, therefore to be criticized, but coped with; not utterly rejected, like the Orthodox, nor wholeheartedly affirmed, like the secular, reform and liberal groups. Zionism therefore demanded that the Jew be accepted as an equal in society because he was a Jew, *not* because his Jewishness was irrelevant. Its suspicion of the liberal stance was based, correctly in my opinion, on the Jews' ambivalence toward Jewishness. Zionism clearly recognized that the Jewishness of the Jew could never be irrelevant, not to the gentile, not to the Jew. It therefore saw more clearly than the liberals the failures of the European Emancipation and the dangers of American liberalism to Jewish self-respect and Jewish interests. Zionists were quick to perceive the readiness of non-Jewish allies of Jewish liberals to take the Jewish liberals at their word: We Jews have no special interests, nothing to fight for in our own behalf. Zionists saw Jews had considerable interests, just like other groups, and exposed the self-deceit (or hypocrisy) of those who said otherwise. The liberal Jew wanted to be accepted into the traditions of society without complete assimilation, on the one side, but also without much Jewishness, on the other. The Zionist assessment of the situation differed, as I said, for it saw that Jews could achieve a place in the common life *only* as Jews; and, rightly for Europe, it held this was impossible.

In its gloomy assessment of the European Emancipation, Zionism found itself in a position to cope with the third component in the Jewish problem, the immense, deep-rooted, and wide-ranging self-hatred of Jews. The Zionist affirmation of Jewish peoplehood, of Jewish-being, stood in stark contrast to the inability of marginal and liberal Jews to cope with anti-Semitism. Cases too numerous to list demonstrate the therapeutic impact of Zionism on the faltering psychological health of European Jews, particularly of more sensitive and intellectual individuals.

The American situation is different in degree, for here anti-Semitism in recent times has made its impact in more subtle ways, but its presence is best attested by the Jews themselves. Yet if a single factor in the self-respect American Jewry does possess can be isolated, it is its pride in the State of Israel and its achievements. Zionism lies at the foundation of American Jewry's capacity to affirm its Jewishness. Without Zionism religious conviction, forced to bear the whole burden by itself, would prove a slender reed. To be a Jew "by religion" and to make much of that fact in an increasingly secular environment, would not represent an attractive option to many. The contributions to Jewry's psychological health by the State of Israel and the Zionist presence in the diaspora cannot be overestimated. It is striking, for example, that Kurt Lewin, Milton Steinberg, and other students of the phenomena of Jewish self-hatred invariably reached the single conclusion that only through Zionism would self-hatred by mitigated, even overcome.

The role of Zionism as a therapy for self-hatred cannot be described only in terms of the public opinion of U.S. Jewry. That would tell us much about the impact of mass communications, but little about the specific value of the Zionist idea for healing the Jewish pathology. In my view, the Israelis' claim "to live a full Jewish life" is a valid one. In Zionist conception and Israeli reality, the Jew is indeed a thoroughly integrated, whole human being. Here, in conception and reality, the Jew who believes in justice, truth, and peace, in universal brotherhood and dignity, does so not despite his peculiarity as a Jew, but through it. He makes no distinction between his Jewishness, his humanity, his individuality, his way of living, and his ultimate values. They constitute a single, undivided and fully integrated existential reality.

Part of the reason is the condition of life: The State of Israel is the largest Jewish neighborhood in the world. But part of the reason is ideological, and not merely circumstantial: Zionists always have rejected the possibility of Jews' "humanity" without Jewishness, just as they denied the reality of distinctions between Jewishness, nationality, and faith. They were not only *not* Germans of the Mosaic persuasion, but also *not* human beings of the Jewish genus. The several sort of bifurcations attempted by non-Zionists to account for their Jewishness along with other sorts of putatively non-Jewish commitments and loyalties were rejected by Zionists. It was not that Zionists did not comprehend the dilemmas faced by other sorts of Jews, but rather that they supposed through Zionism they had found the solution. They correctly held that through Zionist ideology and activity they had overcome the disintegrating Jewish identity-crisis of others.

. . . Like Judaism, Zionism can be understood from within, from its soul. . . . Zionism is to be understood as a solution to Jewish problems best perceived by the Jews who face those problems. The "Jewish problem" imposed by the effects of secularism took the form of a severe and complex crisis of identity, a partial commitment to universalism and cosmopolitan liberalism while claiming the right to be a little different, and a severe psychopathological epidemic of self-hatred. But the way Zionism actually solved those problems is more difficult to explain. If, as I suppose, because of Zionism contemporary Jewries have a clearer perception of who they are, what their interests consist of, and of their value as human beings, then Zionism and the State of Israel are in substantial measure the source of the saving knowledge. But *how* has Zionism worked its salvation on the Jews? Here I think we come to realities only Jews can understand. They understand them *not* because of rational reflection but because of experience and unreflective natural response.

Zionism, and Zionism alone, proved capable of interpreting to contemporary Jews the meaning of felt-history, *and* of doing so in terms congruent to what the Jews derived from their tradition. It was Zionism which properly assessed the limitations of the Emancipation and proposed sound and practical programs to cope with those limitations. It was Zionism which gave Jews strength to affirm themselves when faced with the anti-Semitism of European and American life in the first-half of the twentieth century. It was Zionism and that alone which showed a way forward from the nihilism and despair of the DP camps. It was Zionism and that alone which provided a basis for unity in U.S. Jewry in the fifties and sixties of this century, a ground for common action among otherwise utterly divided groups.

These achievements of Zionism were based not on their practicality, though Zionism time and again was proved "right" by history. The Jews were moved and responded to Zionism before, not after the fact. And they were moved because of the capacity of Zionism to resurrect the single most powerful force in the history of Judaism: Messianism. Zionism did so in ways too numerous to list, but the central fact is that it represented, as Hertzberg perceptively showed, not "secular Messianism" but a profound restatement in new ways of classical Messianism. Zionism recovered the old, still evocative messianic symbolism and imagery and filled them with new meaning. And *this* meaning was taken for granted by vast numbers of Jews because it accurately described not what they believed or hoped for—not faith—but rather what they took to be mundane reality. Zionism took within its heuristic framework each and every important event in twentieth century Jewish history and gave to all a single, comprehensive, and sensible interpretation. Events were no longer random or unrelated, but all were part of a single pattern, pointing toward an attainable messianic result. It was not the random degradation of individuals in Germany and Poland, not the meaningless murder of unfortunates, not the creation of another state in the Middle East. All of these events were related to one another. It was Holocaust and rebirth, and the state was the State of *Israel.*

In so stating the meaning of contemporary events, Zionism made it possible for Jews not only to understand what they witnessed, but to draw meaning from it. And even more, Zionism breathed new life into ancient Scriptures, by providing a contemporary interpretation—subtle and not fundamentalist to be sure— for the prophets. "Our hope is lost," Ezekiel denied in the name of God. "Our hope is not lost," was the response of Zionism. These things were no accident, still less the result of an exceptionally clever publicist's imagination. They demonstrate the center and core of Zionist spirituality and piety: the old-new myth of peoplehood, land, redemption above all. The astonishing achievements of Zionism are the result of the capacity of Zionism to reintegrate the tradition with contemporary reality, to do so in an entirely factual, matter-of-fact framework, thus to eschew faith and to elicit credence. Zionism speaks in terms of Judaic myth, indeed so profoundly that myth and reality coincide.

glossary and abbreviations

Aggadah (Sometimes spelled *Agadah*): Narrative, non-legal teachings of Scripture and Talmud. Adjective used in English writing: *Aggadic/Aggadic.*

Apion: Anti-Semitic Greek writer who lived in Alexandria in the first century C.E.

Betar: Site of a stronghold held by the Jewish armies in the rebellion against Rome led by Bar Kokhba from ca. 132 to ca. 135. Betar was the last stronghold to fall and thereafter symbolized the Jews' capacity to resist to the bitter end.

C.E.: Common Era, corresponding to A.D. Jewish writers sometimes prefer C.E. to A.D., because of the theological implications of the latter usage.

Deut.: Deuteronomy, the fifth book of the Pentateuch.

Essene: Member of a Jewish sect of the first century B.C.E. (Before the Common Era) and C.E., which lived in communes and observed special rules of purity. The Essenes seem to have been close to the sect responsible for the Dead Sea Scrolls.

Ex.: Exodus, the second book of the Pentateuch.

Gen.: Genesis, the first book of the Pentateuch.

Haggadah: In general: Narration, telling. In particular: *The Haggadah* is the narration read at the Passover meal, the *Seder.*

Halakhah: Literally: The way, the manner in which things are to be done. In general: The law. Adjective used in English writing: *Halakhic.* Sometimes spelled *Halachah, halachic.*

Hallel: Thanksgiving Psalms, Nos. 113–118, read on festivals.

Hasid: Pietist. Several groups in the history of Judaism called themselves Hasid (plural: *Hasidim*).

Havdalah: Distinction, separation. The *Havdalah*-ceremony marks the distinction between the Sabbath and the weekday and is said after sunset on Saturday night.

Hellenism: The cultural amalgam of ancient Greece and various Near Eastern cultures, consequent upon the Greek conquest of the Near and Middle East by Alexander the Great and the settlement of many Greeks (Hellenes) in the cities of the area.

Histadrut: The Labor Federation of the State of Israel.

Jehovah: Rendering into English of the sacred name of God, the Hebrew characters for which are YHVH, thus YeHoVaH, with the Y represented as a J. It bears no relationship to the way in which YHVH is pronounced but has nonetheless entered English speech as the Hebrew word for the Lord.

Josephus: Jewish general and historian who led in the first great war against Rome, 66–73 C.E. Josephus surrendered and went over to the Romans some

235

time before the fall of Jerusalem and the destruction of the Temple in 70
C.E., and he afterward wrote a history of the war which laid the war-guilt
on the shoulders of the Jewish zealots.

Kabbalah: Jewish mystical tradition.

Lev.: Leviticus, the third book of the Pentateuch.

Lishmah: For its own sake, without expectation of reward. A *mitzvah lishmah*
is a religious action done for its own sake and without the motivation of
thereby gaining divine recompense.

Lulav and *etrog*: Palm branches and citron used in the celebration of *Sukkot,* the
festival of tabernacles.

Manual of Discipline: One of the scrolls found at the Dead Sea near Qumran,
the Manual of Discipline contains some of the laws of the Essene-like community.

Maror: Bitter herbs.

Masada: Fortress built by King Herod in the first century B.C.E., which served
as the last refuge of the zealot fighters after the destruction of Jerusalem in
70 C.E. Today Masada has been dug up and restored. Situated by the Dead
Sea, it serves as a kind of shrine for the Israeli military forces.

Matt.: Matthew.

Matzoh: Unleavened bread used during Passover, a kind of hard, brittle, tasteless
cracker. Sometimes spelled *matzah.* Plural: *Matzos, matzot.*

Mitzvah: Commandment, religious deed. Sometimes spelled *mizwah, mitzwah,
misvah, miswah,* etc. Plural: *Mitzvot.* A *mitzvah* may be affirmative, requiring that one do a certain deed, or it may be negative, prohibiting a specific
action. A negative *mitzvah,* for example, is that one may not work on the
Sabbath-day. An affirmative *mitzvah* is that one must rest on and enjoy that
day.

Nomos: Greek word for law.

Num.: Numbers, the fourth book of the Pentateuch.

Pharisee: Separatist, a member of a sect in Judaism before 70 C.E. that stressed
belief in "traditions from the fathers" received alongside, and in addition to,
the written scriptures of Moses.

Qoh.: Qohelet, the book called in the Christian Bible "Ecclesiastes."

Seder: Order. Usually refers to the Order of service at the Passover meal.

Shekhinah: The Presence of God that dwells (*Shokhen*) in the world.

Shofar: Ram's horn, sounded in the penitential season marked by the Days of
Awe.

Stare decisis: A juridical principle that holds that one should adhere to and abide
by decided cases.

Sukkah: Tabernacle, a small hut with a roof of boughs or leaves, which allow the
sun and stars to be seen. In observance of the festival of *Sukkot,* or tabernacles, Jews build a *Sukkah* (plural: *Sukkot*) and eat their meals in it, weather
permitting.

Tanakh: The Hebrew name for the Hebrew Scriptures ("Old Testament") formed
of the letters T, for *Torah,* or Pentateuch; N for *Nevi'im,* or Prophetic

writings; and K for *Ketuvim,* or Wisdom-writings, the three divisions of the Scriptures.

Talmud: The corpus of Jewish law produced by the rabbis of the first seven centuries c.e., consisting of the law-code, the *Mishnah,* sponsored by Judah, the Patriarch of Jewish Palestine, in ca. 200 c.e., and the *Talmud,* a considerable commentary on that code, created by the Babylonian and Palestinian rabbis from ca. 200 to ca. 600 c.e., There are in fact two Talmuds, a Babylonian one and a Jerusalemite or Palestinian one, each consisting of the Mishnah and the Talmud of the rabbis of the two respective countries.

Yavneh: A coastal town in the south of Palestine, called Jamnia in Greek and Roman sources. It becomes important in the history of Judaism, because after the destruction of the Temple in 70 c.e., the Romans permitted rabbis, led by Yohanan ben Zakkai, to undertake at Yavneh the work of leading the Jews and reconstructing their religious and communal life.

Yeshivah: A traditional academy for the study of Torah, particularly of the Talmud and post-Talmudic commentaries, laws, and traditions. Plural: *Yeshivot, yeshivos, or yeshivas.*

Zohar: Thirteenth-century mystical treatise.